Sacred Resistance

ECOLOGY & JUSTICE SERIES

Sacred Resistance

Eco-Activism and the Rise of New Spiritual Communities

MARK CLATTERBUCK

editor

ORBIS BOOKS
Maryknoll, New York 10545

Founded in 1970, Orbis Books endeavors to publish works that enlighten the mind, nourish the spirit, and challenge the conscience. The publishing arm of the Maryknoll Fathers and Brothers, Orbis seeks to explore the global dimensions of the Christian faith and mission, to invite dialogue with diverse cultures and religious traditions, and to serve the cause of reconciliation and peace. The books published reflect the views of their authors and do not represent the official position of the Maryknoll Society. To learn more about Maryknoll and Orbis Books, please visit our website at www. orbisbooks.com.

Library of Congress Cataloging-in-Publication Data

Names: Clatterbuck, Mark, editor.
Title: Sacred resistance : eco-activism and the rise of new spiritual
    communities / Mark Clatterbuck, editor.
Description: Maryknoll, NY : Orbis Books, [2025] | Series: Ecology and
    justice | Includes bibliographical references and index. | Summary:
    "Chronicles five eco-activist movements and the spiritualities that
    support eco-activism in the US today"— Provided by publisher.
Identifiers: LCCN 2024038569 (print) | LCCN 2024038570 (ebook) | ISBN
    9781626985988 | ISBN 9798888660539 (epub)
Subjects: LCSH: Environmentalism—Religious aspects. | Ecotheology. | Human
    ecology—Religious aspects.
Classification: LCC BT695.5 .S233 2025 (print) | LCC BT695.5 (ebook) |
    DDC 201/.770973—dc23/eng/20241026
LC record available at https://lccn.loc.gov/2024038569
LC ebook record available at https://lccn.loc.gov/

This book is dedicated to
my son

Ashton Myles Clatterbuck
(2001–2024)

Environmental Justice Warrior
and
Champion of Transgender Rights

CONTENTS

FOREWORD
To Be a Water Protector

Winona LaDuke

Water is life. That's the only truth. Without water, there is no life. And you cannot drink oil. Every generation of people has come to life because of water. We are born of water, and we live on a Mother Earth that is a place of water. Our first environment is the water of our mother's womb.

It's said that we have a covenant with creation, that we do our part and the natural world cares for us. It's a reciprocal relationship of caring and responsibility. We care for the water, and the water gives us life. That's the covenant.

The Anishinaabe universe—Indakiingimin, the very land to which we belong—is half water and half land. This is a fifth of the world's water, and it is the only place we know. The water not only feeds the land but also creates a wealthy aquatic ecosystem full of medicines, Manoomin (or wild rice, the only grain native to North America), deep fisheries, and a way of life, traversed once by canoe and dogsled.

Some days, I wish for those times again, the pre–fossil fuels economy.

The Anishinaabe have struggled to keep our covenant for generations while facing an extractive economy that destroys life—whether rivers, sturgeon populations, wild rice, or the great buffalo herds of the western part of our territory. We have opposed dam projects, clearcuts, nuclear waste dumps, and endless mining projects—and because of our resistance, we are still here, and much of our world remains.

On a worldwide scale, Indigenous people represent 4 percent of the world's population but care for 75 percent of the world's biodiversity. That's the story of a people, a land, and a resistance.

And that is, ultimately, the story of our time. A time of deep conflict between worldviews. It is a land- and water-based worldview, versus a worldview based on the greed of a Wiindigo industrial society where technology has replaced Creation at the center of the paradigm. It is a time when technology has outstripped our understanding and regulations. It is a time out of balance. It is, as the Hopi call it, Koyaanisqatsi.

It is for us to restore balance and reaffirm and restore the covenant.

As a young woman, I had the great opportunity to listen to many wise elders. There were Haudenosaunee, Dine, the Hopi, and Anishinaabe people, and they would say similar things. They would say that we live in the time of prophecies. We were told by our elders that these times would be about a transition between worlds. They spoke of this time as the time of the Seventh Fire and told us that we would need to make a choice between a scorched path and a green path. Then we would light the Eighth Fire. That was the fire of balance and healing. That is our collective hope and our prayer.

Other prophets from the Hopi talked about a time when a web in the sky would signify a new world and a transition. Indeed, with the advent of the World Wide Web and Starlink, we see that world is here. It is time to make a new path, or a path back to harmony with relatives—whether they have wings, fins, roots, or paws.

Over the past fifteen years, world oil geopolitics and the endless demands of a Wiindigo economy have sought to replumb the oil industry, from the largest oil reserves in the world held in Venezuela to the oil of the deep north in the Athabascan Tar Sands. The impact has been devastating as five oil pipelines were proposed to cut across our Anishinaabe territories: the Northern Gateway (Enbridge), Energy East (Trans Canada), Keystone (Trans Canada), Line 3 (Enbridge), and Trans Mountain (originally Kinder Morgan, now owned by the Canadian government). Those pipelines carried oil that was ripped from the ground out of oil sands, the dirtiest oil production in the world, and moved it through pipelines across pristine territories like ours. Our resistance was strong, and three of the five pipelines never made it through. That's because of the commitment of Water Protectors.

We resisted with our prayers and hearts, always hoping that some regulatory process would protect our water and people. By 2021, we knew that there would be no regulatory system, nor any state or federal agency, that would save us. So we stood in prayer, shoulder to shoulder. We stood in hearings. We stood together, facing arrests at the highest rate of any Water Protector movement to this date, while we watched as our lands, people, and waters were scarred.

We are still wounded.

And yet, through it all, we are still here to tell the story. We are still here to be Water Protectors, to watch over our rivers, our aquifers, and this sacred place where the Creator has placed us all.

In 2022, a year after Enbridge completed Line 3, Akiing, an Indigenous community organization, bought the former Enbridge office in downtown Park Rapids, Minnesota. It was once a Carnegie Library. Andrew Carnegie made his fortune from Ojibwe iron ore, so it was a fitting turn in history that Anishinaabe would rematriate this land and our story. Today, the Giiwedinong Museum tells the story of the Anishinaabe, our treaties with the Creator and other nations, and the story of the Water Protector movement.

Let our great and epic story continue. Let us pray for the water, sing for the water, take actions for this water, and create societies where water is revered as a living being. There is no word for reconciliation in Anishinaabemowin. Instead, our word is gwayukizhichigewin: to make it right. That time is now, when we come together to make it right.

Acknowledgments

A highly collaborative project like *Sacred Resistance* depends on the generous participation of many people, beginning with the writers. Without exception, the authors who contributed chapters to this project were writing about their movements while still involved in the ongoing demands of grassroots activism. Intensive years-long campaigns like those described here carry enormous costs, particularly for movement leaders. Carving out time to write these chapters took place amid the stressors of ongoing strategy sessions, community gatherings, marches, rallies, direct actions, press conferences, conflict mediation, court cases, and too many sleepless nights. Despite these daunting demands, a shared desire to inspire new campaigns of spiritually anchored eco-activism compelled each writer to embrace the task of telling these powerful stories in defense of a sacred Earth. For their courage and sacrifice, I am grateful.

I'm also grateful to each of the movements that welcomed me into their communities to hear their stories, share in their work, and take part in their rituals of resistance. I'm especially indebted to my dear friends in Lancaster Against Pipelines and the Adorers of the Blood of Christ. You have radically expanded my understanding of both family and spiritual community.

Financial and logistical support for this project came from a number of sources, beginning with a generous research grant from the Louisville Institute. I'm grateful to Montclair State University for a sabbatical to conduct crucial research for this project. I specifically want to thank my colleagues in the Religion Department, my fellow codirectors of the Native American and Indigenous Studies Program, and students in my courses who helped me to think more deeply about these case studies through our many classroom conversations. This project was also sustained by the generous support and steady encouragement of Don and Bobbie Gallagher.

My deepest gratitude goes to my partner, Malinda, and daughter, Hannah, for all the ways they supported me through this process, even when various challenges threatened to derail it—from our family's six-year involvement in an all-consuming pipeline resistance campaign to the trials of COVID. But even more, I thank them for helping me through the darkest days of our shared grief following the death of our son and brother, Ashton Myles Clatterbuck. They gave me the strength to finish this project when my own strength was not enough.

This book is dedicated to Ashton. He lived a life of fierce compassion and tireless community organizing. Environmental justice and transgender rights were two of his greatest passions. He led marches, spoke at rallies, directed support groups, published opinion pieces, endured multiple arrests, and poured his life into direct-action campaigns to build a kinder, safer, greener world for all of us. He was fearless, principled, inspiring, kindhearted, quirky, and wise beyond his years. He was an incomparable force for good in this world.

He died by suicide in 2024 at the age of twenty-two. Despite his boundless energy for change, our Earth-killing system of capitalism, the cruelty of MAGA politics, toxic theologies of hate, and pervasive anti-trans bigotry combined to create an unlivable environment for him. This book is for Ash. This book is for young Earth defenders everywhere. It's for all trans kids living in dangerous times, who are simply asking for a world they can live with. It's for all young people who are losing hope that tomorrow can be better than today. They are the ones who keep me tethered to the work of sacred resistance.

Introduction

Mark Clatterbuck

How It Started

This is a book about spiritual communities engaged in creative, impactful, nonviolent campaigns of environmental activism. Every contributor to this project hopes that it supports the spread of sacred resistance movements that are rippling across the country today. This collection of case studies is deliberately designed to be accessible to a broad audience. It is especially well suited for college classrooms, seminaries, and religious communities, as well as book clubs or individuals who are interested in the power of grassroots movements to defend the sacred Earth in an age of climate crisis. The case-study format was chosen to spark lively group discussions, offer models of ritual resistance, and stretch our collective imagination in the service of nonviolent change-making.

The voices and stories captured in these pages are inspiring, honest, complex, and often surprising. They are filled with pain and hope: pain over the industrial violence being inflicted against local communities and the natural world, and hope that people of moral courage can imagine, and then create together, a different vision for the future.

To state the obvious, not all spiritualities or religious traditions lead to ecojustice activism. In fact, some actually condemn it. While attending a youth-led climate march a few years back, a local street preacher tried to drown out the speakers with an apocalyptic tirade. When I asked him why he was so upset, he said that God's going to "burn it all up anyway," so why waste time protecting a doomed planet when there are souls to save from hellfire? Other detractors of spiritually grounded eco-activism argue that the work, even if noble for others, belongs outside the domain of religious duty. When an order of Earth-loving Catholic Sisters in my hometown joined a direct-action campaign to block construction of a new fossil fuel pipeline, Catholic priests in the diocese scolded them for taking part in the movement, condemning their participation as a politically motivated distraction from their true religious calling.[1]

But perhaps the most pervasive reason for religious opposition to ecojustice work is less theological or ecclesiastical, and more political. Pew Survey findings from 2022 show how US political polarization has become deeply entwined in religious groups' views on global warming and broader environmental concerns.[2] For example, Donald Trump's most dependably supportive religious demographic of white Evangelical Christians consistently expresses the greatest skepticism about human-caused global warming, while self-described agnostics and atheists, in addition to non-Christians, not only express the greatest concern about human-made climate change but overwhelmingly identify as Democrats. In my own rural Pennsylvania

---

[1] Despite the outsized impact generated by antienvironmental voices within Christian circles, important efforts are underway to recover the Earth-loving spirituality to be found in the texts, voices, and theologies of Christianity through the centuries. One of the most intriguing recent works of constructive Christian ecotheology is Mark I. Wallace, *When God Was a Bird: Christianity, Animism, and the Re-enchantment of the World* (New York: Fordham University Press, 2019).

[2] See Becka A. Alper, "How Religion Intersects with Religious Americans' Views on the Environment," Pew Research Center, November 17, 2022.

county of Lancaster, where Republicans outnumber Democrats two-to-one, it's hard for many religious folks to escape the identity politics that drive antienvironmentalism, even if their own personal faith or connection to the land would otherwise make them receptive to the work.

But, even among religious communities that express a deep concern for the natural world, there is often a yawning chasm between concern and action. A growing corpus of literature is exploring this dynamic, including *Inspired Sustainability: Planting Seeds for Action* (2016) by Erin Lothes Biviano. Through focus groups consisting of ecoconscious individuals belonging to a wide range of religious communities, Lothes Biviano explores how even participants who express strong convictions about protecting the environment routinely fail to translate those sentiments into action—a pattern she calls "the green blues."[3]

In some ways, this project picks up where *Inspired Sustainability* ends. The communities explored in *Sacred Resistance* have managed to make the leap from theoretical concern to concrete action, offering examples of how religious communities and individuals can overcome the obstacles that so often lead to "the green blues." This book examines how these communities turned conviction into action, including how underlying spiritual assumptions motivated and informed that action. It also explores how multiple spiritual traditions operating within a single eco-activist movement interact with one another, often in simultaneously tensive and highly effective ways.

This project is a natural outgrowth of my own involvement in a spiritually grounded ecojustice movement. That movement is the subject of the second chapter. The threat of a fracked gas pipeline through rural Pennsylvania, where my family

---

[3] Erin Lothes Biviano, *Inspired Sustainability: Planting Seeds for Action* (Maryknoll, NY: Orbis Books, 2016).

resides, motivated a diverse coalition of local residents to organize in opposition. My partner Malinda and I were among the cofounders of Lancaster Against Pipelines (LAP), the nonprofit that led the grassroots fight. At the time, she was pastoring at a progressive Mennonite church where our family attended and whose mission included a strong commitment to environmental stewardship. Like us, the vast majority of LAP members were motivated in large part by spiritual conviction to join the resistance—Mennonites, Quakers, Presbyterians, Amish. As time went on, a Buddhist sangha and members of a local Reform Jewish congregation joined the fight, as well as the Adorers of the Blood of Christ, an order of ecojustice Catholic Sisters whose farmland lay in the pipeline's path. Together, we built an interfaith Chapel of Resistance in the middle of a cornfield, directly in the path of construction. That humble sacred structure became the site of weekly vigils, hymn sings, prayer services, rallies, and nonviolent direct actions resulting in more than two dozen arrests.

Given the movement's saturation in religious ceremonies and spiritual rhetoric, I was struck by the participation of so many neighbors who described themselves as nonreligious even while being deeply engaged in the mission, convictions, and actions of the movement. This included regular participation in explicitly religious ceremonies of resistance, like taking part in a Stations of the Cross blockade during Lent or a disruptive eucharistic feast in the middle of an active construction zone. Despite five years of costly resistance, the pipeline was installed. But what endured was an extraordinary community of people transformed through shared sacrifice in service to a sacred cause. This project was born of my experience in that sacred cause.

This book was also born of Standing Rock. As recorded in the following chapters, each of the movements featured in this collection are children of the #NoDAPL phenomenon. The global impact of Standing Rock on environmental activism is hard to overstate. It's no mere coincidence that all the central themes examined in this project—spirit-grounded activism, rituals of resistance, a strict ethos of nonviolence, intersectional awareness, the conspicuous leadership of women—all had their predecessors at Standing Rock.

For one week in the fall of 2016, my sixteen-year-old son Ashton and I joined the thousands of Water Protectors who converged at Camp Oceti Sakowin in North Dakota to fight the Dakota Access Pipeline. Our own pipeline fight in Pennsylvania was in full swing, and we felt compelled to stand in solidarity with the Native-led resistance growing at the edge of the Standing Rock Sioux Reservation. The prayers and ceremonies left a lasting impression on me. At sunrise each morning, we were awakened in our tents to the sound of a drum and voice crying, "It's time to wake up! We're not here to camp, we're here to pray!" Ceremonies of water, fire, sweetgrass, and songs filled the air from morning to night.

The combination of moral authority, fearlessness, and mass actions at Standing Rock unmasked the intimate complicity that weds violent extractive industries and the US settler colonial state. My son and I witnessed a sacred Lakota pipe ceremony interrupted by bulldozers desecrating ancestral graves and centuries-old sacred sites. We watched as private security guards unleashed attack dogs on mothers, elders, and children who risked their bodies to stop the assault. We watched local police leaning against their patrol cars, doing nothing as the bloody scene unfolded. Through it all, the elders, the mothers, the children, and their fathers chased the bulldozers for two miles across the prairie, using only their bodies and their prayers and their songs.

Standing Rock was grounded in the conviction that we're engaged in a spiritual struggle to protect this sacred Earth. In the first chapter, you'll hear voices from the Anishinaabe-led #StopLine3 movement who describe the specter of ecological violence as the spirit of Wiindigo, a monster born of greed that consumes its victims.[4]

The stories that follow are filled with everyday spiritual warriors who dared to confront the threat of Wiindigo when it came knocking at their door. They are stories of powerful, prayerful, painful sacrifice arising from newly formed communities of deeply shared values. These are the stories of sacred resistance.

Five Movements

The primary concern of this book is eco-activism, rather than ecotheology. There is a growing corpus of excellent literature dedicated to green theologies, whether examining existing theologies or constructing new ones. These works often argue that a commitment to environmental justice is not only consistent with the teachings of the world's religions but constitutes a moral imperative within them.[5] There are also a number of fine

---

[4] There are many excellent works by Native American authors on how ongoing industrial violence against the Earth is directly linked to this nation's history of genocidal violence against Indigenous people and theft of tribal lands. A few include: Jace Weaver (Cherokee), ed., *Defending Mother Earth: Native American Perspectives on Environmental Justice* (Maryknoll, NY: Orbis Books, 1996); Winona LaDuke (Mississippi Band Anishinaabeg), *All Our Relations: Native Struggles for Land and Life* (Cambridge, MA: South End Press, 1999); Dina Gilio-Whitaker (Coleville Confederated Tribes), *As Long as Grass Grows: The Indigenous Fight for Environmental Justice, from Colonization to Standing Rock* (Boston: Beacon Press, 2019); Nick Estes (Lower Brule Sioux), *Our History Is the Future: Standing Rock versus the Dakota Access Pipeline, and the Long Tradition of Indigenous Resistance* (London: Verso, 2019).

[5] As one example, in his encyclical *Laudato Si': On Care for Our Common Home* (2015), Pope Francis writes that Christians who lack environmental concern need to have an "ecological conversion." He then adds,

works highlighting faith groups that are deeply engaged in low-stakes activities designed to lighten humanity's footprint on the natural world, such as solar panel installation, recycling efforts, gardening, and water conservation.[6]

While *Sacred Resistance* certainly contains theological reflection and examples of eco-concern that stop short of civil disobedience, this project is primarily concerned with the lived experiences of frontline spiritual communities engaged in direct-action campaigns for environmental justice. More specifically, this collection is organized around five recent case studies of grassroots environmental activism across the United States in which participants self-consciously understood their resistance work as spiritual action. Readers are invited to bring their own analysis, questions, and theological considerations to these stories through group discussion and personal reflection. Here is a quick overview of the case studies.

Anishinaabe-Led #StopLine3, Tar Sands Oil Pipeline, Minnesota

For the Anishinaabe people, northern Minnesota is known as Akiing, "the land to which the people belong." For thousands of years, the Indigenous people of the region have understood their relationship to the natural landscape in spiritual terms, rendering protection of the land a sacred duty. After white settlers forcibly seized control of the territory, tribal citizens nonetheless retained a legal right to hunt, fish, plant, and gather on their

---

"Our vocation to be protectors of God's handiwork is essential to a life of virtue; it is not an optional or secondary aspect of our Christian experience" (§217).

[6] See, for example, Sarah McFarland Taylor, *Green Sisters: A Spiritual Ecology* (Cambridge, MA: Harvard University Press, 2007).

ancestral lands through a series of nineteenth-century treaties between the Anishinaabe people and the US government. This included the right to grow and harvest Manoomin (wild rice), which plays a central role in Anishinaabe society and culture. The 2013 announcement by Enbridge to force a major tar sands oil pipeline through treaty territory—including through tribal rice fields and traditional hunting grounds—represented a direct assault on Anishinaabe treaty rights, cultural integrity, and tribal sovereignty. It also posed a grave threat to Mississippi River, the lifeblood of the region, by pumping thirty-two million gallons of tar sands oil daily through numerous river crossings.

A coalition of Native and non-Native groups in the region organized a massive grassroots campaign to resist the project. Their movement drew inspiration from #NoDAPL at Standing Rock, which provided a powerful model of spiritually grounded, Indigenous-led pipeline resistance. Enbridge had anticipated the opposition, putting $8.6 million in escrow to pay law enforcement to serve as private security at their construction sites and to fund police suppression of the grassroots resistance. The #StopLine3 movement built a multipronged campaign, pursuing legal, regulatory, educational, and public relations strategies. It also organized a huge direct-action campaign that involved mass training sessions, six resistance camps, and a steady stream of disruptive actions that resulted in more than one thousand arrests of peaceful pipeline opponents.

The first chapter examines the diverse spiritualities animating the #StopLine3 campaign. Coauthors Winona LaDuke (Anishinaabe) and Julia Nerbonne tell the story of Anishinaabe women building a traditional Midewin lodge in the pipeline construction corridor to offer prayers of protection for the land and water until they were arrested midceremony. Readers also learn about the founding of Firelight Camp, another ceremonial site established by Indigenous women to confront the desecration of Line 3. The authors explore the extensive interfaith collaborations that developed during the campaign, the ongoing failure of courts to defend Native American religious rights, and the efforts of faith communities to shape environmental policies at the state and federal levels to better align with spiritually informed respect for the Earth.

Adorers of the Blood of Christ and Lancaster Against Pipelines, Fracked Gas Pipeline, Pennsylvania

As noted earlier in this Introduction, the second chapter tells the story of Catholic Sisters who joined a grassroots direct-action movement to block construction of a new fossil-fuel pipeline through rural Pennsylvania. When an Oklahoma-based pipeline company announced plans in 2014 to build a high-volume fracked gas pipeline through two hundred miles of Pennsylvania's farmlands, forests, watersheds, and communities, local residents created Lancaster Against Pipelines (LAP) to block the project. Although LAP was a federal nonprofit with no formal ties to religion, spiritual rhetoric permeated the movement. Leaders openly regarded resistance work as a sacred duty, framing the standoff as a battle between ultimate values. Appeals to the sacred, faith, and care of Creation were ubiquitous themes of speeches, emails, and social media posts. LAP's work was also marked by a strict commitment to peaceful action as informed by the region's deep roots in Anabaptist pacifism.

The Adorers of the Blood of Christ were among the property owners whose farmland lay in the pipeline's path. A pontifical institute of vowed Catholic Sisters, the Adorers embrace a strong ecojustice ethic as a core element of their religious charism. Moved by LAP's shared values, and compelled by the courage of Indigenous Water Protectors at Standing Rock, the Sisters partnered with LAP's direct-action campaign to fight the Atlantic Sunrise Pipeline. At the center of their shared resistance was a rustic outdoor prayer chapel that they built directly in the construction corridor. The Chapel of Resistance, as it came to be known, gave visible expression to the Sisters' spiritual opposition to the pipeline. It quickly became a pilgrimage site for spiritually motivated ecojustice seekers, a gathering place for weekly vigils declaring climate justice as a spiritual imperative, and a physical blockade against pipeline construction that resulted in twenty-nine arrests during a series of nonviolent direct actions.

The alliance between these two groups offers a poignant example of how new, tightly bound communities are emerging in grassroots ecojustice movements around a shared set of ultimate values that transcend institutional religious identities. Catholics, Mennonites, Quakers, Buddhists, Jews, nonreligious, and even antireligious folks joined together at the chapel each week for prayers, songs, testimonies, silence, and the reading of religious texts, united in a shared commitment to defend the sacred Earth. The chapter also examines the movement's efforts to block the pipeline through religious freedom protections in federal court, as well as the gender divide within the Catholic Church over environmental justice concerns.

The Mauna Kea Thirty Meter Telescope Blockade, Hawai'i

The Native Hawaiian movement to block construction of the Thirty Meter Telescope (TMT) on Mauna Kea's summit, on the Big Island of Hawai'i, is the subject of the third chapter. TMT is an extremely large telescope (ELT) project funded by an international coalition of universities, scientists, and governments. For more than a decade, the project has faced persistent opposition from Kanaka 'Ōiwi (Native Hawaiians), who regard the project as a desecration of the sacred mountain. Opposition to the TMT is also driven by a number of other factors. For many ʻŌiwi, the project merely extends the legacy of US imperialism on the Hawaiian islands, represents a disregard for Native Hawaiian tradition and culture, and threatens significant disruption to the mountain's already endangered ecosystem.

Dr. Marie Alohalani Brown, professor of religion at the University of Hawaiʻi (Mānoa) and the chapter's author, is a Kanaka ʻŌiwi and one of the kūpuna (elders) who held space at Mauna Kea to protect the mountain from desecration. She focuses her attention on the blockade and encampment along the summit's access road that effectively halted construction through 2019 and into early 2020. Those efforts raised international awareness about the threats TMT posed to Native Hawaiian religious practices, cultural ways, sovereignty, and the island's delicately balanced ecosystem. Due largely to pressure generated by the resistance movement, construction remains stalled to this day and faces an uncertain future as funders continue to withdraw their support amid the controversy.

Dr. Brown explains why Kanaka ʻŌiwi regard Mauna Kea as sacred, how Hawaiian cultural beliefs informed the tone and tactics of the resistance movement (as exemplified in the movement motto "sacred mountain, sacred conduct"), and how traditional Hawaiian pule (prayer or chants) and hula grounded the movement while doubling as powerful tools of nonviolent resistance.

Interspiritual Resistance, Atlantic Coast Pipeline, Virginia

The successful, spiritually anchored campaign to derail the Atlantic Coast Pipeline (ACP) is the subject of chapter 4. In keeping with the long-standing American tradition of locating the most toxic industrial threats in low-income communities of color, Dominion Energy chose to locate the ACP's sole Virginia-based compressor station—with its ear-splitting noise and dangerous levels of air pollution—in the majority (84 percent) Black community of Union Hill. As the authors put it, "The project was racist, land destroying, water contaminating, air poisoning, community fracturing, and climate destroying." These stories, therefore, offer both a poignant case study in environmental racism and an inspiring model for successful spiritually oriented community organizing.

The chapter was coauthored by two women who were deeply involved in the six-year fight that ended in 2020, when Dominion and Duke Energy suspended their plan to build the six-hundred-mile gas pipeline through parts of West Virginia, Virginia, and North Carolina. Heidi Dhivya Berthoud is a founding member of Friends of Buckingham, a grassroots nonprofit created to oppose the ACP, as well as cofounder of Virginia Community Rights Network. Her passion for environmental justice is rooted in the spirituality of Wicca and other Gaia-centered goddess traditions, as well as the ancient wisdom of Integral Yoga. Swami Dayananda is a Hindu monastic serving the Satchidananda Ashram–Yogaville, whose childhood in Japan was permeated by Shinto and Buddhist influences. Her friendship with the Baptist pastor of a local African American congregation formed the foundation of an unlikely pipeline-fighting alliance between Yogis and Baptists. Together, they tell a story of extraordinary interspiritual coordination of ecojustice activism to defeat a $4 billion industrial threat.

Their account spotlights the movement's unwavering commitment to nonviolence, even while examining how individual participants wrestled with conflicting understandings of the concept when planning strategies of resistance. The writers also highlight the steep costs associated with years-long direct-action campaigns. We learn that the degree of sacrifice involved with such grassroots movements is a key contributing factor in generating the transformative power often experienced within eco-activist communities, leading participants to frame the work in spiritual terms.

Earth Quaker Action Team, Mountaintop Removal Coal Mining, Appalachia

The book's final case study examines the successful movement that was led by Earth Quaker Action Team (EQAT) to pressure PNC Bank to stop financing mountaintop removal coal mining in Appalachia. Lina Blount and Eileen Flanagan, the coauthors of the chapter, are both longtime leaders in EQAT, with extensive experience in community organizing and nonviolent direct-action campaigns. Quakers have utilized the tactic of noncooperation to confront social injustice for centuries. First in England and then in the American colonies, many Quakers defied oppressive laws and faced severe persecution, including imprisonment and execution, for their faith-driven opposition to religious intolerance, slavery, the oppression of women, and other injustices.

Rooted in this long tradition, EQAT was founded in 2010 to advocate for environmental justice using nonviolent direct-action tactics guided by Quaker values. The organization made the strategic decision to turn its attention on PNC Bank, a historically Quaker business and one of the largest financial backers of Appalachian mountaintop removal coal mining. They named the campaign "BLAM!" for "Bank Like Appalachia Matters!" The five-year campaign organized a series of 125 direct actions across thirteen states, guided by the Quaker values of integrity, truth-telling, nonviolence, decentralized leadership, and interfaith collaboration. Many of their actions took place on-site at PNC banks. EQAT members would suddenly flood a lobby while holding signs announcing PNC's deadly support for mountaintop removal coal mining. The group would form a circle, have a seat on the floor, and enter into a time of Quaker-style "silent worship" before closing with a sacred song or social movement anthem. The tactic often caught bank staff, security personnel, and police officers off guard, shifting the power from those who had the legal authority to arrest to those holding moral and spiritual authority.

In the end, PNC withdrew its support for mountaintop removal coal mining in Appalachia, demonstrating the power of spiritually anchored eco-activism. Following the success of BLAM!, EQAT is now leading the direct-action wing of an international effort to disrupt financial support for fossil fuels by the global asset manager Vanguard, the largest financial backer of fossil fuels in the world. Once again, Quaker values are guiding the movement's organizational decision making, campaign strategies, and direct-action tactics. The twin beliefs that there is "that of God" in everyone and that action-for-justice is, itself, a form of worship animate all of their work.

Five Themes

The Sacred

The resistance referred to in the title of this book is described as "sacred" for good reason. I toyed with a number of other options, including "holy," "religious," and "faith-based." Yet each of these labels proved problematic. The word "holy" panders too much to notions of purity or legalism, failing to capture the spirit of gritty engagement with dangerous forces that marks each of these movements. The term "religious" was a nonstarter for the many movement participants who do not identify with any organized religion. "Faith-based" felt too exclusively associated with Christianity or, more broadly, traditions marked by loyalty to theological statements of faith—a poor fit for those practicing less dogmatic paths like Indigenous ceremonial ways or Wicca, among others.

More than anything else, a stated commitment to defend the sacred unites the five campaigns that are examined in this book. While attending mass actions organized by each of these movements, I encountered calls to "defend the sacred" painted on banners, declared during marches, and uttered in prayers. The term is used across these movements not merely to indicate that the health of our planet is worth fighting for, but it is worth sacrificing everything to protect. Although the five movements featured in this book target different threats (pipelines, telescopes, coal mining), take place in different parts of the so-called United States (Minnesota, Pennsylvania, Hawai'i, Appalachia, Central Virginia), and are shaped by different spiritual traditions (e.g., Hindu, Quaker, Indigenous), they share a common conviction that the Earth is sacred and, therefore, action to protect the natural world is a fundamental moral and spiritual duty of every human. In this context, the work of resistance itself is understood as sacred conduct. As the Catholic Sister Bernice Klostermann says of her involvement in pipeline-blocking direct actions, "They were such sacred moments."

These case studies introduce us to individuals who have made enormous sacrifices to prevent desecration of the lands, waters, forests, ancestral rice fields, and mountains that they regard as sacred. In the process, they have sacrificed jobs, relationships, homes, family time, sleep, and their own physical and mental well-being. Many sacrificed their reputations or future career prospects by risking arrest and jail time. Some risked felony charges.

The urge to "defend the sacred" functions in these movements as that which is worth pursuing and protecting above all else, the priority around which all other aspects of life are organized. It is of "ultimate concern" akin to the sense articulated by the theologian Paul Tillich, for whom the very definition of faith is a concern that claims ultimacy and "demands the total surrender of [the one] who accepts this claim."[7] While at Mauna Kea, I asked a young Native Hawaiian participant what brought her to the encampment and blockade. Without hesitation she replied, "I felt like this was my destiny. And I feel so honored to fulfill my destiny. People search a whole lifetime to figure out their 'why.' I always felt like I knew it was coming."

This collection of case studies, therefore, challenges traditional boundaries that are often used to define the category of religion, expanding common notions of what "counts" as religion in American life. For example, these movements are filled with individuals who speak of the sacred, describe their activism as a spiritual imperative, frame their arrestable behaviors of resistance as ceremony, claiming all of it as an expression of their avowed religious commitments—whether Roman Catholic or Buddhist or Anishinaabe. Others, however, make identical claims about the spiritual imperative driving their eco-activism, all while explicitly rejecting any affiliation with organized religion. What does this suggest about the nature of religion in the US popular imagination today?

These case studies also shine a spotlight on legal battles involving spiritually motivated civil disobedience, which far too often is neither recognized nor safeguarded under religious liberty protections in US federal courts. Despite the fact that four of the five movements examined in this project filed

---

[7] Paul Tillich, *Dynamics of Faith* (New York: Harper, 1957), 1.

religiously motivated legal challenges to stop the environmental threats fueling their campaigns, not a single judge acknowledged the merits of their religion-based claims. A growing number of legal observers have noted the increased willingness of US federal courts to extend religious liberty protections to groups engaged in conservative social issues (e.g. abortion bans, or denying transgender youth basic antidiscrimination protections) while, at the same time, failing to acknowledge the religious liberty claims of those seeking religious liberty protections for their work on more progressive social issues (e.g. ecojustice, or immigrant rights).

In these ways and more, this project contributes meaningfully to broad conversations on the category of religion itself—namely, what counts as religion, in which contexts, and who gets to decide?

Rituals of Resistance

Another key theme of this project is the relationship between ecojustice work and spiritual ceremonies. In each of the chapters that follow, we find eco-activism taking the form of ritual behavior in at least two ways.

First, there's a theoretical sense in which eco-activism functions as ritual. Due to the fact that participants routinely understand their commitment to defending the Earth as a sacred duty, virtually all activity related to ecojustice work is understood in sacralized terms. As a consequence, explicitly religious activities like prayer and meditation on behalf of the Earth are regarded as sacred rituals, and even activities typically considered secular are performed as holy acts in the service of a sacred task. In the chapter "Circles of Protection," karma yoga assumes the form of writing the movement's monthly newsletter. While at the Mauna Kea blockade, I spoke with a young Native Hawaiian activist who, through tears of joy, described the task of cleaning the portable latrines as a sacred chore.

The second way in which resistance-as-ritual is explored in this book is more concrete. Namely, one of the most striking aspects of these movements is the variety of ways that performing sacred ceremonies doubled as ritualized acts of civil disobedience to defend Earth. Direct-action tactics have long been used in environmental activist circles to block or delay destructive industrial projects. These include structural blockades, body blockades, lockboxes, tree sits, tripods, and many more tactics.[8] What we're seeing among spiritually grounded campaigns of resistance is a new and distinct tactic that centers the performance of sacred rituals in the context of direct-action campaigns.[9]

In the first chapter, we meet Anishinaabe women establishing a prayer camp in a pipeline construction zone at the headwaters of Mississippi River, as well as building a traditional *Midewiwin* prayer lodge in a wooded location likewise targeted for desecration by the pipeline. Inside the lodge, the women offered prayers for the Earth until police arrested them midceremony. In the second chapter, readers encounter a rustic cornfield chapel built directly in the path of a high-volume transmission pipeline to give visible expression to their inner conviction to "honor the sacredness of all Creation." In the third chapter, we meet Native Hawaiian elders on the sacred mountain of Mauna Kea who

---

[8] For more, see *Earth First! Direct Action Manual*, 3rd ed. (Chico, CA: AK Press, 2015).

[9] For an excellent recent work on the ritual behavior of eco-activist and radical animal rights communities, see Sarah M. Pike, *For the Wild: Ritual and Commitment in Radical Eco-Activism* (Oakland: University of California Press, 2017). Although the movements examined in Pike's book are not explicitly religious, many of her findings resonate deeply with the experiences described in the following case studies.

effectively blocked construction of the Thirty Meter Telescope by transforming the lone access road up the mountain into a ceremonial site of sacred drumming, chants, and hula, anchored by an encampment of elders. In the fourth chapter, a Wiccan spiral dance forms a "circle of protection" against yet another pipeline project in Virginia. Finally, in the fifth chapter, a spontaneous Quaker-style prayer meeting doubles as a bank lobby blockade, disrupting the immoral financing of mountaintop removal coal mining in Appalachia.

Prayerful, joyful, disciplined acts of ritual resistance provide a stark juxtaposition to the violent acts of industrial destruction facing the landscapes we all call home. This contrast is a key reason why these acts are so powerful. They are holy theatre, transforming sites of environmental destruction into outdoor stages where the faithful enact an alternative vision for the future. A future where we love water more than oil. A future where laws respect the inherent right of forests and rivers to flourish. A future where the National Guard and law enforcement defend local communities against large-scale acts of industrial contamination, rather than facilitate our collective annihilation by serving as private security for toxic corporate actors. A future where the actions of fossil-fuel billionaires and multinational corporations are who and what we criminalize, rather than prayerful protests to protect the water, land, and air that we depend on for life itself. Participants in the actions describe feelings of joy, empowerment, and solidarity with fellow resisters, aligned across religious and spiritual traditions by shared moral outrage and a profound sense that the Earth is sacred. Many of the voices that fill these chapters regard civil disobedience as the only remaining option to exercise agency in the face of regulatory, political, and judicial systems that have been designed to legalize—rather than prevent—large-scale corporate destruction of the Earth.

Nonviolence

A strict commitment to nonviolence marks every movement described in this book. Leaders at the Mauna Kea telescope blockade required all participants to observe kapu aloha, which is behaving with love and compassion in both words and actions, exactly as one would behave during a ceremony. While confronting the Atlantic Coast Pipeline in Virginia, yogis appealed to Gandhi's example of ahimsa while Baptists looked to Rev. Martin Luther King Jr. as a model of nonviolent resistance. Leaders of EQAT called members to see "that of God" in everyone, urging peaceful and respectful behavior, no matter how tense a direct action might become. The Catholic Sisters at the Chapel of Resistance in Pennsylvania urged participants to confront pipeline workers with "nonviolence" and even "reverence," asking the question "How do I find God in my enemy?"

Despite unanimity among the movements concerning the importance of nonviolence as a spiritual and strategic principle, the following case studies offer conflicting points of view when it comes to defining that principle in practical terms. For some, cursing at a pipeline worker or turning one's back on a fossil-fuel representative during a public meeting are unacceptable acts of violence. Others believe that there is room to embrace far more disruptive, aggressive tactics within a nonviolent ethos, arguing that the scale of assault against the natural world demands a decidedly bold defense.

When an Indigenous woman elder fighting the Line 3 pipeline screams at pipeline workers, "Rapists! Murderers! Killers of Mother Earth!" one Catholic observer is taken aback, uncomfortable with the confrontation. But further reflection leads the troubled listener to reassess her initial disapproval, instead discovering "the heartbeat of God" in the elder's spontaneous expression of outrage and pain. Indeed, many of the activist voices you'll .

hear in the following pages are frustrated with the prevailing reticence of many religious communities to embrace confrontation despite the urgency of the climate crisis. Some regard the tendency of religious congregations to "avoid controversy" and "follow the rules" as complicity in ecoviolence. They note that corporate perpetrators of violence against the Earth have rigged the system to "legalize" their acts of destruction, all while hiding behind laws that increasingly criminalize grassroots opposition that dares to interfere with construction, confront workers, or disobey industry-serving police. As they see it, religious folks who claim to love the Earth but refuse to challenge the very rules of engagement that facilitate Earth's destruction—all under the pretense of protecting their religious reputation—are displaying not sanctity but cowardice.

For some activists in these movements, a commitment to peace may even justify destroying tools of violence, whether damaging a warhead that's intended for innocent civilians or disabling a bulldozer that's installing a planet-killing pipeline. As one Catholic Worker puts it, "There's a place for yelling and property destruction" within spiritually grounded peace work, adding, "No justice, no peace. In the name of good order, a lot of atrocities have been left unaddressed."

The voices that organically arise in these pages, therefore, offer a powerful exploration on the nature, meaning, and limits of nonviolent resistance in an age of catastrophic threats to the natural world, vulnerable communities, and a livable future for our children.

Intersectionality

The inseparability of environmental activism from other arenas of social justice work is another key theme of this project. Kimberlé Crenshaw is generally credited for coining the term "intersectionality" in 1989 as a powerful lens for analyzing the ways in which intersecting minority identities are related to systems of oppression. Those identities include race, economic status, gender, sexuality, class, religion, and age, among others. Crenshaw's initial application of the concept was in reference to the complex pattern of discrimination suffered by Black women, arguing that isolated examinations of discrimination against women and against Blacks fail to account for the harms inflicted on individuals and communities suffering from overlapping systems of oppression. In Crenshaw's analysis, intersectionality is not simply a matter of belonging to multiple identities. Instead, it's about institutions and systems using identity to exclude, oppress, and exploit for the benefit of those who already enjoy privilege and power.[10]

Acknowledging the grim reality of intersectional oppression, this book situates spiritually inspired eco-activism in the broader context of social justice issues roiling US society today. Each movement examined in this book demonstrates how exploitation of the natural world is directly linked to violence against communities of color, women, victims of poverty, LGBTQ+ individuals, children, religious minorities, and other marginalized people.[11] These case studies also identify three systems as being primarily responsible for these overlapping patterns of oppression: settler colonialism, white supremacy, and US capitalism.

---

[10] Crenshaw first articulated her theory of intersectionality in Kimberlé Crenshaw, "Demarginalizing the Intersection of Race and Sex: A Black Feminist Critique of Antidiscrimination Doctrine, Feminist Theory and Antiracist Politics," *University of Chicago Legal Forum* 1989, no. 1 (Article 8): 139–167.

[11] See Amanda J. Baugh, *God and the Green Divide: Religious Environmentalism in Black and White* (Oakland: University of California Press, 2016), for an important ethnography on the role that race, ethnicity, and class play in the history and current state of religious environmentalism.

This helps to explain why Native Hawaiian elders opposing the TMT on a sacred, ecologically sensitive mountain talk about US imperialism as much as they talk about cultural erasure and ecological devastation. It's also why the #StopLine3 campaign in Anishinaabe territory is simultaneously an ecojustice campaign, an anticolonial treaty rights campaign, and a movement to fight the epidemic of Murdered and Missing Indigenous Women (MMIW). This is because the forced installation of fossil fuel pipelines across America disproportionately—and intentionally—target not only Indigenous lands but the Indigenous women, girls, and two-spirit individuals living on those lands due to the rampant sexual violence associated with the "man camps" that operate along construction corridors. It also explains why EQAT members fighting mountaintop-removal coal mining in Appalachia spent so much time reflecting on gender equality within their movement while simultaneously confronting the billionaire bankers funding the region's ecological destruction. Intersectional theory likewise informed the Virginia-based fight to block the Atlantic Coast Pipeline, where African American Baptists saw the pipeline not only as an assault on water and air but as an extension of racist US economic development policies consistently locating the worst industrial harms in communities of color. All of these movements understand that, when fighting for justice in any arena, chances are pretty good that we're battling the same forces responsible for oppression in every other arena.

A study of spiritually grounded eco-activism in the United States requires paying attention to how a growing number of religious communities are situating that fight within a larger web of social justice campaigns. These narratives provide compelling portraits of what spirit-based intersectional theory looks like when put into practice.

A commitment to exploring the nature of intersectionality in ecojustice work also accounts for my decision to center the voices of women in these five case studies. This is why all the contributors to this collection of essays, with the exception of myself, identify as women. It's also why the voices featured in interviews throughout the chapters are overwhelmingly those of women. This was an intentional decision reflecting the fact that all of these movements were led primarily by women. My choice to foreground the voices and experiences of women was also informed by the reality that women disproportionately serve on the front lines of direct-action environmental justice campaigns globally, despite being at far greater risk of experiencing violence in these positions compared to their male counterparts. Centering women's voices in the telling of these stories is all the more important given the role that entrenched patriarchy plays in perpetuating corporate violence and in propping up the male-dominated legislative, legal, military, and law enforcement systems that defend that exploitation, as these case studies repeatedly highlight.

New Spiritual Communities

One of the most captivating aspects of the following case studies is the variety of interreligious and extrareligious spiritual communities that were formed in the crucible of grassroots eco-activism. Black evangelical Baptists joined Hindu swamis to challenge a fracked gas pipeline. Roman Catholic nuns, Plum Village–inspired Buddhists, and self-proclaimed religious nones stood side by side singing "Amazing Grace" while blocking bulldozers at a makeshift cornfield chapel. Jewish faith leaders joined Indigenous women elders conducting a water ceremony to disrupt pipeline construction at Mississippi River. Furthermore, these tightly knit communities often consisted of individuals who, before the campaigns began, were largely strangers to one another.

Each of the writers in this volume gives special consideration to the formation of new spiritual communities that were organically grown in the soil of their movements, radically transcending traditional theological and sectarian divides. These close-knit and rapidly formed new communities are bound not by creedal continuity but rather by a shared commitment to defend a sacred Earth. These dynamic, extrainstitutional communities appear to be consistent with broader trends in religious self-understanding taking place in America today, as indicated by the following observations.

First, these stories offer striking examples of ecojustice functioning as a religious value that overrides theological and institutional differences that typically act as barriers to interfaith community building. Second, the interfaith collaborations displayed in these movements are not limited to community service or campaign event planning. Rather, in the words of participants themselves, the shared experience of ecojustice work itself operates in the realm of worship, leading members of diverse faith traditions into shared religious experiences and mutually transformative ritual activity. Movement members describe how their interfaith encounters via grassroots eco-activism have opened up new ways of seeing the Divine, experiencing the world, and understanding the meaning of their own lives.

Third, the newly formed spiritual communities described in this book often include individuals who do not identify as religious and, in some cases, denounce organized religion altogether. This is why I use the term "extrareligious" alongside "interreligious" to describe the nature of these emergent new communities. Despite their stated position on the category of religion, they constitute a seamless part of these new communities while performing explicitly religious rituals, singing traditional sacred songs, offering prayers of protection, or dancing in sacred hula ceremonies.

A fourth dynamic that deserves further examination is how these newly formed ecospiritual communities operate in relation to participants' existing relationships with more traditional religious bodies. The following narratives provide anecdotal evidence of participation in eco-activist communities deepening members' association with their church, synagogue, or ashram. At the same time, we also have evidence of movement members finding greater fulfillment in eco-activism than they experienced in preexisting religious commitments, sometimes displacing previous religious loyalties.

Finally, these case studies offer a rare opportunity to explore, in very personal terms, the role that shared sacrifice—including shared trauma—may play in creating and reinforcing new spiritual communities. Direct-action campaigns require steep risks and bring heavy sacrifices for those on the front lines. Participants regularly encounter armed security forces, highly militarized police officers, and laws that are hypercriminalizing even peaceful protests in many states. Arrests and jail time are common consequences, as the following stories demonstrate. Grassroots campaigns make enormous demands on members' time, friendships, family life, financial resources, and emotional and physical well-being. Battling global warming in our highly polarized political context also carries social risks, fomenting divisions within social circles and families. This collection of case studies offers examples of savvy industry reps exploiting such divisions in local communities and religious congregations in an effort to undermine collective resistance.

For Indigenous communities, the pain of industrial projects is compounded by the fact that ecoviolence disrupts both individual and communal relationships to ancestral lands. That disruption is often experienced as spiritual assault and cultural dislocation, further extending the intergenerational trauma rooted in centuries of violent dispossession and US-led genocidal campaigns against tribal nations on their own ancestral homelands. These dynamics are recounted by voices in both the #StopLine3 movement and the battle over Mauna Kea.

While shared pain can foment divisions within a community, each of the following case studies illustrates how the experience of protracted, collective sacrifice can also serve as a potent binding agent. As Heidi Dhivya Berthoud explains,

> Many in our local resistance movement talk of still dealing with PTSD. What it takes to be an activist is a heart cracked open by the pain of feeling the sadness, suffering, existential threat, and injustices of the climate crisis and then answering the compelling call. This alone is a powerful unifying force.

Exploring hearts "cracked open" by pain is an unavoidable theme of this project, with special attention to the ways in which that shared sacrifice engenders feelings of spiritual connection.

A Brief Note on Methodology

A number of factors influenced my decision to include the following case studies in this collection. Beyond the central criteria of movements driven by spiritual conviction and marked by religious rhetoric, I was looking for campaigns that had made the leap from environmental advocacy to eco-activism by employing direct-action tactics in their defense of the Earth. I was also interested in identifying movements that had attracted a critical mass of participants and had succeeded in substantially delaying or outright blocking the targeted threat.

Furthermore, I wanted to feature movements that represented different regions of the country, were shaped by a diversity of spiritual traditions, were battling a variety of industrial threats, and were composed of diverse racial demographics. Existing research at the intersection of religion and ecology tends to skew largely toward communities that are Christian and white. I was eager for this project to amplify a more diverse collection of voices and traditions.

During the process of choosing these five movements for inclusion in the project, I spent time on the ground with each community while their respective campaigns were in full swing. I played the role of researcher (conducting interviews, taking field notes and photographs, and making audio recordings when permission was granted) as well as movement participant (attending direct-action training workshops, participating in rituals of resistance, and occasionally filling roles during actions). During these visits, I met the inspiring movement leaders who agreed to author the following chapters for inclusion in this project. David Parry, professor of communications and media studies and a social movement photographer, joined me for many of the trips to produce a visual record of these intensely embodied direct-action campaigns. Beyond the images appearing in this book, a larger collection of high-quality color photographs from these movements can be found at sacredresistancebook.com.

The central themes examined in this project emerged organically through my firsthand observations and conversations with participants. All of the movements were grounded in a commitment to defending the sacred, performed communal rituals as acts of resistance, embraced a strict ethos of nonviolence, and self-consciously understood their ecojustice work as taking place within a framework of intersectionality. In the process of collective resistance, each also produced a new, tightly bound interspiritual community.

Sacred Resistance is not a product of so-called objective or disinterested scholarship. It is, instead, a self-conscious work of advocacy on behalf of grassroots community organizing and direct-action resistance to corporate ecoviolence. By providing examples of creative, bold, nonviolent, spiritually anchored resistance, I hope these case studies inspire a new generation of spiritually grounded eco-activism in our time of deepening climate crisis.

All of the contributors to this collection are leaders in their respective movements. They're also practitioners of one or more spiritual traditions that deeply inform their environmental activism. Their accounts, therefore, spring directly from the trenches of frontline grassroots activism. While each of the writers thinks deeply about movement theory, the focus of these chapters is not theory but practice. As such, the voices and lived experiences of movement members are given priority over the critical analysis of the authors. Put another way, stories from the front lines, more than theorizing from the sidelines, form the heart of this project.

I shared with each writer the list of recurring themes that I observed during my field visits, asking that they give special attention to the ones that most resonated with their own movement. We also made the decision not to shy away from disagreements and contradictions that emerged within movements, hoping to offer readers and their communities real-life examples of how to navigate the inevitable complexities and challenges that emerge while building communities of sacred resistance. In addition to the writers' own firsthand experiences, hundreds of conversations and interviews with fellow movement members provided the material to create these multivocal and deeply layered narratives.

1

WEAVING TOGETHER RESISTANCE
Treaty Rights and Sacred Action to Stop Line 3

Winona LaDuke and Julia Nerbonne

It is sunset on Fishhook Lake in northern Minnesota. Hundreds of faith leaders from across the country have gathered at Northern Pines resort as part of the Treaty People Gathering in resistance to the Line 3 Pipeline. We are in a circle at the water, singing. Some sing clearly, while others hum along:

> Ne-be Gee Zah-gay-egoo
> Gee Me-gwetch wayne ne-me-goo
> Gee Zah Wayn ne-me-goo[1]

We share tobacco, or Asemaa, in a circle, and each offers it with their prayers to the water. The sound ripples across the lake as we offer our gratitude and our commitment to the water.

---

[1] "Water we love you. We thank you. We respect you." Ojibwe words and tune written by Dorene Day, Waubanewquay, Marten Clan, as inspired by the international water prayer taught by Dr. Massaru Emoto at an international water conference. Dorene wrote it on the request of her grandson Omashkoonce when crossing Mississippi every day on their way to school. To hear a recording of the song, see "Nibi Song," Mother Earth Water Walk (website). To hear Dorene discussing the history and meaning of the song, see "The Water Song - The Nibi Song," D-Day, on YouTube.

Tobacco and prayers are offered at the headwaters of Mississippi, Treaty People Gathering. (PHOTO BY DAVID PARRY / USED WITH PERMISSION)

Cameras click. But it doesn't matter. We know something sacred is taking place. Words of different religious leaders follow in turn and remind the group of why we are gathered.

Finally, three stars come to light the sky. Jewish song leaders gather in the shallows of the lake to mark Havdalah, or the separation between Shabbat and the week to come. They share sacred wine, the sweet smell of spices, and the braided candle of the light that reminds us of the interplay of light and shadow that will lead us. Through this ritual we are reminded of the transcendent vision that Shabbat imparts, which is separated from the six days of daily life and work in the world.

Baruch ha-mavdil bein kodesh le-chol.[2]

---

[2] "Blessed are you, Lord, who distinguishes between sacred and profane."

Through sharing in the ceremony, these Jewish leaders welcome the multifaith group as they look forward in anticipation to the days ahead.

Tomorrow will be a big day. Our group will join thousands of others who have come to the White Earth Reservation in northern Minnesota to participate in the Treaty People Gathering, the largest mass protest against the Line 3 pipeline. We will learn about the impact of Line 3, explore Enbridge's broken promises, and hear directly from Native leaders about the age-old treaties that are the law of the land. On Monday, many will march to headwaters of Mississippi River, where Line 3 construction threatens to destroy this sacred river.[3] Some will risk arrest. Others will be there to witness and pray.

History of the Land and People

For thousands of years, Native communities gathered and lived in the land that is now northern Minnesota. This is known as Akiing, "the land to which the people belong" in the Anishinaabe language, and Mni Sota for the Dakota. This is the land both peoples understand and where these peoples have made prayers and agreements with the Creation for generations. Those prayers are a covenant. Northern Minnesota is the most biodiverse region in the state, with an abundance of lakes, pines, hardwoods, and prairies, all of which provide for the people. It is known as the Creator's Garden.[4] Other vegetables and foods—corn and potatoes and other crops—traveled by canoe and foot north from

---

[3] Mississippi River, as opposed to "the Mississippi River," is a common Anishinaabe way to refer to a relative. Water is not an object, but a living relative.

[4] Term first shared with Winona LaDuke by a James Bay Cree elder. Get a taste for what the Creator's Garden offers us through the storytelling of Joseph Pitawanakwat on YouTube.

Mexico to the lands of the Anishinaabe. These foods supple-
mented an economy based on rich wild rice, or Manoomin,
sweetened by hundreds of thousands of pounds of maple sugar
annually. This is indeed a wealthy land.

It is Indakiingimin, "the very land to which the people
belong." Both the Anishinaabe and the Dakota share the concept
of belonging to land. And between the two are shared territories.
In that place, the buffalo existed in multitudes. It is said that one
could ride a horse for three days and see, to your right and to
your left, the same herd. The peoples, both Dakota and Anishinaabe, moved with the food: the maple sugarbushes, the gardens,
the medicines, the buffalo, and the wild rice.

The relationship between the people was reaffirmed in treaties. The One Dish One Spoon Treaty between the Anishinaabe
and Haudenausaunee to the east, for example, acknowledged
that the people fed with one spoon from one shared land. So
they agreed to share the lands.[5] The Sweet Corn Treaty to the
west established a similar shared agreement between the Turtle
Mountain Anishinaabe and the Sisseton and Yankton Dakota.[6]
Those treaties are still intact.

When the white settlers arrived to this land, the Anishinaabe
continued to move seasonally throughout the region, integrating
European American fur traders, particularly the French, into
their communities. However, greed, smallpox, and whiskey
changed the equation. While the Anishinaabe continued to be
the major producers of food for the non-Indians in the region—

---

[5] See Victor P. Lytwyn, "A Dish with One Spoon: The Shared Hunting
Grounds Agreement in the Great Lakes and St. Lawrence Valley Region," *The
Algonquian Papers* 28, no. 16 (1997): 210–227 (Archives of the Papers of the
Algonquian Conference, online).

[6] See Kade M. Ferris, "The Sweetcorn Treaty of 1858," Turtle Mountain
Chippewa Heritage Center, November 13, 2019 (online).

providing corn and potatoes to the trading posts, forts, and villages—greed destabilized the uneasy balance.

A series of treaties from 1837 to 1864 redefined the way property was held in the region. In these treaties, the Anishinaabe signed nation-to-nation agreements with the United States of America, exchanging land title to millions of acres in northern Minnesota for cash and annuity payments, while retaining the right to hunt and fish. While the land was then commodified and broken into parcels as "property," it was essential that the Anishinaabe reserved the right to continue to hunt, fish, gather, and use the land that they relied on for their livelihoods. As the US Supreme Court ruled in *Minnesota v. Mille Lacs Band of Chippewa Indians* (1999), tribal people in federally recognized tribes retained "usufructuary rights" to the land, including the rights of the Anishinaabe people to hunt, fish, and gather wild rice throughout the territory as part of the 1837 Land Cession Treaties with the Ojibwe and Dakota.[7]

The treaties made with the Anishinaabe and Dakota became treaties of repression, particularly after the American government starved four hundred Anishinaabe at Sandy Lake in 1850, forcing them to travel in the winter from their homes along Lake Superior. Treaties signed after that period show the absolute brutality of the US government, as well as its disregard for both international law and the Northwest Ordinance (1787) requirement that "the utmost good faith shall always be observed" toward Native people.[8]

---

[7] *Minnesota v. Mille Lacs Band of Chippewa Indians*, 526 U.S. 172 (1999).

[8] The Northwest Ordinance (An Ordinance for the Government of the Territory of the United States North-West of the River Ohio), art. 3 (July 13, 1787).

#StopLine3 participants call on Enbridge, lawmakers, and the courts to honor the treaties by halting pipeline construction.   (PHOTO BY DAVID PARRY / USED WITH PERMISSION)

Recognizing Indigenous territories is not something that US state governments have done willingly. Indigenous nations have been forced to utilize the courts for this purpose. The State of Minnesota—the public lands as well as federal lands within the state—is carved out of the reservations and the treaty territories. The Chippewa National Forest, for instance, is wholly carved out of the Leech Lake Reservation; the Itasca Park and the Tamarac Refuge are carved out of the White Earth Mississippi treaty territories. A third of the White Earth Reservation is held by state, county, and federal agencies. Stealing land from Native people is how America was made. As historian Roxanne Dunbar-Ortiz reminds us in *An Indigenous Peoples' History of the United States*: "The history of the United States is a history of settler colonialism—the founding of a state based on the ideology of white supremacy, the widespread practice of African slavery, and a policy of genocide and land theft."[9] The making of America, however, did not make Native peoples vanish, despite mythology like Manifest Destiny and a made-up legacy of Paul Bunyan.

Although the 1855 Treaty ceded eleven million acres of land, several smaller reservations were secured. The reservations of Gull Lake, Pokegama, Rabbit Lake, Nett Lake, Sandy Lake, Rice Lake, Leech Lake, and Mille Lacs were all a part of that treaty. The Anishinaabe continued to harvest and hunt in the entire 1855 Treaty territory, and some families never went to a reservation. Despite continued erosion of their livelihood and rights, the Anishinaabe people continued the cultural practices of syruping, collecting Manoomin, and hunting and fishing. Don Wedll, treaty rights expert and tribal historian from the Mille Lacs band, explains the legal basis for the Anishinaabe continuing to use the land. "You have to explicitly take these rights away," he says, adding, "Tribal people could not have understood [a world without] hunting, fishing, and gathering because that was like breathing the air. [They did not understand the words] 'All right, title, and interest' to mean [they] gave up the right to breathe the air. That is not something that the Anishinaabe would do."[10]

History of the Line 3 Resistance

Fast-forward to the mid-twentieth century and the massive expansion of our industrialized economy. A fossil fuel economy has grown exponentially. With the advent of the Arab oil embargo and the creation of the Organization of the Petroleum Exporting Countries (OPEC), Canada and the United States—

---

[9] Roxanne Dunbar-Ortiz, *An Indigenous Peoples' History of the United States* (Boston: Beacon Press, 2014), 2.

[10] Don Wedll, interview by Winona LaDuke, October 16, 2023.

two of the most inefficient users of fossil fuels—looked to deepen North American oil production. Venezuela, with the largest oil reserves in the world, has not always been politically aligned with the United States, so corporations looked to Canada with its Athabasca tar sands.

Tar sands, also known as oil sands, require a massive amount of processing, water, and toxins in order to be extracted, making tar sands oil one of the dirtiest fuels in the world. Then they needed pipelines to move this dirty fuel. Those pipelines were first installed in Canada by the Interprovincial Pipeline Company (IPL), and in the United States by the Lakehead Pipeline Company. In 1968, Lakehead began operation of its thirty-four-inch diameter, 1,031-mile-long Line 3 Pipeline and commenced the movement of crude oil from Hardisty, Alberta, in Canada to Superior, Wisconsin, in the United States. In 1998, IPL Energy officially became Enbridge, a name that combines "energy" with "bridge," and the company endures to this day. Enbridge built the Athabasca Pipeline in 1999, connecting Alberta's oil sands to its mainline system at Hardisty.

Today, Enbridge is the leading pipeline operator in the Fort McMurray to Edmonton and Hardisty corridors, with twelve oil sands projects connected to the Enbridge system. Enbridge moves 75 percent of all tar sands oil—what the Center for Biological Diversity describes as "dirtier than the dirtiest coal"— to US markets.[11] By the 1990s, Lakehead and then Enbridge were transporting 22 million gallons, or 524,000 barrels, of oil a day and had reported twenty-four ruptures, totaling 5.7 million gallons of leaked oil.[12] In 1991, Line 3 leaked 1.7 million gallons,

---

[11] See "Worse for Climate Change Than Coal" in the article "Oil Shale and Tar Sands," Center for Biological Diversity (online), accessed January 7, 2024.

[12] Dan Kraker and Cody Nelson, "Minnesota's Line 3 Oil Pipeline Proposal: The Basics," MPR News, June 18, 2018.

approximately 40,000 barrels, of oil into Prairie River, a tributary of Mississippi. This was the largest inland oil spill in US history.[13] After this spill, Enbridge reduced the flow of oil significantly.

With the Kalamazoo Spill in 2010, the second-largest inland oil spill in US history, the reality of aging pipeline infrastructure became apparent. That spill went on for seventeen hours as the monitors in Alberta failed to notice it. The public was outraged at Enbridge, and the EPA—in something called a Consent Decree—ordered Enbridge to either close down or replace Line 3.[14]

As America expanded so-called domestic oil production—despite being stolen from Native lands and the treaty territories—the Bakken oil fields began to boom, and Enbridge looked to diversify the pipeline systems to bring more dirty fuel to the markets. The company knew that a new Line 3 was required and also wanted to begin a new pipeline from the Dakotas, called the Sandpiper pipeline, which would bring 225,000 barrels per day across the 1855 Treaty territory in new pipes through a new pipeline right-of-way.[15] Learning of this pipeline proposal in 2013, Native people and many lakeshore owners became deeply concerned and organized to challenge the Sandpiper at the Public

---

[13] See the oil spill incident report in "Lakehead Pipeline Company; Grand Rapids, Minnesota," *Incident News*, March 3, 1991, NOAA.gov. See also Julie Siple, Bill Wareham, Dan Kraker, and Cody Nelson, "Rivers of Oil, Episode 2: The Largest Inland Spill," MPR News, June 20, 2018.

[14] For more on this oil spill, see "EPA Response to Enbridge Spill in Michigan," EPA.gov, which reports, "On July 26, 2010, a 30-inch pipeline belonging to Enbridge Inc. ruptured near Marshall, Michigan and contaminated Talmadge Creek and the Kalamazoo River with hundreds of thousands of gallons of crude oil. EPA ordered Enbridge to dredge submerged oil and oil-contaminated sediment from the Kalamazoo River. From 2010 to 2014 over 1.2 million gallons of oil were recovered from the river."

[15] See "Sandpiper Pipeline Project, Minnesota," Hydrocarbons Technology (online), accessed January 13, 2024.

Utilities Commission (PUC). The PUC had never fully considered the implications of these pipeline projects, and this was the first time it faced massive opposition to any project since the battle against the Prairie Island Nuclear Power Plant and nuclear storage facility was waged by Minnesota citizens and Native people (specifically the Dakota people of Prairie Island, where the nuclear plant and storage facility is sited).

Much of the dirtiest infrastructure for America's energy independence is forced on Native communities, who ironically are the least electrified and have the least infrastructure in the country.

With aging pipelines and the understanding that pipelines may be "out of sight" but have impacts, Enbridge began a massive public relations and lobbying campaign aimed at Minnesota, the first state on Enbridge pipeline's stretch to Michigan. This new "Line 3" pipeline would carry 760,000 barrels of tar sands oil per day, roughly the carbon equivalent of fifty average coal plants, or greater than all annual emissions combined for the state of Minnesota.

This new pipeline was immediately opposed by the seven Anishinaabe reservations of northern Minnesota, by non-Native local community people (including many lakeshore owners), and by climate justice organizations across the country. Following the defeat of the Sandpiper Pipeline (Enbridge withdrew its application when the court ordered an environmental impact statement), Enbridge purchased approximately 30 percent of the Dakota Access Pipeline.[16] By the end of 2016, at the height of the #NoDAPL resistance at Standing Rock, it was clear that new pipeline projects were no longer getting a free pass.

Across Minnesota, grassroots organizing work began to engage with the public process to defeat the new Line 3 pipeline.

---

[16] Alyssa Julie, "Enbridge Acquires Significant Stake in Controversial Dakota Access Pipeline," Global News, February 15, 2017.

Youth climate intervenors, Native nations, and both white and Native-led environmental organizations legally participated in the permitting process, and tens of thousands of hours were spent organizing voices from around the state to oppose the project's approval. Of the 71,986 written public comments that were submitted in reference to the project, 94.8 percent opposed Line 3.[17]

After the publication of a study illustrating that the risk of the pipeline outweighed the public need, even the Department of Commerce legally appealed the decision to permit the pipeline.[18] Yet Enbridge prevailed. In 2018, the pipeline and route were approved by the PUC. Among the more shocking outcomes was a ruling that permitted Enbridge to create an escrow account to fund the police to suppress the resistance.

In the fall of 2020, a number of last-ditch efforts emerged to block minor construction permits. But construction ultimately began in December 2020. Having learned from the massive resistance that the Dakota Access Pipeline faced at the edge of the Standing Rock Reservation in North Dakota along the Missouri River, Enbridge launched a full-scale occupation of northern Minnesota, where five construction spreads spanned the region with equipment, large encampments of construction

---

[17] For a summary of public comments on Line 3, see "Findings of Fact, Conclusions of Law, and Recommendation," State of Minnesota, Office of Administrative Hearings for the Public Utilities Commission: *In the Matter of the Application of Enbridge Energy for a Certificate of Need for the Line 3 Project in Minnesota* (OAH 65-2500-32764), and *In the Matter of the Application of Applicant Enbridge Energy for a Routing Permit for the Line 3 Project in Minnesota* (OAH 65-2500-33377). Filed April 23, 2018. PDF archived at mn.gov.

[18] The Minnesota Department of Commerce previously hosted this study on their website. Since the authors began writing this chapter, the link to the study has been removed from public access.

workers (known as "man camps"), and a huge number of police and their agents. Approximately three hundred miles of pipeline were installed. A horizontal directional drill bore under sixty-two rivers and through some of the best wild rice in the region.

Alongside construction, half a dozen resistance camps sprung up along the route. On June 7, 2021, over twenty-five hundred people gathered on the White Earth Nation to declare themselves treaty people and prepared to demonstrate their opposition to the construction of the pipeline through large-scale direct action.[19]

During the ten-month construction process, Enbridge paid $8.6 million in escrow to the police departments to facilitate the pipeline policing.[20] Over one thousand people were arrested for activities blocking access to construction. And despite promises that they would not alter the water during construction, the Minnesota Pollution Control Agency has said that Enbridge is responsible for twenty-eight frac-outs (accidental releases of drilling fluid), found at a dozen river crossing locations. Those included thirteen releases into wetlands and one into a river, when roughly one hundred gallons spilled into the Willow River in Aitkin County.[21]

During the construction season, Minnesota was in a deep drought—yet the Department of Natural Resources was willing to amend Enbridge's permit, allowing them to pump five billion gallons of water from lakes, rivers, and municipal wells. This was

---

[19] Louise Hall, "Jane Fonda Slams Biden as Not 'Bold or Fast' Enough on Climate Crisis as She Joins Oil Line Protest," *The Independent,* June 8, 2021.

[20] Alleen Brown and John McCracken, "Documents Show How a Pipeline Company Paid Minnesota Millions to Police Protests," Grist, February 9, 2023 (online).

[21] Kirsti Marohn, "Minnesota Lawmaker Demands Data on Line 3 Frac-Outs," MPR News, February 23, 2022.

almost ten times more than the original amount the company had requested.[22]

By the summer of 2023, it was clear that Enbridge had breached four or more aquifers, causing immense groundwater disruption to a place where ground and surface water are still drinkable.[23] Billions of gallons of water have breached out of deep aquifers that serve an integrated hydrological system. The Minnesota Environmental Partnership describes just one of these breaches: "The fact that an aquifer could be breached in January 2021, go unnoticed by regulators for months, and not be repaired until January 2022 shows there has been a complete breakdown of our state's environmental protections and regulatory system."[24]

On October 31, 2021, Enbridge started pumping oil through the new corridor, and the company is now planning an expansion of the line through Wisconsin and Michigan in a project known as Line 5. That line will ultimately bring much of the oil from the Canadian tar sands back to Canada for refining in Sarnia. Line 5 crosses under the Straits of Mackinac. Essentially, this Canadian pipeline company has a noose of oil pipelines surrounding a fifth of the world's water.

Voices of Resistance

In the following pages, we bring you voices of Native and non-Native women from Minnesota who were part of a spiritual movement to protect the water through resisting the Line

---

[22] Kirsti Marohn, "Line 3 Foes Worry Increased Pumping Could Threaten Minnesota Water," MPR News, June 24, 2021.

[23] Jennifer Bjorhus, "Fourth Aquifer Rupture Discovered along Line 3 in Northern Minnesota," *Star Tribune* (Minneapolis), July 28, 2023.

[24] "Understanding the Line 3 Aquifer Breach and Spills," Minnesota Environmental Partnership, September 23, 2021 (webinar).

3 pipeline. We use a series of stories to shed light on spirituality in protest movements and show that, in the end, the Line
3 resistance movement was not simply tactical. It was born out
of a spiritual movement that was not only rooted in Anishinaabe
spirituality but sprang from a deeply human desire to connect
with and protect our life source as expressed through multiple
faith lenses.

We show how Anishinaabe spirituality and the practice of
land tenure are one and the same. Humans belong to the land;
the land does not belong to us. We fight for the land like we
fight for our closest relatives. In a place where the world is half
land and half water, we become, by necessity, Water Protectors.
We share stories of others who came into the Indigenous-led
movement and how their own inherent connection to Earth and
others grew through a multifaith experience of solidarity. Indeed,
every tradition can find language to connect to the movement to
protect the sacred.

We examine how fundamentally colonial legal structures
and assumptions about property rights prevented authentic
treaty rights, leading to widespread destruction. We ask the
fundamental question: can recommitting to Indigenous understandings of sacred land relationships put us on the green road?

The Sacred in the Line 3 Movement was not always a
comfortable space. While we deeply listened for the truth, or
"the heartbeat of God" as described by members of the Hildegard Catholic Worker house, we were forced to confront anger
and grief. These diverse and differently expressed feelings of rage
were complicated and led to competing ideologies and theories
of change. The conflicts that arose were a natural and emerging
part of the decentralized movement.

While Line 3 was ultimately built, we continue today to
build the movement that emerged in this fight.

The Land to Which We Belong: Mississippi Lodge

In this section, we describe our own personal experience as authors being arrested at a sacred lodge in Palisade, Minnesota. It is early November 2020, and Mississippi is peaceful. About ten miles north of Palisade, on the Great River Road, women pray by the banks, where generations of women before us have prayed.

Our Anishinaabe people have no church. Instead, they/we have lodges: teaching lodges, Midewin lodges, sweat lodges, and ceremonial lodges. At this place, we have made a prayer and teaching lodge so that we can listen, speak, and feast with the spirits, remembering our river and acknowledging all that is around. Oval in shape, twenty by ten feet, it is made of ironwood branches lashed together with rope. In the center of the lodge is a fire.

It is December 2020, and the land is deeply frozen. Orange flags now mark the future location of the Line 3 pipeline as it traverses the forest and crosses Mississippi. On the north side of the road, a massive metal machine reverberates and screeches as it grabs trees and tears them out of the ground by the roots. A fire burns in the prayer lodge. The women, including both authors, are gathered. Again, praying for water, for health, and yet feeling the Wiindigo of Enbridge come closer.[25]

The Minnesota Department of Natural Resources (DNR), the agency responsible to care for the land, has been training

---

[25] According to Kaitlin Smith, in most Algonquian traditions, "The wendigo is human in origin and becomes a monster through a process that results either from acts of starvation-induced cannibalism or from possession by a spirit. In the course of the transformation from human to wendigo, the person exhibits increasing selfishness, violence, hunger, and greed—particularly for human flesh." Smith, "More Than Monsters: The Deeper Significance of Wendigo Stories," Facing History and Ourselves, November 30, 2021 (facinghistory.org).

conservation officers to arrest anyone who disrupts pipeline construction. They are prepared for a season of resistance, and an extra paycheck as well. Enbridge has set up an escrow account to cover all the expenses of deploying these officers.

It's not surprising to look outside of the lodge and see a line of Minnesota DNR officers coming our way equipped with zip-tie handcuffs and loudspeakers. Despite the fact that this is public land and we are Mississippi Band Anishinaabe protected by the American Indian Religious Freedom Act, the ceremonial lodge does not protect us. As Native women, we are ordered by the officers to finish prayers and depart. When we do not, we are arrested and charged with resisting arrest and trespassing on a construction site. As non-Native allies, we are removed immediately and charged with misdemeanor trespass on a construction site under Statute 609.605.1 (b)(9).

Since Native religions are land-based religions, and much of that land is sacred—as well as full of copper, iron ore, and uranium—the conflict over Native freedom of religion always meets with corporate challenges. Native people continue to be killed over the same natural resource issues a hundred years after the Osage murders chronicled in David Grann's *Killers of the Flower Moon*. But we stand with our prayers, saying clearly that our prayers and faith should have the same protections that the Christian churches are accorded. It's time to pray. Together.

Many months pass that are filled with weekly acts of resistance. Bail funds are established. Many are jailed and released. By September 2021, 1,000 people have been charged with various crimes. Ninety-two are on the hook for felony charges, and 349 face gross misdemeanors according to the Pipeline Legal Action Network.[26]

---

[26] See Colleen Connolly, "Line 3 Activists Face Felony Charges for Attempted Assisted Suicide: Protestors say Local Prosecutors Are 'Over-

Midewiwin lodge on Anishinaabe treaty land seized for pipeline installation.
A number of women, including coauthors Winona LaDuke and Julia Nerbonne,
were arrested here by state law enforcement officials while performing ceremony.
(PHOTO BY MARK CLATTERBUCK / USED WITH PERMISSION)

Fast forward to Aitkin County Courthouse. It is February 9, 2022, and we are gathered for an evidentiary hearing. Winona takes the stand to describe the history and purpose of the lodge:

> About six or seven thousand years ago we were given different instructions. As Anishinaabe people having lived for a very long time in this territory we had to learn how to live right.... The Midewiwin lodge was a set of instructions on how we should heal our people ... and so in those teachings some of us were instructed to follow this healing lodge path.

charging' in an Effort to Deter Exercise of Free Speech Rights," *Minnesota Reformer,* September 6, 2022.

I have constructed many lodges. That's what you do when you're in the Midewiwin society. You make new lodges every year or you make lodges for different ceremonies. I with my sister Tania built the lodge on the Mississippi River. I'm what's known as a Chippewa of the Mississippi. That's my legal designation and so I continue to be in the territory of the Chippewa of the Mississippi and so I did build a lodge on the shore of Mississippi.

As an Ojibwe woman it is my responsibility to take care of the water. Often we will have a lodge and ceremony specifically for the water, and this is a place that we had many ceremonies for the water there in the Mississippi River. And in our Midewiwin scrolls we see this place on the Mississippi River.

We constructed the lodge in November of 2020, and then we prayed and then we had a feast. You know it took a lot of work to build [so we] had a good feast and then we brought in our ceremonial items and we danced in that lodge. Ojibwe women danced and then we invited in some of our fellow [allies] ... people of different religious ceremonies, you know, traditions that we understood would understand our spiritual practice and appreciate it.

[SPEAKER]: And so, you mentioned inviting Julia Nerbonne, who's sitting here?

Winona: Yeah. This woman right here.[27]

---

[27] Transcript of *State of Minnesota vs. Julia Ariadne Frost Nerbonne*, US District Court, Ninth Judicial District, File No. 01-CR-20-1024, Evidentiary Hearing, February 10, 2022, 38–43.

Many more months pass before trial. The cases of white allies are dismissed, and still it will be more time until a final ruling is issued on the Anishinaabe women. Ultimately, all charges are dropped without reference to the lodge or to the American Indian Religious Freedom Act.

The Land to Which We Belong: Fire Light Encampment

I am here by invitation of the Sovereign Anishinaabe Nation to stand and support their efforts to uphold their inherent responsibility to the future generations and protect Lands, Waters, Manoomin and the Anishinaabe way of life. This is being done in peace and prayer, supporting the defense of Indigenous Sovereignty, treaty-reserved rights, and the free prior and informed consent of the Anishinaabe nation for anything impacting them.

—The Fire Light Solidarity Statement[28]

It is June 8, 2021. Dozens of tents occupy a boardwalk that has been built into the wetlands surrounding a small channel, the headwaters of Mississippi River. It is blisteringly hot now, and the biting midges are on the move. One can wade across this stream in just a few big strides. From the road, it looks like little more than a ditch, and yet there, at the edge of the wetland, burns a sacred fire around which several elders sit in camping chairs.

For Anishinaabe people, the fire is the hearth of life and represents our prayers. We keep the fires going at ceremonies for our prayers, for the spirits, and to keep our people warm. A long time ago, and still today, people would travel with coals from a fire to another place, often bringing fire with them in a horn.

---

[28] See the Fire Light Treaty Case website, accessed January 8, 2024.

That's how precious fire has been to our people. It remains this way today.

Nearby is a tent for food and gear. About one hundred people have gathered to occupy the space on the boardwalk and in the ditch. Someone has been organizing a picture with a drone, handing out lettered T-shirts and getting people organized. They lie down in order. The T-shirts in the photograph read, "WE ARE ALL TREATY PEOPLE." Sheriff Halverson of Clearwater County is parked by the side of the road and is talking with some of the women organizers. A Native elder talks to a small group that is gathered to learn about the teachings. This is day seven of what will become an eight-day occupation of the Enbridge Line 3 construction easement at the headwaters of Mississippi. Earlier in the week, over two thousand people from across the country had answered the invitation of Native leaders and gathered on the White Earth Reservation in northern Minnesota for the Treaty People Gathering. On Monday, following an interfaith prayer circle, one thousand people marched to the site of this crossing, where a small group of individuals began an occupation of the easement.

Native organizer and camp leader Nancy Beulieu describes the formation of the Fire Light Camp on a blog posting she wrote for MN350.org:

> Immediately following the Treaty People Gathering we, along with Jane Fonda, met at the Mississippi bridge near the LaSalle State Park where we marched, sang, and prayed for the Nibi. Soon after, we followed our hearts and occupied the Line 3 easement in a prayer ceremony. We invited our treaty partners/allies and held space collectively in peace and prayer. We asserted our collective treaty rights along with our right to freedom of religion and together we held space for eight peaceful

days. We stopped construction for those eight days. I'm sure Mother Nature thanked us.

Our non-Native treaty partners prayed with us and amplified our struggle and gave voice to our story. This story includes all of us, mitakuye owasin indinawe maaganidog in the Ojibwe language, which means all my relations. We showed the world what it looks like to honor treaties and to live in peace as neighbors as the treaties intended. We followed our original instructions and became guardians of all that is sacred. We were protectors of the Nibi and keepers of the 1855 Treaty.[29]

Gaagigeyaashiik (Dawn Goodwin), another one of the leaders of Fire Light Encampment, lives on Upper Rice Lake and is enrolled in the White Earth Reservation. She has been an artist and worked in education for decades and has been deeply involved with the pipeline resistance movement for over ten years. Influenced by the Occupy movement, she cut her teeth on activism as part of the Red Lake, Nizhawendamin Indaakiminaan Camp in Leonard, Minnesota, in 2013.

Several years following this, she avidly followed what was taking place at Standing Rock. Ultimately, she was increasingly involved in protecting her own homelands and waters such that she resigned her job in adult education in 2019. Since then, she has been devoting all her time to the Water Protector movement. In 2019, she organized an education event for local law enforcement on treaty rights and the pipeline project. In 2021, she became a founder of Manoomin Genawendang Endazhigabeshing, "Wild Rice Protector Camp," a place where Water Protectors have gathered for rest, organizing, and cultural rejuvenation.

---

[29] See "Camp Firelight" on the MN350.org website.

I remember back in 2016 getting the call from my sister Joye at Standing Rock, asking all of us to come out. It was like this was the moment for us, for me, to be powerful. It was [new and it was] intense.... The Line 3 resistance movement was similar. And I was ready, guided by the Spirit but also by the knowledge that treaty rights were being put at risk. Even though most of Line 3 construction would not be directly through our reservations, we knew that we had the right to travel and occupy our land. And so now, more than ever, we needed to make sure that we were honoring our treaties, not just protecting the Water.

Fire Light Encampment and ceremonial grounds at the headwaters of Mississippi, located in the pipeline construction corridor.
(PHOTO BY DAVID PARRY / USED WITH PERMISSION)

As it was with the building of the Midewin lodge on Mississippi at Palisade, Gaagigeyaashiik knew that her people reserved the right to practice their religion throughout the region. In

Anishinaabe culture, lighting a sacred fire is not taken lightly. The lighting of this fire on the banks of Mississippi was named by a local elder, Fire Light, to bring truth to the light. Lighting a fire helps to discern a way forward, and so Nancy and Gaagigey-aashiik and their partners brought the sacred prayers that had inspired them at Standing Rock to the headwaters of Mississippi. Fire Light was born in the heat of the summer at the culmination of a march with thousands of people from across the country who had come to bear witness to what Enbridge was doing at the headwaters.

> When we gathered, we entered into prayer by lighting a sacred Fire. This is one of the things that was protected by our treaty rights. Our right to use the land and gather spiritually. Some of us were doing a ceremony, others were fasting, and because we needed at least four days to complete the ceremony we negotiated with Sheriff Halverson to be able to stay and complete the ritual. Some say that this was just a move to block the pipeline, but it was about honoring our treaty right to gather. So the way we left was really important. Sheriff Halverson said he was protecting our right to peacefully and lawfully protest, and he did honor our treaties and right to peacefully assemble.

When asked about how she saw the spirit emerge at Fire Light, Gaagigeyaashiik recalls a day when she arrived at camp to see a line of robed Buddhists praying on the bridge. They were there for quite a while, she recalls. The amazing thing to her was that she hadn't asked them, and she didn't know them. They, like her, were called to hold space at the water. Something about the universality of this place and this time in history made it feel like things were exactly like they should be.

Although there was some disagreement about tactics, after eight days, the camp leaders made the decision to disband the camp peacefully to avoid a situation where violence and the use of force was brought to that location. For Gaagigeyaashiik it was important to center the ceremony where the fire's light was literally bringing truth to the world. Fifty-one people were peacefully arrested that day. They later organized a collective defense using treaty rights and recorded their story on the Fire Light Treaty Case website.

Listening for the Heartbeat of God

Michele NaarObed lives in the Hildegard House, a Catholic Worker community in Duluth, Minnesota, that she cofounded, which is committed to following the model of Jesus in connecting with and serving the deepest needs of society.[30] The community honors Hildegard of Bingen and her vision of listening deeply to those least heard in society as they work to welcome immigrants and women survivors of sexual violence into a safe space. Michele grew up in a small town in the Hudson River Valley in New York. She is the daughter of Italian immigrants and has been part of the resistance community for many decades.

Michele's work with victims of sexual assault in Minnesota raised her awareness about the disproportionately high abuse suffered by Indigenous women. She also learned that the epidemic of abuse and sexual violence against Native women and girls in the United States is directly connected to the recent spike in oil and gas extraction that targets Native lands across the country. Reflecting on her work, she explains,

---

[30] Michele Naar and her husband, Greg, were gifted the suffix of Obed by a Catholic Sister upon their wedding. Obed means "servant of God." She is now Michele NaarObed.

I learned a lot about the Indigenous connection, [and] why Indigenous communities here are so vulnerable to sex trafficking. How did that happen? And then, you know, I heard about the man camps. And then I heard about why missing and murdered Indigenous women [MMIW] multiply around these areas where man camps are, and these man camps are in areas where pipelines are being built.

She links oil industry violence against Indigenous women to a larger pattern of violence perpetrated by large corporations everywhere.

That's all part of these gigantic industries, whether it be the fossil fuel industry, the pharmaceutical industry, all these mega corporations, transnational corporations that have waged war—and then we come into the wars being waged now in our backyard. But it's been waged in Native communities' backyards for a long time.

While Michele frequently speaks about the economic and political dimensions of this violence, she believes that it has spiritual roots:

This whole thing, this is a spiritual war we're in right now. And it's what Indigenous people will call the Wiindigo spirit. We might call it Satan. I don't know, but it's a spiritual war. And so we take a little bit from our traditions, the best of our traditions, that hold us together as humans—even beyond human, as living entities—to help us confront this warfare that we're in. It's trying to claim everything. I heard many Indigenous people speak about [how] everything starts with prayer and ends in prayer. And I thought, *That's what we should be doing as Catholic Workers.* It starts in our faith, and we act out of our faith. Our faith is our prayer, and our prayers are our faith. Our prayers are our action; our actions are our prayer. It all flows together.[31]

Michele has a history of serving time in prison for civil disobedience as a moral act as part of Jonah House in Baltimore. During the Line 3 conflict, she was arrested as part of a small group of Catholic Worker "valve turners" who shut down a portion of the Line 3 pipeline in February 2019.[32] As she prepares her next "necessity defense," she reflects on what being part of the Stop Line 3 movement felt like for her and how she experienced the lack of justice at the hands of the State of Minnesota.

It was June 28, 2018. She describes the day so many of us remember like it was yesterday.[33] The audience is packed into the Public Utilities Commission. After four years and over sixty-eight thousand public comments opposing the new Line 3 pipeline, finally there will be a decision:

> For days, I was down there [with everyone] . . . and saw the bullshit that they got away with and the lies that they were telling. I saw all of those expert witnesses, especially the young [speaking out against the pipeline]. They even had one of the commissioners in tears, [but] Enbridge got their certificate of need and their route at the end.

Michele goes on to describe how it felt when Anishinaabe elder Tania Aubid responded as the last of the five commissioners voted to approve the pipeline. Cloaked in an American flag, she stood up and broke the silence:

---

[31] Michele NaarObed, interview by Mark Clatterbuck, May 27, 2021.

[32] Dan Kraker, "'Valve Turners' Target Oil Pipeline Equipment in Itasca County," MPR News, February 4, 2019.

[33] Elizabeth Dunbar and Dan Kraker, "PUC Backs Enbridge Line 3 Oil Pipeline, Sets Route," MPR News, June 28, 2018.

"You have just waged war on the Ojibwe people."

And then she left, alone.

Then the commissioners began to discuss the route. Michele explains,

> I can remember my [Anishinaabe] friend from Fond Du Lac didn't want to look at the route map. "What does it look like?" [she asked]. It doesn't look good, I responded. Then she said, "Stop talking."

Afterward, Michele asked her friend why she wanted her to stop talking. She replied,

> "Because I don't want the ancestors to hear this." This is really deep. And then I started to take some time to really think: What would the ancestors want to hear? What would God want to hear? What would the angels want to hear? What would the spirit world want to hear? What can I say? What can I do?

Michele and her Catholic Worker friends decided that they would send a message of resistance to Enbridge by shutting down the current line. On February 3, 2019, four Catholic Workers entered a pump station in Itasca County. After calling Enbridge to let them know of their plans, they scaled the fence and attempted to shut off the flow of oil by turning a valve. They were ultimately arrested and posted their story on a Facebook page titled "The Four Necessity Valve Turners." While they were motivated and inspired by Indigenous women with whom Michele had become so close, they wanted to do this action in a way that made it clear they had responsibility to Indigenous leadership, but were also not going to burden them with the repercussions of the action. They decided to confront Enbridge away from the reservations so that the tribe would not have to suffer the blowback. Michele explained,

We did it in our Catholic Worker tradition of prayer and song and nonviolence—and staying with it after we did it. We took responsibility for what we did. We didn't feel that we were committing the crime. We thought that they were committing a crime. And so we tried the necessity defense in court ... [arguing] that we broke the letter of the law because we were trying to fill the spirit of the law. This is what Jesus said: I didn't come here to break the law. I came here to fulfill the law.

Once construction commenced, Michele spent many weeks at the Welcome Water Protector Camp at Palisade near the lodge, living in community and helping out. There, she became reconnected with Tania, where they had many discussions about the role of religion in the movement. During this time, Tania describes how Native religion was once illegal in the United States:

1978 [with the passage of the American Indian Religious Freedom Act] is when we could finally practice our religion freely. Before then, we were jailed, put in asylums and everything like that. Still today some of their old-school thinking is in the air. And that's why they wanted to try to squash what we were doing with the prayer lodge over by Mississippi River. ... When we put that up ... [we brought together] a collective of people who knew the history of the place, and that was why the lodge was built there.

Just like the fire at Mississippi headwaters, the lodge at the Palisade Mississippi crossing became a focus for teaching about tradition and responsibility:

We had people coming in from South America, Argentina, and Ecuador. We had people from Hawai'i that showed up [at the lodge] because it was like a safe sanctuary place to see what was actually happening and how far they had gone as far as building that pipeline.

We asked Michele about her experience at the camp with Tania, what she came to learn about her own spirituality, and what she came to learn about the spirituality of Native women at the camp. Since the theme of the Hildegard House is "listening for the heartbeat of God," we asked her what she hears at the Welcome Water Protector Camp. Her answer was different than we had expected:

> I met a lot of different people at the camp … [but what stands out the most was Tania yelling at the pipeline crew]: "Rapists! Murderers! Killers of Mother Earth!" … She would say that over and over again and she would really yell it. … And then sometimes she'd start to [yell at the workers], "Did you go home and beat your wife?" Things like that. But when she was yelling, "Rapists! Murderers! Killers of Mother Earth!" she was describing the pipe as a rape. Some people … judged her for speaking violently … but the thing is that it was the truth. This was rape. This was a murder. This wasn't a business plan, you know? So that really hit me, because I was up there when the drill went under [Mississippi] and I was sleeping right on top of it. And I could feel [the penetration and the violence] of it.

Michele was listening for the "heartbeat of God," and she found it in an unusual place. For Michele, it was in the gut-wrenching calls of Tania Aubid speaking an uncomfortable truth to the construction crew and feeling in her bones the penetration of the drill into the earth. God is angry, and so are we. We feel God's anger. Being part of the pipeline resistance movement was a traumatizing experience for so many. But it was real. Michele

has since been found guilty of a gross misdemeanor for participating in a ceremonial dance and is waiting for sentencing with
the possibility that she could serve nine months in prison. She
is also busy welcoming refugees into her home, and growing a
garden to share in community. Every morning, she rises early to
attend morning prayer.

Sacred Solidarity:
Rise and Repair at the State Capitol

Winter has come again, and it's now 2023. It has been over a year
since oil started flowing through the Line 3 pipeline. Over five
hundred of the one thousand cases continue through the legal
system as criminal trials are underway for Line 3 resistance. A
weekly newsletter titled *Defendant Solidarity Network* broadcasts
Zoom links to omnibus hearings. Cases for white allies using
the American Indian Religious Freedom Act (AIRFA 1978) as
the key argument were dismissed just weeks before trial with no
explanation. The Public Utilities Commission administrators
have finished doling out over $8.6 million in escrow funds paid
by Enbridge to support local policing of the protests.

At the Minnesota state capitol, things are brewing. It's
February 15, and organizers have invited a new coalition to come
together. This is the time to "Rise And Repair," and organizers
have set the stage to bring many of the team back together in
what they describe as a bold agenda to promote "Indigenous
Rights and Climate Justice."[34] Over thirty-five individual meetings are in process, connecting movement actors to their local
legislators. A cohort of Native women move together from one
meeting to the next, describing their experiences to lawmakers.

---

[34] Nicole Ki, "Hundreds Rally at Capitol for Clean Energy Plans
Centered on Indigenous Rights," MPR News, February 16, 2023.

"We never knew" is a common refrain coming from lawmakers. "How can we help?"

In the afternoon, a group assembles on the steps of Christ Lutheran Church. Handmade signs created during a movement sing-along the previous weekend are distributed: "Indigenous Rights," "Land Back," and "Solar For All." Everyone clamors to get their own "Rise Up for Climate Justice" and "Rise Up for Indigenous Rights" rally posters. The group marches forward to the beat of the drum. We cross over the train tracks, up the snowy path, and through the entrance of the capitol, where the drum stops at the door before three hundred people file in. A stage is set up with seating for Elders in the middle of the rotunda. Most circle the edge as speakers take the stage. Young people beg the adults in the group not to leave this crisis up to them alone. "It's inappropriate, actually, for you to leave this burden to us," says Mikayla Freedman with Youth N' Power. Sophia Benrud, from the Environmental Justice Table, instructs people to pay attention to a cumulative impacts bill that would set limits on polluting industries setting up shop in neighborhoods that are already laden with an overwhelming majority of the toxic waste. Great-grandmother Mary Lyons of the Leech Lake Band of Ojibwe reminds us that we are all Indigenous to some place, and that it is our job now to work to see and honor each other and the land.

Bishop Craig Loya of the Episcopal Church takes the stage in solidarity:

> Human beings were created primarily to care for the earth that God has given to us. I am also deeply aware of the way in which Christians have been shamefully complicit in the decimation of the earth and horrific violence against Indigenous peoples. . . . We have failed to live in the right relationships with others and with

the land. We too often have bought into an extractive capitalism that frankly ignores the wisdom in our own teaching, let alone listening to or respecting the wisdom of other traditions and voices.

In this season we have a historic opportunity to renew the long-overdue work of making reparations for what has been broken. We can do that by following the leadership of Indigenous Minnesotans as we work to build a future that cares for the earth, a future that rebuilds communities that have been broken down, a future where we learn how to embrace one another in kinship across all lines of difference, which I believe in my very heart is God's dream for all of us. This is the moment for us to rise up and to repair what we have broken, and to work with all our siblings to build a better future for the earth and all those who come after us. It is an unspeakable gift to be able to walk with all of you on this journey today and as we move into the future together.

A Window of Hope

It is September 14, 2023. It has been almost three years since trespass charges were filed against Winona in Aitkin County and is now five days before a jury trial is scheduled to begin. District Court Judge Leslie Metzen mails the following to Winona's lawyer, dismissing her long-standing charges. We believe the significance of the judge's opinion warrants its lengthy inclusion here:

"IN THE INTERESTS OF JUSTICE," a phrase often spoken but rarely applied to defendants, the less powerful, the voiceless. The State is entitled to justice and the fair and impartial application of the law. I have no concern that the State, with its resources and power does not receive its share of justice in courtrooms throughout this state every day. I have spent nearly 40 years playing my part in our system of justice.

These cases and these 3 defendants in particular have awakened in me some deep questions about what would serve the interests of justice here. As a child growing up in the '50s and '60s what I learned about "Indians" came from TV shows about cowboys and Indians and in school where the Caucasian European view of the world and history was the only one discussed. In the last 20 years I have come to a broader understanding of what we, the now dominant culture, did to try to eradicate our indigenous neighbors. We moved them by force and power and violence off the land where they lived for thousands of years. To make peace, we signed treaties with them that promised many things they never received. When they had been forced to live within reservation boundaries, we stole their children; forced them to attend boarding schools where their language, long hair, spiritual beliefs, and contact with their families were forbidden. Many of them died from disease, violence, and some probably from a broken heart. I know only enough of this history to wonder how those of us in the "dominant culture" could ever have thought any of these actions were okay or justifiable.

I have a simple and rudimentary understanding of some of the beliefs and values of native people. Their reverence for the earth and what she provides; animals and fish to hunt and catch for food. Plants to gather from the forests for food and medicine. And wild rice, Mahnomen [sic], the sacred food on this land that sustained them through the long harsh winters. Their practices in using these substances did not deplete the resources nor did they pollute the land, air, and water.

I have no expertise in the values and beliefs of the tribes that call Minnesota and Wisconsin home but respect and value their presence on this land. Tania Aubid, Dawn Goodwin, and Winona LaDuke are respected members of their tribes and Anishinaabe people. Their presence at various gatherings to protest the construction by Enbridge of the Line 3 pipeline was an expression of their heartfelt belief that the waters of Minnesota need to be protected from damage that could result from the pipeline. Their protest was expressed by performing a jingle dance and beating a drum. Their gathering may have briefly delayed construction, caused extra expense to law enforcement who came to clear their gatherings (much of which was reimbursed to Aitkin County by Enbridge), but the pipeline has been completed and is operating in spite of their efforts to stop it through peaceful protests.

This court also notes that in other counties across northern Minnesota many of the cases involving pipeline protesters were dismissed outright or continued for dismissal with a small fine and an admonition to not commit a same or similar offense. In the interests of justice the charges against these three individuals who were exercising their rights to free speech and to freely express their spiritual beliefs should be dismissed. To criminalize their behavior would be the crime.[35]

---

[35] Judge Leslie Metzen, "Order to Dismiss" and "Memo," District Court, State of Minnesota, Ninth Judicial District, Nos. 01-CR-21-87, 01-CR-21-119, 01-CR-21-86, 01-CR-20-1056, September 14, 2023. See

Finally, a representative of the state is speaking real truth, for a change. But let's center the real story. For thirty-two months, these Native women endured the threat of being jailed at the hands of a hostile state. And yet they wouldn't settle. And because they refused to step down, we all have a collective chance to inch toward justice.

Moving Forward

> Ne-be Gee Zah-gay-egoo
> Gee Me-gwetch wayne ne-me-goo
> Gee Zah Wayn ne-me-goo[36]

It is the summer of 2023, and again we gather at the banks of the headwaters of Mississippi. Many who came to participate in the Line 3 resistance have departed Minnesota. Some have joined the fight against Cop City in Georgia, where an activist was killed by police. Many Minnesotans who joined the movement have returned to focusing on their communities, children, day jobs, and the work of life.

On occasion, we still get together on the water to breathe together and to sing the familiar song once again. The Nibi Song was written by Dorene Day as a way to honor the water each day she crossed Mississippi with her grandson. During the pipeline resistance movement, people from many faiths came together to honor and protect life. Rather than appropriating the water ceremony or using it in nontraditional ways, we started singing the Nibi Song. "Water we love you. We thank you. We respect you."

---

also Christopher Ingraham, "Judge dismisses remaining Line 3 charges against Indigenous activists, citing longstanding government mistreatment," *Minnesota Reformer*, September 15, 2023 (online).

[36] "Water we love you. We thank you. We respect you."

And with that respect came deep pain and deep connection. The song brings healing not only for the water but within us. The water within us.

The Nibi Song was written to be sung every day, to remind us where we came from and what is important. For many, the Line 3 fight has changed us. We didn't succeed in stopping the pipeline. Three years later, we are still angry. We continue to carry the trauma of generations and to fight for a community that truly embodies the deep respect that we have learned from being together. We know now what we are up against.

In 2024, we gather at the newly opened Giiwedinong Museum of Anishinaabe Treaty Rights and Culture, where we will honor the story of Water Protectors and continue educating ourselves about the history of treaties in Minnesota.[37] The museum serves as a basket of Water Protector stories, oral histories, and treaty interpretations from the Anishinaabe worldview.

We will be back at the Capitol to work on a Minnesota state resolution about the rights of water and Manoomin/Psin.[38] We will fight for a property deed tax that will help to fund Land Back efforts. And we will challenge the state to require consent—not just consultation—for fossil energy permits that travel through treaty lands.[39]

As we stop to honor the water and each other, we will listen "For the heartbeat of God" and for the voices inside each of us that are calling us to be our best selves as we work in our communities, on this land to which we belong.

---

[37] The Giiwedinong Museum was created by Anishinaabe women and the nonprofit organization Akiing. The museum is located in the former Carnegie Library, which was then used as an Enbridge office. With the end of the Enbridge occupation of the North Country, they sold many of their properties including this one. Museum website at giiwedinong.org.

[38] Manoomin is Ojibwe and Psin is Dakota for wild rice.

[39] See Rise and Repair Alliance at riseandrepair.org.

2

CATHOLIC SISTERS AND CORNFIELD ACTIVISM
The Fight for Green Religious Rights

Mark Clatterbuck

The Sisters of the Adorers of the Blood of Christ
in Pennsylvania put a chapel right there where
the Atlantic Sunrise gas pipeline would come
through in order to block the pipeline. This is
literally putting your faith on the line.

—Yeb Saño (2020)
Executive Director, Greenpeace Southeast Asia

In July 2017, under a blistering sun, more than three hundred
local residents joined a community of Roman Catholic Sisters
in a Pennsylvania cornfield to dedicate a rustic outdoor chapel as
both sacred space and pipeline blockade.* The land on which this
Chapel of Resistance was built has been farmed by the Adorers

---

* A version of this chapter appeared in Mark Clatterbuck, "Catholic
Sisters and Cornfield Activism: The Fight for Green Religious Rights," *Journal
for the Study of Religion, Nature and Culture* 16, no. 2 (2022): 264–299. Copy-
right © 2022 Equinox Publishing Ltd. Used with permission.

of the Blood of Christ (ASC) since the 1920s. The Adorers are an international Catholic order of vowed religious women, some of whom live in community across the street from that cornfield. Between the chapel dedication in the summer of 2017 and the day that gas started to flow through the contested pipeline in the fall of 2018, a series of prayerful protests took place at that ritualized site of resistance. These protests resulted in the arrests of twenty-nine friends of the Sisters.

In many ways, the Adorers' story is a continuation of the one told by Sarah McFarland Taylor in *Green Sisters* (2007). Taylor's book chronicles the faith and work of the Sisters of Earth Network, a loosely affiliated community of earth-conscious Roman Catholic women religious throughout the United States and Canada. In other ways, the Adorers, who are not formally tied to the movement described by Taylor, offer important new insights into the ongoing phenomenon of Earth-conscious Sisters. This essay explores the organizational, liturgical, and legal dimensions of the Adorers' faith-based resistance by examining their rich partnership with local grassroots organizers, their performance of rituals as a tool of resistance against corporate exploitation of the natural world, and their invocation of religious liberty protections to pursue environmental justice in federal court. I conclude by considering the ways in which the Adorers' activism has exposed a deep divide between their own ecologically informed faith and an all-male Catholic hierarchy that consistently displayed indifference, and occasional hostility, toward their embodied green theology.

This is an unapologetically personal story for me, one that arises from my twin roles as scholar and activist. As a founding member of Lancaster Against Pipelines, the grassroots movement that partnered with the Adorers in the work of sacred resistance, my relationship to the Sisters is not merely as a professor of religion but also as a fellow advocate for environmental justice. Therefore, while much of the material for this project was generated through the traditional scholarly avenues of conducting interviews, scouring archives, poring over newspaper articles, digging through social media posts, and reading reams of legal briefs, my role as LAP's liaison to the Adorers means that my work is also informed by the hundreds of phone calls, thousands of emails, and countless face-to-face conversations that have passed between me and the Sisters while planning the interfaith vigils, frontline actions, press conferences, public lectures, and courtroom appearances described in the pages that follow. I share these observations both to locate myself in the story and to shed light on the methodology that informs my analysis.[1]

Spirited Eco-Activism Comes to Rural Pennsylvania

In early 2014, the Oklahoma-based pipeline giant Williams/Transco announced plans for a new $3 billion project called the Atlantic Sunrise Pipeline (ASP). The centerpiece of the project was a new 198-mile, forty-two-inch, high-pressure transmission line designed to carry fracked gas from Pennsylvania's Marcellus Shale region to processing facilities along the East Coast. The majority of the gas was contracted for markets in India and Japan.[2] The ASP construction process alone carried staggering

---

[1] Many of the quotes appearing in this chapter arose from a series of in-person interviews, both individual and group, that I conducted among the Adorers in July 2021 at their Ruma Center (Illinois) and in September 2021 at their De Mattias Center (Pennsylvania). During my time at Ruma, Sr. Regina Siegfried generously arranged for my access to the Order's archives. I'm deeply grateful to the many Adorers who shared their stories with me for this project. I also wish to acknowledge grant support for this project from the Louisville Institute.

[2] Dennis Witmer, "A Perspective on Natural Gas Markets: From Mount

environmental impacts:[3] 331 waterbody crossings, 251 wetland crossings, the permanent fragmentation of forty-five interior forests, the clear-cutting of more than twenty-six hundred acres of land, and further degradation of the Susquehanna River, which, in 2016, was ranked the third-most-endangered river in the United States.[4] The ASP also violated the conservation easements of more than forty preserved farms in Lancaster County alone,[5] while disproportionately targeting the county's Amish landowners, whose religious teachings, conveniently for Transco, discouraged them from challenging the company's eminent domain seizures in court.[6]

Since becoming operational in October 2018, the pipeline continues to threaten even greater ecological harms. Thousands of new fracked-gas wells will likely be drilled in Pennsylvania to service the new line, with each well consumptively using an average of 4.25 million gallons of water in its lifetime.[7] These new wells will require the disposal of toxic fracking fluid in containment ponds and injection wells, both of which routinely poison underground aquifers and local drinking water supplies. All of

---

Nebo to JKT," Lecture delivered at Millersville University, Pennsylvania, November 4, 2015; Alan Armstrong, "Williams Reports First-Quarter 2014 Financial Results," Williams, April 30, 2014.

[3] Federal Energy Regulatory Commission, *Draft Environmental Impact Statement*, vol. 1: *Atlantic Sunrise Project*, Docket No. CP15-138-000 (May 2016).

[4] American Rivers, "America's Most Endangered Rivers," Medium, April 11, 2016.

[5] Karen Martynick, "Comments to the Federal Energy Regulatory Commission," FERC Public Hearing, Manheim Township High School, Lancaster, PA, June 13, 2016.

[6] Mark Clatterbuck, "Amish Exploitation," Public Comment to the Federal Energy Regulatory Commission, Docket No. CP15-138-000, June 27, 2016.

[7] Andrew Kondash and Avner Vengosh, "Water Footprint of Hydraulic Fracturing," *Environmental Science and Technology Letters* (September 15, 2015): 276–280.

this activity will substantially increase methane emissions, which are already accelerating global warming at an alarming rate. Beyond the environmental harms, natural gas extraction through the process of hydraulic fracturing, more commonly known as fracking, also poses significant public health risks such as low birth weights, preterm births, increased rates and severity of asthma, congenital heart defects, migraines, chronic sinus symptoms, and severe fatigue. Studies have also identified increased cancer rates among children in heavily fracked regions of the country.[8] In June 2020, the Pennsylvania attorney general's office released a 243-page grand jury report detailing acute public health risks and environmental harms as a direct result of gas industry activity in the state, including the persistent contamination of drinking water.[9]

For all of these reasons, local residents founded a nonprofit called Lancaster Against Pipelines (LAP) to educate the public about the dangers posed by the ASP and to organize a grassroots resistance to derail the project.[10] My partner and I were among the founding members and served on the leadership board through the movement's five-year campaign. At first glance, Lancaster County appears to be an unlikely place for large-scale environmental activism. Donald Trump, who made climate denial and unfettered fossil fuel production centerpieces of his political agenda, won Lancaster County by a 20 percent margin in 2016 and a 15 percent margin in 2020. The county is home to

---

[8] Concerned Health Professionals of New York and Physicians for Social Responsibility, *Compendium of Scientific, Medical, and Media Findings Demonstrating Risks and Harms of Fracking (Unconventional Gas and Oil Extraction)*, 6th ed. (2019).

[9] Josh Shapiro, "Report 1 of the 43rd Statewide Investigating Grand Jury," Violations and Harms of the Pennsylvania Fracking Industry, Allegheny County Common Pleas, CP-02-MD-5947-2017, June 22, 2020, 22–47.

[10] For more on the LAP community, see https://www.facebook.com/lancasteragainstpipelines/.

one of the nation's largest Amish populations, a deeply conservative religious community that avoids the spotlight and generally eschews the political fray.[11] Given the rural landscape and stoic German heritage of the county, residents have a reputation for keeping their heads down and minding their own business, hardly a recipe for grassroots activism. But from 2014 to 2018, Lancaster County was home to one of the most vibrant pipeline battles in the country. In the final two years of the campaign, roughly a thousand residents pledged support for civil disobedience to resist the pipeline. Of those, six hundred attended locally run direct-action training workshops. By the time the pipeline became operational, LAP had organized over twenty nonviolent mass actions against the project resulting in fifty-three arrests.

In September 2016, I received a phone call from Sister Sara Dwyer, a vowed member of the Adorers of the Blood of Christ, who led the Order's Office of Justice, Peace, and Integrity of Creation. Dwyer told me that the courageous, prayerful activism of tribal elders fighting the Dakota Access Pipeline (DAPL) at Standing Rock, North Dakota, which was reaching a crescendo at the time, had inspired the Adorers to elevate their own opposition to fossil fuels from passive noncompliance to active resistance. As I explore later in this chapter, environmental justice has long played a central role in the Order's charism. According to Dwyer, the Order's leadership decided that the best way to support the #NoDAPL movement was to openly join the pipeline resistance taking place in Lancaster County, Pennsylvania, where members of the Adorers have lived and managed farmland since the 1920s.

---

[11] Although the majority of Amish choose not to vote, the Republican Party has made a concerted effort in recent years to increase voter turnout among the group as evidenced in the 2016 establishment of the Amish PAC. Julie Zausmer, "The Famously Secluded Amish Are the Target of a Republican Campaign to Drum Up Pennsylvania Votes for Trump," *The Washington Post* (October 9, 2019).

In her book *Inspired Sustainability*, Erin Lothes Biviano asks a compelling question: when it comes to religious communities that are committed, in principle, to environmental justice, why do so many fail to translate those convictions into action?[12] She suggests three key obstacles that account for this disconnect between faith and action: the knowledge gap, the caring gap, and the action gap.[13] Conversely, she identifies "the power of group energy" and "collective conversion" as key drivers for helping communities, who have already mastered the knowledge and caring gaps, to make the final leap across the action gap.[14] This was certainly the case for the Adorers, whose quiet opposition to the gas pipeline was transformed into bold, public defiance in solidarity with the Indigenous Water Protectors at Standing Rock.[15]

Moved to action by the courage and boldness of the Native Water Protectors at Standing Rock, Sister Sara wanted to know how the Adorers and LAP might work together to resist construction of the Atlantic Sunrise Pipeline in our own community. Just as the Indigenous-led #NoDAPL movement wed prayer and ceremony to a sacrificial defense of the Earth to form a seamless garment of communal activism, the Sisters were ready to nourish the grassroots work of LAP with the deep waters of their own spirituality.[16] She explained that the Adorers felt drawn to the

---

[12] Erin Lothes Biviano, *Inspired Sustainability: Planting Seeds for Action* (Maryknoll, NY: Orbis Books, 2016).

[13] Biviano, *Inspired Sustainability*, 58–59.

[14] Biviano, *Inspired Sustainability*, 111–145.

[15] For more on the #NoDAPL movement, see Nick Estes, *Our History Is the Future: Standing Rock versus the Dakota Access Pipeline, and the Long Tradition of Indigenous Resistance* (London: Verso, 2019). For an important study placing the Standing Rock resistance within the centuries-long Indigenous fight for environmental justice, see Dina Gilio-Whitaker, *As Long as Grass Grows: The Indigenous Fight for Environmental Justice, from Colonization to Standing Rock* (Boston: Beacon Press, 2019).

[16] While a shared reliance on ceremony and spiritual convictions link

spiritual values evident in LAP's work. Despite being a federal 501(c)(3) without formal religious affiliation, LAP's educational events, rallies, flyers, press statements, and social media posts regularly referenced "sacred resistance," "spiritual strength," and "moral clarity." A number of key positions in the organization were filled by local religious leaders, lay and clergy. At the height of LAP's direct-action campaign, four of its seven board members were associated with Community Mennonite Church of Lancaster (CMCL), including one who was a pastor on staff at the time. In 2017 and 2018, CMCL held Easter sunrise services at two different blockade sites along the pipeline route and hosted a LAP-sponsored direct-action training workshop in their sanctuary. The LAP ethos was a natural fit with the Adorers' own faith-based opposition to the pipeline. An article in the *New Yorker*, "The Renegade Nuns That Took on a Pipeline," quotes Sister Sara Dwyer calling LAP's founders "the religious leaders of our day."[17] A shared understanding of ecojustice as a sacred calling was the foundation for the relationship that developed between the Adorers of the Blood of Christ and Lancaster Against Pipelines during their multiyear direct-action campaign. Indeed, a reverence for creation and a penchant for sacred rebellion have been in the Order's DNA from its founding.

---

the #NoDAPL movement in North Dakota and the ASP resistance in Pennsylvania, crucial differences distinguish the campaigns. The former was led by Indigenous communities who have experienced centuries of state-sanctioned violence and overt racism and whose ceremonial traditions have been systematically suppressed by federal and state governments throughout US history; the other was led primarily by white Christians who continue to enjoy extraordinary social, legal, and political privileges in the United States. As such, Indigenous Water and Land Protectors routinely face much greater risks on the front lines on environmental justice campaigns compared to their white allies.

[17] Eliza Griswold, "The Renegade Nuns That Took on a Pipeline," *The New Yorker*, April 10, 2019.

The "Obedient Rebel": A Charism of Action

Sister Bernice Klostermann, a vowed member of the Adorers for sixty-one years, recently told me, "Religious women are known, as a group, to do things that need to be done. If you're looking for change, look at religious women and how they push forward."[18] This certainly has been the case for their own Order, which was founded in 1834 by Saint Maria de Mattias in Italy. Following a mystical vision at the age of sixteen, Maria developed a deep devotion to the transforming power of Christ's blood. This devotion, combined with her captivating public preaching and organizational prowess, produced a prolific life of service.

Maria's efforts were particularly focused on the education and spiritual formation of women, leading her to establish nearly seventy schools primarily for women in underserved, rural communities. The community of women she inspired during her lifetime continued to grow following her death in 1866, eventually spreading throughout Europe, the United States, South America, Asia, Africa, and elsewhere around the world. Historically, the Order's ministries have focused heavily on the education of women and children, orphanages, and caring for the sick and elderly. Today, the Adorers comprise roughly eleven hundred Sisters living in twenty-five countries. Their work remains dedicated to social action, especially in the pursuit of antiracism efforts, immigration reform, and care of the environment.

Despite the crucial support she received from Gaspar de Bufalo and other clergy who supported her in establishing the Adorers, Maria de Mattias was often denounced by the Catholic hierarchy, who disapproved of her wildly popular preaching and

---

[18] Kristen Forgotch, Leona Hunter, Bernice Klostermann, Anne Marie Meadowcroft, Helene Trueitt, and Martha Wachtel, interview by Mark Clatterbuck, De Mattias House, Columbia, Pennsylvania, September 3, 2021.

the large crowds that she attracted.

Maria's biographer Michele Colagiovanni, who titled the story of her life *Obedient Rebel*, records how she was regularly derided as a would-be priest.[19] The archpriest of Acuto reportedly declared with disgust, "One of these days, she will go to the confessional or you'll see her secretly saying Mass!"[20]

St. Maria's fearless commitment to underserved communities through actions considered unconventional by the standards of her time continues to animate the work of the Adorers in the US region today. "When you study our history, not only in relation to the Earth but across the board, when it comes to power, we were the ones who tried to raise the voice," says Sister Sara Dwyer. "[Our foundress] went against the power structures of the church even to get established as a congregation. And when you look at our history, we've always kind of pushed the boundaries." She says the Adorers have long understood their mission "to listen to the word of God, to be grounded in the word of God, but to rebel against anything that's oppressive."[21] Sister Bernice Klostermann agrees and ties this historical orientation to the Order's current work for climate justice:

> Our whole constitution, through St. Maria de Mattias our foundress, calls us to do what we can "to bring about the beautiful order of things." ... At that time, it was education of women, and helping women. Now, it's the call for the environment.[22]

---

[19] Michele Colagiovanni, *Obedient Rebel: The Story of Maria de Mattias*, trans. Pauline Grady, ASC (St. Louis: Christian Board of Publication Press, 1991).

[20] Colagiovanni, *Obedient Rebel*, 81.

[21] Dani Brought, Sara Dwyer, Maria Hughes, Janet McCann, and Mary Alan Wurth, interview by Mark Clatterbuck, Adorers of the Blood of Christ Ruma Center, Ruma, Illinois, July 29, 2021.

[22] Forgotch, Hunter, et al., interview.

Caption: *The Adorers of the Blood of Christ have been caring for their farmland in Lancaster County since the 1920s. Environmental justice is a core part of the Order's religious mission.*   (CREDIT: ADORERS ARCHIVE / USED WITH PERMISSION)

This "call for the environment" was, in fact, a key part of what first brought the Adorers to rural Lancaster County in the 1920s. The newly established community eagerly embraced farm life, planting the fields and tending the orchards in their bulky habits and wimples. Sister Maria Hughes, who served on the Adorers' US region leadership team until 2023, when she was installed as General Superior in Rome, emphasizes the impact that the "farming sisters" of Pennsylvania have had on the Order through the years. She refers to the "seed" of charism that resides in each person at birth, which is then nurtured during one's life. Considering that so many of the Sisters grew up in farming families, Hughes believes that the legacy of tending the land has shaped the Adorers' work right up to the present time, nationally and around the world.[23] This deep connection to the

---

[23] Brought, Dwyer, et al., interview.

land among the Lancaster County Sisters is viscerally expressed in Sister Leona Hunter's reaction to the moment when pipeline construction began on their farmland:

> The most intense time of being with the LAP group for me was when ... the big machinery was coming in to work, and when I saw that hitting the earth and tearing it apart, I just felt like part of me was being ripped apart. The Earth was being violated and it really, really touched me. I actually cried when I saw that, and it brings tears even now.[24]

In 1985, the Order's Provincial Assembly in Ruma, Illinois, established an Earth Stewardship Committee to support sustainable local agriculture during the farm crisis in the Midwest.[25] At their 1995 International General Assembly, the Sisters committed themselves to "radical initiatives for our planet's welfare and to a lifestyle which is ecologically responsible."[26] In 1997, the Order hosted a global Earth Summit at their rural center in Ruma to explore the relationship between ASC spirituality and ecology. At that summit, Adorers from across the US were joined by participants from Europe, Asia, South America, and Africa.[27]

In 2005, the Adorers formalized their environmental priorities in a "Land Ethic" that declares, in part:

> As Adorers, we honor the sacredness of all creation; we cultivate a mystical consciousness that connects us to the Holy in all of life. As women, we celebrate the rhythms

---

[24] Forgotch, Hunter, et al., interview.

[25] Adorers of the Blood of Christ, "Earth Stewardship Committee: Early History (1985–1991)," Adorers Archives, Ruma, Illinois.

[26] Liz Quirin, "Women Religious Hold World Summit on Environment," *St. Louis Review*, August 29, 1997.

[27] Quirin, "Women Religious Hold World Summit on Environment."

of creation. . . . As prophets, we reverence Earth as a
sanctuary where all life is protected.[28]

The document instructs members of the Order to "choose simple
lifestyles that avoid excessive or harmful use of natural resources"
and to "seek collaborators to help implement land use policies and practices that are in harmony with our bioregions and
ecosystems."[29] The Order has pursued such collaborators around
the globe. Adorers serving in Guatemala, for example, have spent
the past decade supporting La Puya, a grassroots resistance movement working to protect local drinking water from dangerous
gold mining operations. La Puya's efforts have included a four-
year human blockade of the US-based El Tambor mine. Sister
Dani Brought, who served the community as a healthcare
administrator, joined the resistance and provided medical care for
villagers following brutal attacks by riot police and vigilantes.[30]

Putting faith into action lies at the heart of the Adorers'
mission. Sometimes that commitment has come at a terrible cost.
In 1992, five of the community's members were martyred in Liberia
during the course of their mission activity as educators and healthcare workers.[31] Their witness of ultimate sacrifice in fulfillment of
the Order's charism continues to guide and inspire the Sisters' lives
of service today. When paired with their conviction that care of
Creation is a gospel imperative—or as Sister Dani Brought explains,

---

[28] Adorers of the Blood of Christ, "Land Ethic," https://adorers.org/
asc-land-ethic/.

[29] Adorers of the Blood of Christ, "Land Ethic."

[30] See Mary Jo McConahay, "On the Front Lines of Mining Protests
with the Maya," *National Catholic Reporter*, March 23, 2015.

[31] For an examination of how these Sisters' deaths shed light on the
changing nature of martyrdom in contemporary Christianity, see Elizabeth
Kolmer, "The Death of Five Adorers of the Blood of Christ and the Changing
Meaning of Martyrdom," *US Catholic Historian* 24, no. 3 (Summer 2006):
149–164. Kolmer's sister and cousin were among the victims.

"We are called as Adorers to live the word of God. And the first word of God is creation"—it is hardly surprising that eco-activism is a core mandate of their continuing witness today.[32]

Sister Anne Irose offers a striking articulation of her Order's commitment to environmental justice and action-driven faith. After spending decades among the Aymara and Quechua communities in Bolivia, she believes that the Catholic Church has a great deal to learn from Indigenous ways of interacting with the natural world. Her theological orientation is unabashedly rooted in Latin American liberation theology, a tradition that gives priority to orthopraxis over orthodoxy and embraces an ecclesiology from below, rejecting hierarchical top-down models of the church. During her time in Bolivia, she was immersed in *communidades de base*, a lay-driven movement of ecclesial base communities. Years after returning to the United States, she still speaks longingly of these small groups that are "directed by laypeople" where often "there are no priests around," explaining, "There's no sermon. Everybody shares the word of God. And it's always for action—to look, to see, to judge what the word of God is calling us to do and then to act, go forth, and to do!" For Sister Anne, the work of the church is dependent on the community, not on the hierarchy. "It's wherever *we* are. We are the church, and we are empowered by this word which is so forcefully present in the entire world."[33]

---

[32] The Adorers' example of bold and courageous work for environmental justice confirms many of the observations raised by John E. Carroll in his book *Sustainability and Spirituality* (2004). In his analysis of women religious engaged in ecojustice work, he identifies several factors that are found among the Adorers: a deep sense of place, a willingness to challenge the status quo born of an inherently countercultural monastic lifestyle and frontlines work among marginalized communities, a commitment to living out their values despite the costs, and extensive—sometimes dangerous—international service.

[33] Anne Irose, interview by Mark Clatterbuck, Adorers of the Blood of Christ Ruma Center, Ruma, Illinois, July 30, 2021.

For Sister Anne, faith does not exist in the abstract. Instead, it is rooted in the natural world and must always be expressed in action.

The Cornfield Chapel

Given the Adorers' history of costly public service and passionate commitment to environmental justice, it was hardly a surprise when the Sisters refused Transco's financial offers to secure permission to build a climate-warming fossil fuel pipeline on their Pennsylvania farmland. This time, it was a group of local environmentalists who became their "collaborators" to "reverence the Earth as a sanctuary." Over lunch one day in the spring of 2017, at their St. Maria de Mattias community house, the Sisters met with members of LAP to craft a partnership of resistance to Transco's pipeline, a project that both groups considered a violation of the sacred. By the end of the meal, everyone around the table had agreed to build a rustic outdoor prayer arbor in the middle of the Adorers' cornfield, directly in the path of the proposed pipeline. Beyond serving as a public proclamation of their faith, this Chapel of Resistance, as some of the Sisters called it, would also be a place where people from any religious tradition, or none at all, could gather to pray, celebrate the Earth, and live out their own convictions about the sacredness of the land.

Within weeks, LAP started construction on the chapel. The project was overseen by Jon Telesco, a local builder, animal rights activist, and key leader in Lancaster's pipeline fight. It included an altar, an arbor, and wooden outdoor pews surrounded by a low rope fence. When LAP and the Sisters posted an open invitation for a dedication service at the site, gas industry advocates reacted swiftly. The region's largest pro-industry newsletter responded with an inflammatory screed that began, "Here's a story of some Catholic nuns who have forsaken their vow to serve Christ, and instead have taken up a vow to serve radical environmentalism—which is apparently their new religion."[34] In the months that followed, the same influential newsletter accused the Adorers of "sacrificing Christ on the alter [*sic*] of politics"[35] and routinely referred to these vowed Catholic women as "Sisters of the Corn," a reference to Stephen King's famous short story "Children of the Corn" in which a cult of murderous children worships a demonic cornfield deity.[36]

Transco's lawyers also wasted no time in responding to news of the dedication. Within days of the announcement, the company filed an emergency motion in US District Court for the Eastern District of Pennsylvania, seeking immediate seizure of the Sisters' land, even before the land was condemned through eminent domain.[37] Testimony accompanying the motion declared, "It appears that Landowners—in conjunction with Lancaster Against Pipelines—are seeking to obstruct construction of the Project and/or interfere with Transco's possession of the Rights of Way [by] dedicating the 'prayer chapel' on the Rights of Way."[38]

Transco had good reason to be worried. Flyers advertising the event featured stylized praying hands blocking bulldozers, accompanied by the following event description:

---

[34] Jim Willis, "Catholic Nuns Use Radicals to Build Chapel in Path of PA Pipeline," *Marcellus Drilling News,* July 7, 2017.

[35] Jim Willis, "Lancaster Nuns Continue to Agitate against Already-Installed Pipeline," *Marcellus Drilling News,* March 26, 2018.

[36] Jim Willis, "Sisters of the Corn Say Fight to Stop Atlantic Sunrise Not Over," *Marcellus Drilling News*, August 31, 2017; Jim Willis, "End of the Road for Sisters of the Corn re Atlantic Sunrise Pipe," *Marcellus Drilling News,* February 20, 2019.

[37] *Transco v. Adorers,* "Document 8: Plaintiff's Emergency Motion," US District Court for the Eastern District of Pennsylvania, June 20, 2017.

[38] *Transco v. Adorers,* "Document 8-2: Statement of Aaron Blair," US District Court for the Eastern District of Pennsylvania, June 20, 2017, 2.

The cornfield Chapel of Resistance in rural Lancaster County, Pennsylvania, became the visible symbol and epicenter of the Adorers' religious objection to a climate warming fracked gas pipeline that was forced on their farmland by eminent domain.   (PHOTO BY CHARLES MOSTOLLER / USED WITH PERMISSION)

> The Adorers carry a deep spiritual connection to the Earth as reflected in their "Land Ethic." People of good-will, from all faith traditions, are warmly invited to participate in this dedication service marking this as a Site of Sacred Resistance against corporate exploitation of Creation.[39]

To the Sisters' relief, the judge denied Transco's bid to immediately seize their land and dismantle the chapel. Two days later, more than three hundred people joined LAP and the Adorers to dedicate the space. The austere wooden benches were filled to capacity, with additional lawn chairs packing the perimeter.

---

[39] Lancaster Against Pipelines, "Chapel Dedication Flyer," July 15, 2017.

Sister Janet McCann, the Adorers' US regional councilor and point person for the Order's partnership with LAP, delivered the homily. She said of the Sisters' chapel blockade, "This is not a political statement but a spiritual stand as people of faith."[40] The two-hour service concluded with a ribbon-tying ceremony as congregants showed their solidarity by offering silent intentions while leaving colorful strips of material on the rope fence encircling the Chapel. In doing so, the Sisters were realizing their vision for a sacred site where inner convictions about the sacredness of Earth took visible form in acts of ritual performance. Two large signs, one planted on each side of the chapel entrance, greeted congregants as they gathered for the service. One contained the Sisters' Land Ethic. The other displayed LAP's Pledge to Resist, which concluded with a communal "vow to protect our communities through nonviolent Civil Disobedience" by putting "our bodies between the land we love and those seeking to destroy it."[41]

Following the dedication service, the Sisters and their allies began holding weekly prayer vigils at the chapel. Clergy and lay leaders from a variety of local Protestant churches took part.[42] The vigils were intentionally interreligious and steeped in the tradition of nonviolent social activism. Passages from the *Tao Te Ching* and the Qur'an mingled freely with readings from Martin Luther King Jr.'s "Letter from a Birmingham Jail." The founder of a local engaged Buddhist sangha became a regular attendee. Local Jewish congregants held a Rosh Hashana service at the chapel later that fall. Members of the Lancaster Friends Quaker

---

[40] Janet McCann, "Chapel Dedication Homily," Columbia, Pennsylvania, July 9, 2017.

[41] McCann, "Chapel Dedication Homily."

[42] For a story celebrating this ecumenical activism, see Anne Sensenig, "Lancaster Protests Pipeline with Quilt, Worship, Bodies," *Mennonite Creation Care Network Newsletter*, November 11, 2017.

Meeting began convening there on Saturday mornings for silent meditation.

The chapel soon became a pilgrimage destination for faith-based activists far beyond Lancaster County. Groups of Catholic sisters from across the region journeyed to the site, leaving packets of songs and prayers for future pilgrims. Volunteers with the Catholic Worker movement, including a group from New York City, made regular visits to the consecrated cornfield; some were later arrested during peaceful mass actions at the chapel. Many eco-pilgrims left colorful prayer ties to symbolize their solidarity with the Adorers. One group installed a wooden birdhouse inscribed with the words, "One day a family of beautiful choir singers will move in this house to help defend this chapel and to remind you of why you stand strong." An offering of eclectic items sprang spontaneously around the altar: handwritten notes of support, printed prayers, small stones, loaves of bread, fresh produce, flowers, and a pair of Pennsylvania Dutch cornhusk dolls. One woman left a pair of well-worn shoes, the date of her baptism scrawled across them with a Sharpie.

One of the most intriguing aspects of the movement was the extent to which self-identified nonreligious individuals participated in the Cornfield Chapel phenomenon. I regularly spoke with vigil attendees, including some who participated in direct actions at the site, who openly aired their distaste for traditional religious practice while feeling entirely at home singing hymns and offering prayers alongside these ecopassionate Catholic nuns. A shared commitment to the sacredness of Earth seemed to transcend sectarian divides, creating an extraecclesial community bound together by a shared "ultimate concern" for the natural world, to borrow Paul Tillich's famous phrase. One local resident, who had abandoned organized religion years earlier, was so drawn to the Earth-loving faith she encountered at the chapel that she asked to be baptized under the arbor. She later publicly testified at a chapel vigil that, although her mother used to call her "a heathen," a deep love for the land and attachment to the chapel proved her mother wrong. As Sister Sara Dwyer observed about this striking alliance of religious and secular lovers of the land, "That's one of the beautiful things. People of any religion or no religion can get behind the sacredness of Earth."[43] This partnership between the Adorers and non–religiously affiliated environmental advocates appears to be consistent with a larger national movement as reflected in the Nuns & Nones initiative established in 2016 that brings together Catholic sisters and diverse spiritual seekers who, despite their dogmatic differences, share a deep commitment to community, spirituality, and justice.[44]

Another remarkable feature of the Adorers-LAP partnership is the extent to which the Sisters credit this grassroots activist movement for helping the Order live more fully into their own charism. Dwyer recently spoke to me about her first experience participating in LAP's direct-action campaign, which took place at a frontline pipeline blockade that local activists had dubbed "The Stand." "When I went to the Stand for the first time," said Dwyer, "I was on fire, because you all were on fire. . . . For me, it was just like a sacramental moment."[45] For Sister Janet McCann, the partnership with LAP was

> a way that we [Adorers] can publicly give witness to what we have on paper, and what we say we believe. It was a way to give witness to that. We've talked often that we could not have done what we did on our own. . . . Fear is contagious, but so is courage. We received that gift from LAP a lot throughout this process.[46]

---

[43] Kelly Adams (dir.), *Atlantic Sunrise* (2019).

[44] See www.nunsandnones.org.

[45] Brought, Dwyer, et al., interview.

[46] Brought, Dwyer, et al., interview.

Sister Anne Marie called the Adorers' collaboration with LAP a "godsend" through which "God was telling us something—that we had to speak out."[47] For Sister Bernice Klostermann, her encounter with LAP came as a sacred calling: "My faith says, 'Do what you can.' For me, the call came from Lancaster Against Pipelines."[48] She described her participation in direct actions at the chapel in overtly religious terms: "They were such sacred moments. Such sacred moments."[49]

The chapel's ability to become both an interreligious and extrareligious space of eco-activism was made possible partly by the Adorers' belief that God's love, presence, and activity transcend dogmatic loyalties and sectarian divides. Sister Bernice Klostermann has described the rich confluence of religious and secular participants at the chapel like this: "It's the God within each one of us that reaches out to the God in the other person, no matter what we call them or how we worship."[50] Regardless of our varied religious backgrounds, she believes that we need to ask critical questions about shared values and what brings people together. This is why Bernice says that, during vigils and actions at the chapel, "We never looked at what our differences were. We looked at what was common to all of us."[51]

Sister Mary Alan Wurth was born and raised on a farm in central Illinois, holds a doctorate in physiology, and has been an Adorer for sixty-three years. She believes the unifying principle at the chapel was a shared commitment to what St. Maria de Mattias called "the beautiful order of things." Wurth explained that, while protecting "that beautiful order" certainly draws on each person's

---

[47] Forgotch, Hunter, et al., interview.
[48] Forgotch, Hunter, et al., interview.
[49] Forgotch, Hunter, et al., interview.
[50] Forgotch, Hunter, et al., interview.
[51] Forgotch, Hunter, et al., interview.

"particular spirituality," it also relies on what she calls "a universal spirituality."[52] Sister Anne Irose develops this theological concept even further. "The Christ of the universe, the universal Christ, is not the historical Jesus," she explained, adding, "Jesus was great, but *this* is the universal Christ from the very beginning. From the very beginning was Father, Son, Spirit. In whatever way we explain it, from the very beginning was that Spirit."[53] She contends that the divine nature found in Jesus the Christ is the same divine nature found in Creation. In this way, the communion experienced among fellow defenders of the natural world is inherently spiritual and transcends religious affiliation.

As the Adorers' grassroots resistance in partnership with LAP gained more participants and wider media coverage, Williams/Transco redoubled their efforts. Despite the company's earlier failure to access the Adorers' land by way of a court-sanctioned land grab, it nonetheless persisted in its efforts to seize the property through eminent domain. The Sisters responded by invoking the Religious Freedom Restoration Act (RFRA) in US District Court.[54] Their complaint asserted that forcing a fossil fuel pipeline on their farmland was "antithetical to the deeply held religious beliefs and convictions of the Adorers," whose "religious practice includes protecting and preserving creation, which they believe is a revelation of God, the sacredness of which must be honored and protected for future generations."[55]

RFRA won unanimous support in the US House and near-unanimous support in the Senate (97-3) on its way to becoming

---

[52] Brought, Dwyer, et al., interview.

[53] Irose, interview.

[54] The Adorers' years-long legal battle against the ASP has been led by Lancaster County attorneys Dwight Yoder and Sheila O'Rourke of Gibbel Kraybill & Hess.

[55] *Adorers v. FERC and Transco*, US District Court for the Eastern District of Pennsylvania, amended complaint, August 11, 2017, §1.

law in 1993. It stipulates, "Government shall not substantially burden a person's exercise of religion even if the burden results from a rule of general applicability," unless the burden is determined to be the least restrictive means of furthering a compelling governmental interest.[56] The Sisters argued that being coerced by the government, through eminent domain, to use their own property for a privately owned climate warming pipeline was a direct violation of their deeply held religious convictions. The court disagreed.

In a sharply worded opinion defending Transco's seizure of the Adorers' land, District Judge Jeffrey Schmehl bluntly dismissed the Sisters' RFRA claims.[57] That opinion was accompanied by a court order validating Transco's "substantive right to condemn" the Adorers' land.[58] The order included a heavy-handed enforcement provision, authorizing the US Marshal Service "to investigate and to arrest, confine in prison and/or bring before the Court" anyone who interfered with Transco's seizure of the land.[59] Clearly aware of the Sisters' partnership with LAP, the judge warned that the Sisters themselves would be subject to arrest and confinement in federal prison if they authorized "third parties" to interfere with pipeline activity on their property.[60]

Rituals of Resistance

Pipeline construction on the Sisters' farmland was set to begin on Monday, October 16, 2017. Undeterred, the Sisters posted a Call to Action on their website inviting supporters to join them

---

[56] Religious Freedom Restoration Act of 1993, 42 USC § 2000bb, §3.

[57] "Memorandum Opinion," *Transco v. Adorers*, US District Court for the Eastern District of Pennsylvania, Document 29, August 23, 2017, 22.

[58] "Order," *Transco v. Adorers*, US District Court for the Eastern District of Pennsylvania, Document 30, August 23, 2017, §3.

[59] "Order," *Transco v. Adorers*, §3.

[60] "Order," *Transco v. Adorers*, §3.

"in holy Vigil" at their Chapel of Resistance.[61] LAP also issued a public call for action, which welcomed supporters to "hold a prayerful, songful vigil at the very edge of Williams' desecration corridor."[62] They warned that "those who choose to place themselves in the pipeline easement should be prepared to face arrest by US Marshals who, despite their duty to serve and protect the citizens of this nation, will be serving, instead, the financial interests of a private, for-profit, out-of-state, billionaire-run, fossil fuel industry."[63]

The evening before Transco broke ground on the Adorers' land, a solemn vigil was held at the chapel. The weight of the approaching conflict was evident in the songs, prayers, and reflections chosen for the service. Sister Bernice Klostermann was among those who spoke, raising the poignant question, "How do I find God in my enemy?" She called on congregants to move with both nonviolence and reverence when confronting pipeline workers in the days ahead.[64] The next morning, just after sunrise, roughly one hundred supporters of the Sisters were gathered at the chapel. Pipeline security personnel, local police, state troopers, and US marshals were also on site. After a time of singing, leaders of LAP spoke of the "moral crisis" posed by the pipeline, urging participants to engage in peaceful, disciplined resistance. A variety of roles were assigned to ensure an orderly day of protest: police liaisons, legal observers, song leaders, medics. A large military-style support tent had been erected beside the chapel space to provide participants with food, water, cots, and medical attention if needed.

---

[61] Adorers of the Blood of Christ, "Call to Action," October 2017.

[62] Lancaster Against Pipelines, mass email, "Call to Action" at chapel, October 14, 2017.

[63] Lancaster Against Pipelines, mass email.

[64] Bernice Klostermann, message at chapel in Columbia, Pennsylvania, October 15, 2017, audio recording by author.

It was midmorning when construction activity began. In an interview with Lancaster's local newspaper after the event, a Transco spokesperson conceded that the company chose the Adorers' land as the first location to break ground along the two-hundred-mile construction corridor as a direct result of the Sisters' public opposition.[65] When the first excavator rolled onto the field, it was swarmed by local allies of the Sisters who formed a human blockade in front of the machinery, bringing it to a standstill. The group carried a rustic wooden processional cross draped with colorful ribbons, along with banners proclaiming "You Will Not Spoil This Land" and "You Will Not Endanger Our People." For more than an hour, familiar hymns and well-known movement songs filled the air, from "Amazing Grace" and "This Little Light of Mine," to "Solid as a Rock" and "Which Side Are You On?"[66]

Later that morning, the police issued their final warning for pipeline opponents to leave the portion of the Sisters' farmland that Transco had recently seized for its right-of-way. Twenty-three people remained, ranging in age from sixteen to eighty-six, singing until the last person was arrested.[67] They were handcuffed, transported to local police stations, and ultimately detained in Lancaster County Prison until the following day. Three pastors from three different denominations were among those arrested, along with the coordinator of a local engaged Buddhist community rooted in the teachings of Thich Nhat Hanh.

---

[65] Ad Crable, "Contested Land Owned by Nuns Is First Spot for Atlantic Sunrise Pipe Burial in Lancaster County," LNP Lancaster Online, November 3, 2017.

[66] Lancaster Against Pipelines, "Chapel 23 Arrests," October 16, 2017, video file, https://www.facebook.com/lancasteragainstpipelines/videos/758510657674699/?__so__=channel_tab&__rv__=all_videos_card.

[67] Ad Crable and Lindsey Blest, "Authorities Release Names of 21 Protesters Arrested after Blocking Start of Atlantic Sunrise Gas Pipeline Construction," LNP Lancaster Online, October 17, 2017.

*Catholic Sisters and members of LAP carry a cross into the pipeline corridor on
the Adorers' farmland. Palm Sunday, Lancaster County, PA.*
(PHOTO BY DAVID PARRY / USED WITH PERMISSION)

In the months that followed, community members joined
the Adorers and LAP in a series of additional direct actions.
Central to the Sisters' campaign was the use of religious ceremonies as acts of sacred resistance. Less than a week following that
initial action, dubbed the Chapel 23, six individuals, including
members of the Catholic Worker movement, were arrested while
disrupting pipeline construction by way of a quilt blockade at
the chapel site. The fifty-foot quilt contained hundreds of handmade squares, each designed by a different local resident and
collectively expressing the community's opposition to the pipeline. Given the rich quilt-making heritage among the region's
Mennonite and Amish communities, the months-long process
of crafting the individual squares, and then sewing them
into attachable panels to stretch across the full length of the

construction corridor, can be understood as a quintessentially Lancaster County ritual.

One week later, eighty local residents marched with several Sisters into an active work site adjacent to the chapel carrying a processional cross, singing hymns, and offering homemade bread to a confused crew of welders and backhoe operators. Sister Sara Dwyer, who led the procession, explained to the outdoor assembly how the modified eucharistic meal was simultaneously a celebration of the Earth's bounty, a ritual of repentance for humanity's violence against the natural world, and a public call to halt construction of the pipeline. The congregational trespassers joined hands in a large circle, offering prayers and hymns until Pennsylvania state troopers descended on the site with tactical zip-tie handcuffs to arrest everyone in the construction zone. The ceremony concluded before any arrests were made.

The Adorers chose Palm Sunday for another demonstration of liturgical resistance. Defying industry warnings to stay off the dormant worksite on their own farmland, the Sisters were joined by a large congregation in raising a ten-foot wooden cross in the middle of the right-of-way. Participants also created a large, heart-shaped prayer labyrinth out of straw bales directly in front of the cross. Together these sacred objects made a pipe-line blockade out of the heart-and-cross logo that serves as the Adorers' official symbol. During the ceremony, which doubled as a direct action, the Sisters led the congregation in praying the Stations of the Cross around the labyrinth. They also issued an open invitation for supporters to use the new labyrinth as a public site of meditation in the days ahead, despite Transco's demand to stay off the property. Additionally, two signs were posted in the middle of the construction zone beside these newly installed religious structures. One was the Adorers' Land Ethic. The other contained this straightforward proclamation: "We continue to affirm our religious right—and duty—to challenge Transco's unholy and unconstitutional seizure of our land for a climate-warming fossil fuel project in direct violation of our deeply held religious convictions."

Friends of the Adorers block pipeline construction on the Sisters' farmland with songs and prayers. Twenty-three were arrested on site, ranging in age from sixteen to eighty-six years old. The Cornfield Chapel is in the background. Lancaster County, PA.
(PHOTO BY DAVID JONES / USED WITH PERMISSION)

In July 2018, a crowd of supporters joined the Sisters for a service marking the chapel's one-year anniversary. After a time of songs, prayers, and reflections at the chapel, the congregation processed into the construction corridor to encircle the cross and straw-bale labyrinth where Sister Mary Alan Wurth led a call-and-response. The chant declared solidarity with the forests, the rivers, and the ecosystem, and with pipeline resistance movements around the country—from Camp White Pine in Pennsylvania, to Camp Turtle Island on the White Earth Chippewa (Anishinaabe) Reservation in Minnesota, to the Standing Rock Sioux (Lakota and Dakota) Reservation in North Dakota. The Sisters closed the ceremony by leading congregants in a ritual scattering of wildflower seeds, symbolizing their hope that new life would spring from that sacred site of resistance despite the deadly fossil fuel pipeline being planted in their field.

In her book *For the Wild*, Sarah M. Pike identifies two kinds of rituals that are routinely found among eco-activist communities: rituals of conversion that initiate individuals into the realm of environmental activism and subsequent rituals of protest enacted to defend the natural world.[68] For the Sisters, their conversion was understood primarily in the context of the Catholic theological tradition. Pope Francis himself called for 'ecological conversion' in his 2015 encyclical *Laudato Si'*.[69] For many others in the movement, however, conversion to environmental activism was understood in less overtly theological terms, particularly for those who identified as having no religious affiliation. Even so, I argue that, for many of these individuals, their experience of ecological conversion and subsequent participation in eco-activism was no less religious than the experience of the Sisters.

I offer this claim with three observations in mind. First, the language of the Lancaster County pipeline resistance movement was awash in religious rhetoric, among secular and religious participants alike. Almost without exception, members of the movement described their turn to activism in familiar religious language: it was a sacred calling, a sacred duty, the most important thing in their lives, that which gave them meaning, their highest priority. As a consequence, high-stakes protests, including actions that carried a high probability of arrest and potential jail time, were embarked upon with a kind of joyful

---

[68] Sarah Pike, *For the Wild: Ritual and Commitment in Radical Eco-Activism* (Oakland: University of California Press, 2017), 16.

[69] Pope Francis, *Laudato Si': On Care for Our Common Home, The Encyclical of Pope Francis on the Environment*, with commentary by Sean McDonagh (Maryknoll, NY: Orbis Books, 2016), §§216–221.

eagerness that struck many outside observers as incongruous for a group of local residents who had, for the most part, never taken part in acts of civil disobedience before this pipeline fight.

Second, the movement's protests were consistently performed in a manner akin to religious devotion. All of the mass actions conducted at the chapel—including those that blockaded heavy equipment, confronted pipeline security personnel, and defied police orders—were carried out by individuals holding hands and singing spiritual songs, with eyes closed and faces turned upward as if in prayer. Their highly choreographed direct actions essentially functioned as religious ceremonies of rapturous disruption. This may explain why so many of the participants in the chapel actions balked at being called "protesters" or "activists," insisting instead that they were simply fulfilling a sacred obligation. Their experience of protest as religious ritual, rather than political action, is consistent with a growing body of testimony from social justice movements across the United States, including #NoDAPL and BLM.[70]

Third, the Adorers-LAP partnership cultivated a powerful sense of communal belonging among participants that produced striking parallels to a tightly knit religious community. During my years serving as LAP's liaison with the Sisters, I heard many members liken their experience in the movement to finding their true family. The group frequently gathered to celebrate the birth of babies, mourn deaths, and celebrate birthdays of its members. Participation in the work proved personally transformative for many. Others found a sense of belonging and shared purpose

---

[70] See Lily Oyster, "Field Notes from Standing Rock: Non-extraction as Spiritual Practice," *Cross Currents* 69.2 (June 2019): 128-136; Alexander Zaitchik, "On Native Grounds: Standing Rock's New Spirit of Protest," *The Baffler* (Spring 2017): 102–116; Hebah Farrag, "The Spirit in Black Lives Matter: New Spiritual Community in Black Radical Organizing," *Transition* 125 (2018): 76–88.

that so exceeded the connections they had previously experienced within faith congregations that they no longer felt compelled to attend traditional religious services. The Sisters, likewise, came to regard the movement as a kind of extraecclesial religious family.

Noting the lack of support that movement people felt from their own church, Sister Sara Dwyer described the "sense of community" that developed around the actions, regardless of religious "labels or stuff like that," until the movement, for many, "now became your faith home."[71]

Then Jesus Asked, "What Is Written in the Law and How Do You Read It?"

While these acts of ritual resistance were taking place in the cornfield, the Sisters continued waging their legal battle in the courtroom. After a US District Court dismissed their RFRA claim, citing lack of subject-matter jurisdiction, the Adorers took their case to the US Court of Appeals for the Third Circuit in Philadelphia. While the environmental impacts of increased fossil fuel consumption were at the heart of the Sisters' RFRA appeal, they were not the only religiously motivated argument presented in the filing. The Adorers also drew attention to the ways that climate change is closely linked to economic inequality, another core religious concern of the Sisters. Their filing argued that "the earth and its inhabitants, particularly the poor, are under serious threat due to global warming and climate change caused by the trapping of greenhouse gases created by the use of fossil fuels," adding pointedly, "The poor and most vulnerable will experience the greatest harm."[72]

---

[71] Brought, Dwyer, et al., interview.

[72] "Brief in Support of Appeal," *Adorers v. FERC and Transco*, US District Court for the Eastern District of Pennsylvania (November 2, 2017), 32.

According to Sister Sara Dwyer, many of the Adorers experienced a turning point around climate justice in the 1990s while
studying the work of Fr. Thomas Berry, among others.[73] They
began to see care of creation as an integral component of broader
social justice concerns. "We began understanding the significance
of humans and earth forming one sacred community," she says.
"Most of the Adorers had connections to the earth either by being
from farm families or serving in farm communities." She situates
the Order's staunch defense of the natural world squarely within
a Catholic pro-life ethos, broadly understood. "We began to see
that our ASC charism for life—and in particular, here in the US,
our 'Land Ethic'—was a moral and religious stance expanding and
deepening our pro-life values," Dwyer said. "We are one with the
Earth, one body of Christ, mutually and intimately interrelated."
For this reason, she expresses frustration for those Catholics whose
pro-life convictions are reserved exclusively for unborn babies,
while having no interest in "education, job training, housing or
other issues that foster life for a mother and child" *after* birth, let
alone the natural environment on which all life depends. "We
Adorers realized that, without clean air, clean water, and good soil,
there is no life—not for humans or creation!"[74]

Despite the Adorers' impassioned appeal for judicial relief,
the Third Circuit sided with Transco and the federal government

---

[73] Thomas Berry (d. 2009) was a Passionist priest and renowned scholar
in the history of religion, evolutionary cosmology, and religion and ecology.
He often referred to himself as a geologian. In her book *Green Sisters*,
Sarah McFarland Taylor explores the critical role that Berry played in the
ecological turn of so many US Catholic women religious since the 1990s.
Sarah McFarland Taylor, *Green Sisters: A Spiritual Ecology* (Cambridge, MA:
Harvard University Press, 2007), 5–8; Mary Evelyn Tucker, John Grim, and
Andrew Angyal, *Thomas Berry: A Biography* (New York: Columbia Univer-
sity Press, 2019).

[74] Dwyer, personal correspondence.

in concluding that the provisions of the Natural Gas Act (NGA) supersede protections offered by the RFRA. The precedent-setting opinion contends that the Sisters effectively forfeited their right to religious freedom protections "because they failed to engage with the NGA's procedural regime."[75] This proved a bitter irony for the Sisters, who had intentionally avoided participation in FERC and Transco's public hearings out of concern that their involvement would give the false impression of cooperation with the pipeline builder. Nevertheless, the court concluded that it was "without jurisdiction to hear the Adorers' claims."[76] For this reason, the three-judge panel did not even consider the Sisters' religious rights argument against the pipeline. Instead, their RFRA claim was dismissed, with startling brevity, in the final footnote of the Court's opinion.[77]

The Adorers responded to the ruling with a scathing press statement:

> While historically, the federal courts have been the stalwart protectors and defenders of religious freedoms in our country, today's panel sided with the interests of the powerful gas and oil industry over the religious freedoms of the Adorers.... The Adorers believe that their faith and religious beliefs will ultimately prevail. At issue is nothing less than the future of our sacred earth.[78]

Soon after the Third Circuit's ruling, attorneys for the Sisters advised FERC and Transco that they would be filing a petition

---

[75] "Opinion," *Adorers v. FERC and Transco*, US Court of Appeals for the Third Circuit, July 25, 2018.

[76] "Opinion," *Adorers v. FERC*, 23.

[77] "Opinion," *Adorers v. FERC*, 23.

[78] Adorers of the Blood of Christ, "Appeals Court Sides with Fossil Fuel Industry," press statement, July 25, 2018, http://adorers.org/appeals-court-sides-with-fossil-fuel-industry/.

before the US Supreme Court to reconsider their RFRA claim.[79]
Despite knowledge of these ongoing legal proceedings—or,
perhaps, because of them—Transco employees entered the
Sisters' property on the morning of October 1, 2018, to topple
their cross and dismantle their prayer labyrinth.

Three weeks later, the Adorers filed their promised petition
before the US Supreme Court. The writ of certiorari filing argued
that "the Third Circuit erroneously decided a legal question that
has not been, but should be, settled by this Court. The decision incorrectly disregarded a clear conflict between RFRA and
the NGA [Natural Gas Act], which must be resolved in favor of
RFRA."[80] As such, the filing contended that the district court
should be forced to reconsider the Sisters' case, and address the
merits of the Order's religious freedom argument rather than
preemptively dismissing it on procedural grounds. Sister Janet
McCann prepared a statement that was read from the steps of the
Supreme Court building as they filed their petition. It concluded,
"We invoke the words of Jesus and ask, 'What is written in the
law and how do you read it?'"[81]

To the Sisters' disappointment, in February 2019, the court
denied the Adorers' petition, allowing the Third Circuit's dismissal
of their case to stand. The Order's attempt to halt construction
of the Transco pipeline through a religious freedom challenge
was never even considered in a court of law. This unwilling-
ness to hear the Sisters' RFRA complaint reinforces a disturbing
trend emerging in US federal courts. Whether a party in a suit
is granted religious liberty protections appears to depend a great

---

[79] Dwight J. Yoder, letter to Secretary Kimberly Bose, public comment
to the Federal Energy Regulatory Commission (August 31, 2018).

[80] "Petition for Writ of Certiorari," *Adorers v. FERC and Transco*, US
Supreme Court (October 22, 2018), 16.

[81] McCann, citing Luke 10:25–28. Janet McCann, "Press Conference
Statement," Washington, DC, October 22, 2018.

deal on whose faith, and which religious convictions, are being threatened. Such unequal application is the subject of a 2019 report by the Law, Rights, and Religion Project of Columbia Law School, *Whose Faith Matters? The Fight for Religious Liberty Beyond the Christian Right*. The study examines how

> Advocates, legislators, courts, and journalists have contributed to a climate in which only the religious liberty claims of conservative people of faith "count" as religious, while the claims and rights of progressive people of faith are dismissed or ignored as "merely" political in nature.[82]

The Adorers' faith-based environmental advocacy is cited in that report as an example of this very trend.[83]

A Church Divided:
Activist Women, Obstructionist Men

While engaged in a predictably uphill battle against the fossil fuel industry and the courts, the Sisters found themselves facing additional opposition from a source much closer to home: the hierarchy of the Catholic Church. Despite the highly visible and openly religious nature of their campaign, the response of the church's male-only leadership ranged from silence to disdain. Tellingly, neither the Diocese of Harrisburg nor any of the ninety parishes within its jurisdiction publicly supported the Adorers' religious defense of their land. The few who did raise their voices tended to express annoyance at the women for daring to speak

---

[82] Elizabeth Reiner Platt, Katherine Franke, Kira Shepherd, and Lilia Hadjiivanova, *Whose Faith Matters? The Fight for Religious Liberty beyond the Christian Right*, report by the Law, Rights, and Religion Project of Columbia Law School, November 2019.

[83] Platt, Franke, et al., *Whose Faith Matters?*, 51–53.

up, rather than at the industry for violating the Order's religious convictions. One Sister, who has spent more than a half-century in vowed religious service to the Catholic Church, told me how the priest of a large local parish personally scolded her in church one day for her activism, snapping, "You shouldn't be involved in these pipeline demonstrations!"[84] About that same time, I broached the subject of the chapel with a Catholic priest I met at a local pizza shop. He simply rolled his eyes and suggested that the Sisters should stick to religion.

The total lack of support from Bishop Ronald Gainer of the Harrisburg Diocese, home of the Cornfield Chapel, has been particularly conspicuous. Through two years of well-publicized vigils, hymn sings, and interreligious services at the chapel located just thirty-five miles from the cathedral, the bishop chose not to attend a single event at the site. Nor has he expressed any public support for the Sisters' internationally recognized work on behalf of the environment.

Despite attracting large crowds and widespread media coverage between 2017 and 2019, the chapel was never mentioned in the *Catholic Witness*, the biweekly diocesan news-letter. This was a remarkable omission considering that the editors routinely found space to promote a steady stream of argu-ably less momentous events: parish flea markets, golf outings, and chicken barbecues. At times, the newsletter's silence on the Sisters' work bordered on the absurd. The edition released during the week of the chapel's nationally publicized dedication service contained a lengthy, impassioned appeal for Catholics every-where to boldly defend religious liberties.[85] Despite the fact that a community of Catholic Sisters within the diocese was, at that

---

[84] Unnamed, personal conversation with the author, Columbia, Penn-sylvania, January 27, 2020.

[85] Erik Zygmont, "Work for 'Holiness of Freedom, Freedom for Holi-ness,' Bishop Says," *Catholic Witness*, July 7, 2017, 11.

very moment, waging a religious freedom battle in federal court, the *Witness* made no mention of the Adorers' struggle.

In July 2018, I contacted Bishop Gainer's office for comment on the Adorers' environmental efforts. At that time, the Sisters' religious freedom lawsuit was in full swing. A ruling from the US Third Circuit Court of Appeals was expected within days. The chapel was continuing to attract a high level of media attention, in addition to the coverage it had already received in the *Washington Post*, the BBC, and CNN.[86] The Adorers-LAP partnership had also been featured in high-profile documentaries by CBS National News and *The Guardian*, alongside independent film productions like *Half-Mile, Upwind, On Foot.*[87]

The decision to sit on such an inspiring story unfolding in their own diocese was particularly baffling to me at the time, considering that the Pennsylvania attorney general's grand jury investigation into clergy sexual abuse was preparing to release its damning report later that summer, a report that would include allegations against forty-five priests within the Harrisburg Diocese.[88] In response to my queries, a clearly agitated diocesan spokesperson curtly informed me that the bishop had never visited the chapel because the Adorers had never invited him. I

---

[86] Julie Zauzmer, "Catholic Nuns in Pa. Build a Chapel to Block the Path of a Gas Pipeline Planned for their Property," *Washington Post,* July 16, 2017; Amanda Watts and Paige Levin, "Nuns to Dedicate Outdoor Chapel Built in the Path of Proposed Pipeline," CNN, July 8, 2017; William Crawley, "Nuns Fighting Fracking; Forced Marriage; Food Safety Post-Brexit," BBC Radio 4, August 6, 2017.

[87] Elizabeth Kineke (prod.), *Protecting the Sacred*, CBS News Video (2017); Charlie Phillips, Lindsay Poulton, Chloe White, and Will Davies (dirs.), *The Climate and the Cross: US Evangelical Christians Tussle with Climate Change, The Guardian* video, 2018; Brian McDermott (dir.), *Half-Mile, Upwind, On Foot,* EmpathyWorks Production, 2019.

[88] Josh Shapiro, "Report 1 of the 40th Statewide Investigating Grand Jury," Catholic Clergy Sexual Abuse, redacted by order of the Pennsylvania Supreme Court, July 27, 2018, 149–206.

later confirmed that the Adorers had, in fact, extended a personal invitation to the bishop ahead of the chapel's dedication service more than a year earlier.[89]

The Catholic hierarchy's dismissal of the Sisters' activism extended all the way to Rome, where the Adorers have been recognized as a pontifical institute since 1878. In the summer of 2018, the Vatican hosted an international conference to commemorate the third anniversary of the encyclical *Laudato Si'*. During the conference, the Sisters hand-delivered a written request to Pope Francis seeking a statement of support for the Adorers-LAP partnership ahead of the chapel's one-year anniversary.[90] The Adorers' request was unexpectedly buoyed by the comments of world-renowned environmentalist Bill McKibben, who was among the conference's plenary speakers the following day. While reviewing strategies for mass mobilization to advance climate justice, McKibben highlighted the Adorers' chapel as a model of nonviolent resistance in the spirit of Jesus's Sermon on the Mount.[91] The crowd erupted in applause. Vatican officials were less enthusiastic. After six months without a reply, the Adorers finally received a brief letter from the Vatican's Dicastery

---

[89] I spent six months requesting an interview with Bishop Gainer for this essay. Despite numerous assurances from diocesan staff that an interview would be arranged, in the end I received the following email from his secretary: "Bishop Gainer must decline an interview." No further explanation was offered. Hilary Smith, Executive Secretary to Bishop Gainer, email message to author, December 27, 2019.

[90] Janet McCann and Mark Clatterbuck, "Joint Letter of Appeal to Pope Francis from the Adorers of the Blood of Christ and Lancaster Against Pipelines (LAP)," June 30, 2018.

[91] Bill McKibben, "How to Inspire a Massive Movement for the Care of Our Common Home," Third Session of the International Conference on the Third Anniversary of the Encyclical Letter *Laudato Si'* (July 6, 2018), see 41:36 into livestream at https://www.youtube.com/watch?v=YrTPS41-g_M&feature=emb_err_watch_on_yt.

for Promoting Integral Human Development instructing them to "first seek the support of the US Catholic Bishops Conference," after which time the dicastery would "discern about whether and what to add."[92]

As it turned out, the US Conference of Catholic Bishops (USCCB) was equally reluctant to support the Sisters. When the Adorers filed their petition for a writ of certiorari before the Supreme Court later that year, they invited the USCCB to prepare an amicus curiae brief supporting their cause. Representatives of the Conference declined to get involved. One constitutional lawyer with extensive experience in religious liberty cases on behalf of the US bishops, and who served in the Trump administration's State Department, replied to the Sisters' request for legal support by writing, "I cannot think of a more wasteful use of legal time and talent."[93] John Whitehead, constitutional attorney and founder of the influential Rutherford Institute, held a very different opinion of the Adorers' petition, saying, "These nuns have every right to tell the government and its corporate partners to stay off the convent's land and respect the nuns' right to exercise their religious beliefs about the sacredness of God's creation."[94] The amicus brief that the Rutherford Institute filed on behalf of the Adorers described the lower court's dismissal of the Sisters' RFRA claim as having potentially "dire effects on the ability of the [Adorers] and countless other persons of faith to live and act according to their religious beliefs."[95]

---

[92] Peter K. A. Turkson, Dicastery for Promoting Integral Human Development, the Vatican, personal letter to Janet McCann and Mark Clatterbuck, December 17, 2018.

[93] Personal email correspondence with the author, October 17, 2018.

[94] Rutherford Institute, "Rutherford Institute Asks Supreme Court to Prevent Gov't from Seizing Nuns' Land, Drilling Pipeline through Convent Land," November 28, 2018.

[95] "Amicus Curiae in Support of the Petitioners," *Adorers v. FERC*

The US bishops' refusal to advance the Adorers' RFRA case is telling, given that the USCCB has filed twenty-seven amicus curiae briefs since 2000 that deal directly with religious liberty protections. They filed four such briefs in 2019 alone. However, a closer look suggests that the US bishops do not defend all Catholic teachings with equal zeal. For example, the church's commitment to protecting religiously motivated infringements on LGBTQ rights (e.g., *Masterpiece Cakeshop v. Colorado Civil Rights Commission* 2017) and faith-based restrictions on women's access to federally mandated reproductive health care (e.g., *Sabelius v. Hobby Lobby* [2014]) account for more than half the religious freedom amicus curiae briefs filed by the USCCB over the past twenty years. The US bishops have not filed a single brief pertaining to religious freedom protections related to environmental justice.[96]

During the interviews I conducted with the Sisters, most expressed very little surprise at the hierarchy's failure to support them. Sara Dwyer situates the hierarchy's response squarely within a long history of gender inequality within the Catholic Church:

> As women in a patriarchal church, we don't have the same kind of voice or access to decision making that the men do.... At a basic kind of level, we [women religious] are equal to the lay people; we're not clerics. So, to be invited to work with a community of lay people like Lancaster Against Pipelines, it didn't surprise me at an organizational level that nobody [within the hierarchy] stood forward. Because, unless the power man says, "Yes,

---

and Transco, US Supreme Court, submitted by the Rutherford Institute, November 28, 2018.

[96] To access a listing of amicus curiae briefs filed by the USCCB Office of the General Counsel in recent years, see http://www.usccb.org/about/general-counsel/amicus-briefs/index.cfm.

you can do this," they're not going to be able to make an independent decision. Whereas, as women religious, we've struggled with that issue, in lots of cases, all of our religious history.[97]

Dwyer joins her community in feeling compelled to act on their charism despite the silence or pushback they experience from male church leadership. She explained to me her belief that "women are more resilient, and . . . more willing to risk, because we don't have the sense of power loss that a guy would feel if he steps across a line. So, if they don't come along, no problem. We're going to do it anyway."[98] In the end, this is why she felt so confident working with Lancaster Against Pipelines.

Although not surprised, Sister Helene Trueitt—who joined the Adorers sixty-four years ago, marched for civil rights in the 1950s and '60s, and played an active role in the pipeline resistance—expressed grave disappointment for the failure of church leaders to support the Sisters' work for environmental justice. She told me,

I felt very bad that our bishop and all the priests in this diocese were not strong enough to say, "I believe in this; I'm going to support those women." But they did not. They have not. And that's such a [thumbs-down sign] for me, being a Roman Catholic.[99]

For all those who admonish women religious to quit lives of activism and stick to prayer, Sister Anne Irose, who lives at the Adorers' Ruma Center in southern Illinois, has a ready response: "The gospel sends us out. Read the word of God! My gosh, it's

---

[97] Brought, Dwyer, et al., interview.
[98] Brought, Dwyer, et al., interview.
[99] Forgotch, Hunter, et al., interview.

like, 'Go forth! Go tell them! Go and tell the world!'"[100] She
points to Mary Magdalene, who didn't wait for others to take
the lead, but proclaimed of herself that "she would be the
disciple, she would be the messenger."[101] "We're all called to be
Mary Magdalenes," she said, and added with a wry nod to the
Catholic hierarchy: "Overlooked, of course. Overlooked. We
know where we stand."[102]

Conclusion

There are signs all across the United States that faith-based environmental activism is on the rise. There is also evidence that the
trend is having a real impact on the fossil fuel industry. In July
2020, Dominion Energy and Duke Energy abruptly announced
cancellation of their $8 billion Atlantic Coast Pipeline after
six years of persistent grassroots opposition. That opposition
was led, in part, by an unlikely alliance between environmen-
tally conscious Hindu yogis at the Satchidananda Ashram and
Reverend Paul Wilson, the pastor of an African American Baptist
congregation in rural Buckingham County, Virginia.[103] Together,
they produced some of the most visible and vocal opposition
to the project through public rituals of resistance, community
education, regulatory pushback, and legal challenges.[104] This
movement is the subject of chapter four of this book.

---

[100] Irose, interview.

[101] Irose, interview.

[102] Irose, interview.

[103] Gregory S. Schneider, "The Baptists and the Yogis Join to Fight a
Pipeline," *Washington Post,* August 18, 2018.

[104] For more on the role of religion in the Atlantic Coast Pipeline fight,
see Sarah Vogelsong, "What Sank the Atlantic Coast Pipeline? It Wasn't Just
Environmentalism," *Virginia Mercury,* July 8, 2020.

Back in Lancaster County, Pennsylvania, the Adorers of the Blood of Christ did not succeed in stopping the pipeline project threatening their community. Even so, their campaign can hardly be called a failure. The ecumenical, interfaith, and secular partnerships they forged with local community members offer a promising model for future grassroots alliances working for environmental justice. Their daring, meticulously orchestrated, and joyfully executed mass actions of liturgical resistance serve as a blueprint for ritual acts of civil disobedience across a wide range of protest settings. Their legal challenges have succeeded in highlighting important possibilities, as well as current obstacles, attending religious freedom protections for faith-based environmental activism. And their message of spirited defiance in the face of multibillion-dollar fossil fuel companies captured a remarkable level of media attention on the coattails of Standing Rock's extraordinary success at framing pipeline resistance as both a moral and spiritual battle.

The Adorers-LAP partnership has also exposed how regulatory agencies and courts routinely privilege corporate profits over local communities, the natural world, and religious rights. Given the extent to which oil and gas industry interests are disproportionately wed to conservative politics in the United States, the prominence of the Sisters' grassroots campaign against a fracked-gas pipeline in rural, deep-red Lancaster County may prove a significant indicator of shifting public opinion on the moral necessity of climate action. Furthermore, the Adorers' pipeline fight offers poignant lessons on the role of gender in faith-based ecojustice work in the United States today. Women have long been at the forefront of grassroots environmental activism worldwide. The Adorers' campaign is one more example of that reality. In addition to highlighting the tone and tactics being used by women leaders in eco-activist movements, the Sisters' work also highlights the kind of male-led resistance that environmental advocates face in virtually every arena of the fight. This dynamic deserves further scholarly attention.

Perhaps the best evidence that the Adorers-LAP partnership posed a legitimate threat to the fossil fuel industry is the response it provoked from Pennsylvania's heavily pro–gas industry legislature. Just as the movement's direct-action campaign was heating up, Lancaster County's state senator Scott Martin—whose district is home to both LAP and the Chapel of Resistance— proposed two separate bills designed to suppress mass protests, with a clear focus on curbing grassroots pipeline resistance. The first was proposed one month after hundreds of local residents dedicated the Adorers' Chapel directly in the path of Transco's pipeline. The bill would have forced protesters to reimburse police response costs incurred at demonstrations where even a single participant was convicted of a crime, however minor. This would apply even to misdemeanor trespass charges arising from acts of civil disobedience. In a clear attempt to discourage faith-based resistance like that taking place in his own district, the bill's language specifically identified "the holding of vigils or religious services" among the kinds of demonstrations being targeted.[105]

The second antiprotest bill Martin sponsored sought to designate natural gas pipelines as "critical infrastructure" and to reclassify even peaceful pipeline protests as felonies.[106] Under

---

[105] SB 323, General Assembly of Pennsylvania, February 22, 2019.

[106] SB 887, General Assembly of Pennsylvania, October 7, 2019. The bill is modeled on legislation drafted by the American Legislative Exchange Council (ALEC) to protect so-called critical infrastructure, a term broadly defined in the bills to safeguard all sites related to the extraction, transmission, and production of oil and natural gas. In the summer of 2019, a version of ALEC's critical infrastructure bill was introduced in the US Congress, signaling efforts by industry advocates to chill oil and gas protest on a national level. The bill, known as the Protecting Our Infrastructure of

this measure, merely walking onto a posted pipeline site without permission would have constituted a third-degree felony, punishable by up to a year in prison and a minimum fine of five thousand dollars. Entering a pipeline infrastructure site with the intent "to impede or hinder operations"—which is often the goal of peaceful demonstrators resisting new pipeline construction—would have been classified as a first-degree felony punishable by up to two years in prison and a minimum fine of ten thousand dollars. In this way, the bill put peaceful, religiously motivated pipeline protests on par with voluntary manslaughter and rape. Both bills have since expired.[107]

To this day, the chapel remains a site of both ritual and resistance. In 2023 and 2024, LAP and the Sisters renovated and expanded the area to include a more permanent heart-shaped prayer labyrinth of paver stones, an Amish-installed post-and-rail fence, and a black locust tree as a symbol of resilience. Individuals and groups continue to use the space as a kind of ecopilgrimage destination for prayer, meditation, and reflection on our collective responsibility to defend the Earth as a sacred duty. The Sisters are currently exploring plans to install a large solar array directly adjacent to the climate warming pipeline that was forcibly installed on their farmland. Their agrivoltaic design

---

Pipelines and Enhancing Safety (PIPES) Act of 2019, would make peaceful, religiously motivated disruption of pipeline construction—like the prayerful acts of ritual resistance performed at the Adorers' Chapel—punishable by up to twenty years in prison. See Alleen Brown, "Trump Administration Asks Congress to Make Disrupting Pipeline Construction a Crime Punishable by 20 Years in Prison," *The Intercept* (June 5, 2019).

[107] In the wake of the Standing Rock resistance of 2016-2017, dozens of state legislatures introduced a range of bills designed to chill mass protest, many explicitly designed to protect the interests of the fossil fuel industry. For more information, see Reid J. Epstein and Patricia Mazzei, "G.O.P. Bills Target Protestors (and Absolve Motorists Who Hit Them)," *New York Times* (April 21, 2021).

envisions growing crops under the panels. If the Sisters have their way, a rural grassroots coalition of spiritual resistance—rather than a multibillion-dollar fossil fuel company—will have the final say about what sort of future we're building together in that sacred cornfield.

3

MANA-FESTING ON A SACRED MOUNTAIN
Rites of Protection and Resistance
to Protect Mauna a Wākea

Marie Alohalani Brown

The term "mana-festing" in my essay's title is a play on the ways that manifesting mana to protect Mauna a Wākea (Mauna Kea) and the kiaʻi (protectors) is integral to the movement. While the Mauna Kea movement's main aim is to stop the construction of the Thirty Meter Telescope (TMT), it is also an act of resistance against the hegemonic forces that want to build the TMT. Mana is a culturally dense concept. It is broadly related to power, although "power" is inadequate to capture fully the nuances of this concept.

To begin, mana has other-than-human origins, which renowned cultural expert Mary Kawena Pukui has variously described as a "power" that is "supernatural," "spiritual," or "divine."[1] Because everything in nature comes into existence with some degree of mana, it is reasonable to describe mana as an entity in its own right, "a thing with a distinct and independent existence."[2] Mana is a capacity, a potential to effect positive or

---

[1] Pukui and Elbert, *Hawaiian Dictionary*, s.v. "mana"; Pukui, Haertig, and Lee, *Nānā*, 1:10.

[2] *Merriam-Webster Dictionary*, s.v. "entity."

negative change; it can be spiritual, intellectual, or physical; it powers and empowers; it is intangible but its manifestations are tangible; it can be embedded in or transferred to something else; it is intrinsic but can be increased or diminished; and it grants authority and defines status.[3]

That mana is a core concept in Hawaiian culture is evidenced by the ancient word for our traditional belief system, "Hoʻomana." This compound word, consisting of "hoʻo" (a causative) and "mana," means "to generate mana." The act of worshiping (prayers, rites) akua (deities) and ʻaumākua (ancestral deities) generates mana for akua and ʻaumākua. In turn, to greatly simplify, akua and ʻaumākua may use their mana to aid us or grant us mana to help ourselves. In other words, because prayers and rites are often performed to secure a desired outcome, such as protecting Mauna Kea, they also manifest the mana needed to ensure that outcome.

The Mauna Kea movement is just one of the many historic struggles in which Kanaka ʻŌiwi ("Hawaiians") resist the injustices they have experienced as a result of settler colonialism and US hegemony.[4] At the same time, however, the movement stands out in several significant ways. First, as one of the more recent stands in Hawaiian history, it benefits from the culminating successes of the movements that preceded it. Second, it is notable for the great number of ʻŌiwi and allies who physically participated in it. Third, the global attention and support it garnered are unprecedented. Fourth, it became a catalyst for the resurgence of Hoʻomana.

---

[3] Pukui and Elbert, *Hawaiian Dictionary*, s.v. "mana"; Pukui, Haertig, and Lee, *Nānā*, 1:10.

[4] "Kanaka ʻŌiwi" is one of several terms the Hawaiian people use to describe who they are, along with "Kanaka," "ʻŌiwi," "Kanaka Maoli," "Kanaka Hawaiʻi," "Poʻe ʻŌiwi," "ʻŌiwi Hawaiʻi," and "Kanaka ʻŌiwi Maoli." I use "Kanaka ʻŌiwi," "ʻŌiwi," and "Hawaiian" in this essay.

The people—'Ōiwi and their allies—who held space on the Mauna did so because they considered the TMT issue to be of the utmost concern, and their motives ranged from the secular to the spiritual-religious. Secular motivations included environmental justice and solidarity with 'Ōiwi against oppression in all its forms. The spiritual-religious belief that Mauna Kea is sacred is rooted in Hawaiian religious traditions. While not all 'Ōiwi identified as practitioners of Ho'omana, this chapter primarily focuses on the ways that Hawaiian religious traditions informed or were incorporated into the movement. Because activism does not happen in a political vacuum but in the context of systematic oppression, I also discuss the strategies TMT supporters adopted to discredit kia'i and the movement, strategies that were oppressive and traumatizing.

My positionality and relationship to the topics I cover in this essay are as follows: I am a professor of religion at the University of Hawai'i at Mānoa, specialist in Hawaiian religion. I am an 'Ōiwi. I practice Ho'omana. I held space on Mauna Kea for five months during the 2019 stand until I had to leave for health-related reasons. Because of my religious beliefs, I feel morally and ethically obligated to protect that which is considered sacred in our culture—and Mauna Kea is sacred. I was among the thirty-eight kūpuna (elders) arrested on July 17, 2019, as we and others held space to protect the Mauna from further desecration.

The historical trauma we 'Ōiwi have inherited as a people is substantial. The physical, spiritual, and intellectual violence we have experienced because of settler colonialism and US hegemony include demographic collapse because of introduced diseases; being marginalized in our own homelands; land dispossession; religious discrimination; destruction of cultural and natural resources; desecration of sacred sites and ancestral remains; loss of language, cultural traditions, and identity from

Flags flying at the TMT blockade on Mauna Kea reflect the entanglement of spirituality, antiimperialism, and ecojustice aims.
(PHOTO BY MARK CLATTERBUCK / USED WITH PERMISSION)

imposed assimilation and blood quantum laws; being reduced to stereotypes; cultural appropriation; sexual objectification; hate speech; and being othered as uncivilized or even subhuman. Despite the successes of previous struggles to rectify some of these injustices—most notably saving the Hawaiian language from the brink of extinction through revitalization efforts, grassroots litigation that forced the US military to stop using the sacred island of Kahoʻolawe for bombing practice, and the resurgence of certain cultural traditions and practices—other injustices continue and we continue struggling to rectify them. The Mauna Kea movement is one such effort.

Overview of the Mauna Kea and TMT Issue

The main objective of the Mauna Kea movement is to prevent the proposed construction of the TMT on the summit of Mauna Kea. Were the project completed, the TMT would be the fourteenth telescope on Mauna Kea and the largest telescope in the world. The uninformed might wonder why this is a problem given that there are already thirteen telescopes on the mountain's summit.

KAHEA, a community-based organization, synthesizes the issue:

> In the 1960s, Hawai'i agreed to share two of our highest and most sacred mountaintops [of Mauna Kea and Haleakalā, respectively on the islands of Hawai'i and Maui] with a small community of astronomers. Today, an expanding industrial footstep of roads, buildings, people, parking, and ever-larger telescopes populate these summits—all the while cultural landscapes and native habitats are being irreplaceably lost.[5]

In short, the larger astronomy community and their backers took advantage of the original agreement.

Mauna Kea is a conservation district and thus falls under the jurisdiction of the Department of Land and Natural Resources (DLNR), which is headed by the Executive Board of Land and Natural Resources (BLNR). In 1968, the State Land Board (now BLNR) "issue[d] a general lease to the University of Hawai'i to build one observatory on Mauna Kea." This lease was for sixty-five years "for lands above the 12,000-foot level" of the mountain.[6] For the next twenty years, the University of Hawai'i ignored the initial agreement and allowed "developers [to] build a number of telescope complexes, without permits," with the apparent complicity of the BLNR. Only when the public outcry

---

[5] KAHEA, "Sacred Summits," n.d., http://kahea.org/issues/sacred-summits. As this organization explains, "KAHEA is an acronym for Ka (the) Hawaiian-Environmental Alliance ("About," n.d.). http://kahea.org/about.

[6] Marion M. Higa, "Audit of the Management of Mauna Kea and the Mauna Kea Science Reserve," I, http://kahea.org/files/1998-audit-of-the-management-of-mauna-kea.

could no longer be ignored did the BLNR finally take action. Its highly questionable decision was to grant the developers an "after-the-fact permit," which set a problematic precedent.[7] A 1997 state audit of the thirty-year management of Mauna Kea summit and the Mauna Kea Science Reserve found that the University of Hawai'i had failed in its duties and that the DLNR had failed to regularly enforce "permit conditions, requirements, and regulations."[8] Despite this critique, the University of Hawai'i developed a master plan in 2000 "allowing for at least 40 new telescopes and support structures." On February 25, 2011, the BLNR approved the University of Hawai'i's Conservation District Use Application (CDUA) for the TMT project and simultaneously approved "a contested case hearing on the TMT-CDUA."[9] Over the next few years, the Mauna Kea Hui and other groups would contest the CDUA. On July 25, 2014, the BLNR approved the University of Hawai'i's "proposed sublease of Mauna Kea lands to [the] TMT Corporation." TMT made plans to prepare the construction site. Less than three months later, the TMT group held a groundbreaking ceremony.[10]

While guests were seated waiting for the ceremony to begin, a core group of Mauna protectors arrived to disrupt it. The protectors' intervention was videoed.[11] Figuring prominently is Joshua Lanakila Mangauil, one of the Mauna leaders. His entire appearance makes a clear statement about his relationship to his culture. His long hair is shaved on both sides of his head and

---

[7] KAHEA, "Mauna Kea Timeline," http://kahea.org/issues/sacred-summits/timelineof-events.

[8] Higa, "Audit," i, ii.

[9] KAHEA, "Mauna Kea Timeline."

[10] KAHEA, "Mauna Kea Timeline."

[11] David Corrigan, "TMT Opponents Halt Groundbreaking Ceremony," Big Island Video News, https://www.youtube.com/watch?v=SZ4Gt35hs-s.

tied at the base of the neck. He wears a brown malo (loincloth), a length of hand-printed kapa (bark cloth) draped about his shoulders, a lei hulu (feather choker), a lei kūpeʻe (shell necklace), and a shark-tooth pendant. In other words, Mangauil is dressed for ceremony, which is significant in two ways. First, he is on a sacred mission to stop the TMT groundbreaking ceremony and educate the participants about the sacredness of the mountain and why the TMT would be an act of violence upon it. Second, in a time when outsiders often assume that nā mea Hawaiʻi (things Hawaiian) other than hula are essentially a thing of the past, Mangauil's attire is an important visual reminder that ʻŌiwi ways of knowing and being continue to inform our lives today. In English laced with Hawaiian, Lanakila calls out the participants for their "hewa" (wrongdoing) and tells them that protectors had gathered at the bottom of the mountain the night before but were denied entry to the ceremony, and that they, the TMT ceremony participants, used the excuse of going to the restroom to sneak into the ceremony, which was to take place higher up on the mountain. His statements are striking for their truth and passion. Other kiaʻi joined him and offered their manaʻo (thoughts) about the hewa that is the TMT and then performed chants. The video went viral on social media and galvanized the ʻŌiwi community and their supporters into action. "Kū Kiaʻi Mauna" (Stand to protect the mountain) became a common rallying cry.

This was the start of the 2014–2015 Mauna Kea stand—a nonviolent direct action.

Mauna a Wākea: A Sacred Mountain

In my conversations with other kiaʻi and on the basis of what I observed, it was clear that many of us were motivated by reasons that can be characterized as spiritual, religious, neither, or both. It is important to note that many people make a distinction between being "spiritual" and being "religious." In common parlance, the use of "spiritual" to qualify a quality, state of being, or practice carries with it a recognition of a transcendent power or powers, that which is "beyond or above the range of normal or merely physical human experience."[12] Thus, one way that "spirituality" can be understood is an individual's recognition of or relationship with a transcendent power or powers whether an individual practices an organized religion or not.[13] Because of the diverse expressions of that which in English is termed "religion," there is no scholarly consensus on how to define it. Religion is generally understood as an organized or structured system of beliefs and belief-related practices. Such vague definitions are useful because they take into account the many ways that this realm of human activity, religion, is expressed around the world.[14] As religion scholar Bron Taylor points out, "Religion is an engagement with the sacred, however this is understood."[15] His qualifying "however this is understood" speaks to the ways that what constitutes the sacred can vary greatly according to a given community, religious tradition, or culture. This is also true for 'Ōiwi.

To better understand what constitutes the sacred according to a Hawaiian worldview and in connection with Mauna Kea, it is helpful to envision "sacred" as a continuum. As a whole, Mauna a Wākea (mountain child of Wākea) is intrinsically sacred because it is the child of two akua, Wākea and Papa, but certain parts of it are sacred for other reasons.[16] By way of comparison, the 'āina (land) is

---

[12] *Merriam-Webster Dictionary*, s.v. "transcendent."

[13] For an extensive discussion of "spiritual" and "religion," see Bron Taylor's introduction to Bron Taylor, ed., *The Encyclopedia of Religion and Nature* (London: Continuum, 2005), ix–x.

[14] Taylor, *Encyclopedia of Religion and Nature*, ix–x.

[15] Taylor, *Encyclopedia of Religion and Nature*, ix.

[16] Kepa Maly and Onaona Maly, *Mauna Kea—Ka Piko Kaulana O Ka*

sacred because the islands are the children of Wākea and Papa, who are also the progenitors of the Hawaiian people. Thus, the ʻāina is an older relative of Kanaka ʻŌiwi and also that which feeds us. But certain areas of the ʻāina, such as mountain summits, are especially sacred because they are wao akua: a wao (region) inhabited by akua. In 1823, missionary William Ellis wrote that there were "many" accounts about Mauna Kea "being the abode of the gods," and for this reason, "none ever approach its summit."[17] Countless chants and moʻolelo (hi/stories) record the names of akua who dwell in the wao akua of Mauna Kea.

These akua include Poliʻahu, Lilinoe, Waiau, Kahoupokāne, Kalauakōlea, Moʻoinanea, Waka, and Moanalihaikawaokele.[18] Consequently, a mountain's upper reaches are off limits to humans, although there are exceptions to this general rule. These exceptions include the construction of religious structures (heiau or ahu) to worship akua, ceremonies to honor akua, and the burial of ancestral remains or a child's piko (umbilical cord)—all of which took place on the slopes and summit of Mauna Kea, and some of these practices continue there today. Thus, the Mauna is also sacred for these reasons.[19] Because the stands to protect Mauna Kea serve a sacred purpose, kiaʻi are exempt from the traditional prohibition regarding human presence in the wao akua.

ʻĀina (Hilo: Office of Mauna Kea Management at the University of Hawaiʻi, 2005), v.

[17] William Ellis, *A Narrative of an 1823 Tour Through Hawaiʻi* (Honolulu, HI: Mutual Publishing, 2004), 304.

[18] S. N. Haleole, "Ka Moolelo o Laieikawai," *Ka Nupepa Kuokoa,* January 24, 1863; Maikoko, "Mele kanikau no Aikahalelo," *Ka Nupepa Kuokoa,* July 25, 1863; Moses Manu, "He Moolelo Kaao no Keaomelemele," *Ka Nupepa Kuokoa,* November 29, 1884; Hooulumahiehie, "Ka Moolelo Walohia no Hainakolo," January 31, February 7, 8, 1907.

[19] Maly and Maly, *Mauna Kea,* v–vi.

Another reason Mauna Kea is considered sacred is related to its great height—it extends high up into the lani, so much so that its summit is often hidden by clouds. The lani (sky, heavens, firmament) is a space that belongs to akua. For this reason, "ka lani" (the heavens or the heavenly one) is an epithet traditionally used for high-ranking aliʻi (members of the ruling class) who had kept the purity of their lineage—descendants of akua—intact through physical unions with close relatives and were therefore considered divine humans.[20]

View from near the summit of Mauna Kea.
(PHOTO BY DAVID PARRY / USED WITH PERMISSION)

Mauna Kea is also culturally significant in that it is a major wahi pana—a place celebrated in moʻolelo (a capacious genre that includes histories, myths, legends, cautionary tales, life writing, etc.), ʻōlelo noʻeau (poetical sayings that can be didactic or commemorative), chants, and songs.

---

[20] Pukui and Elbert, *Hawaiian Dictionary*, s.v. "lani."

The summit area of Mauna Kea has been officially designated as a conservation district, which means it is valued for environmental reasons. Some species of flora and fauna exist only on Mauna Kea, some of which are classified as endangered. Moreover, the Mauna encompasses major aquifers for Hawai'i Island.

TMT and the Public Dismissal of Kanaka 'Ōiwi Religious Traditions

The spiritual-religious impetus behind the Mauna Kea movement has been questioned and attacked.[21] TMT supporters initially attempted to discredit declarations about the Mauna sacredness. At one point, the public controversy was such that anthropologist Leslie E. Sponsel wrote an op-ed about sacred places. He makes three salient points in this op-ed. The first evidences the global prevalence of sacred places: "In addition to human constructions such as churches and temples a wide range of 'natural' phenomena are thought to be sacred by people in more than 7,000 cultures existing in the world today, and especially by indigenous peoples who have dwelled in an area for centuries or millennia." Thus, the significance that we 'Ōiwi place on our sacred places is not an anomaly but part of the human condition. The second point establishes the sacred as existing along a continuum: "A particular sacred place or area can encompass various individual sites and phenomena as integral parts of a whole, thereby comprising an entire sacred landscape, sometimes with different degrees of sacredness in different places." This is true also for Hawaiian culture. The third point speaks to the physical, intellectual, and spiritual violence that people can experience when their sacred

---

[21] See Marie Alohalani Brown, "Mauna Kea: Ho'omana Hawai'i and Protecting the Sacred," *Journal for the Study of Religion, Nature, and Culture* (2016): 150-169.

site is desecrated: "Sacred places ... merit special respect on their own merits as well as out of due respect for the people and their culture and religion that consider them sacred. As such desecration of a sacred place is dehumanizing for those who believe it to be sacred, and also for those who desecrate it."[22] All too often, outsiders weigh the validity of ʻŌiwi affirmations about sacred places through the ethnocentric lens of their own culture and refute our ways of knowing and being. Many TMT supporters are unwilling to accept how its construction would be devastating for ʻŌiwi who consider the Mauna sacred.

By the time the second stand took place, disputes about the Mauna's sacred status had largely ceased. Given that this tactic hadn't worked, TMT supporters tried others. Official statements suddenly acknowledged the sacredness of Mauna Kea and then evoked a "common good" rhetoric: the scientific discoveries the TMT could bring trump the desecration of a sacred mountain. This is a strategy of colonial oppression. As Taiaiake Alfred and Jeff Corntassel explain, "The 'common good' becomes whatever it is defined as by shape-shifting colonial elites."[23] At the same time, TMT supporters claimed that those of us who believe the Mauna to be sacred are antiscience, which is untrue. As ʻŌiwi scientist Rosie Alegado explains, it's "the process, not science." She states, "Painting Native Hawaiian culture as against modern science is a false dichotomy."[24]

Another strategy was to assert that most Hawaiians support the TMT and that those who didn't were merely a very vocal

---

[22] Leslie E. Sponsel, "Sacred Places Are an Integral Part of the Human Condition," *Honolulu Star-Advertiser,* April 9, 2014.

[23] Taiaiake Alfred and Jeff Corntassel, "Being Indigenous: Resurgence against Contemporary Colonialism," 601. *Government and Opposition* 40, no. 4 (2005): 567–614. http://doi.org/10.1111/j.1477-7053.2005.00166.x

[24] Rosie Alegado, "Opponents of the Thirty Meter Telescope Fight the Process, Not the Science," *Nature* 572, no. 7 (August 2019), https://www.nature.com/articles/d41586-019-02304-1.

minority. The governor of Hawaiʻi, David Y. Ige, implicitly sanctioned this tactic when his official website, the Capitol Connection, published an unsigned, three-paragraph piece titled "The 'Silent Majority' Speaks Out" on August 29, 2019, about a month after the 2019 stand began. The title's claim is based on the statement of a single Hawaiian, Oliver Crowell, who asserted that he "knows of many Native Hawaiians who support TMT but are reluctant to speak out since the issue has become so personal."[25] The piece adopts a rhetorical strategy that marks the two Hawaiian TMT supporters it names, Crowell and Chad Kalepa Baybayan, as *just as culturally Hawaiian* as the Hawaiians who oppose the TMT for cultural-religious reasons.

Crowell, eighty years old when the piece was written, is described as "a Kamehameha Schools alumnus." Thus, he attended Kamehameha Schools (KS) when it still operated as a residential school for Hawaiian children. In those years, KS—like other residential schools for Indigenous children in the United States, Canada, and Australia—was the means by which Hawaiian children were assimilated into the hegemonic culture and converted to Christianity.[26] Moreover, many KS alumni oppose the TMT. Thus, the depiction of Crowell as just as culturally Hawaiian as

---

[25] "The 'Silent Majority' Speaks Out," Capitol Connection (online), August, 29, 2019.

[26] In recent years, Kamehameha Schools has greatly changed. Although it is still a residential school, it now promotes Hawaiian ways of knowing and being. For more information on residential schools, see American Indian Relief Council, "History and Culture: Boarding Schools," http://www.nativepartnership.org/site/PageServer?pagename=airc_hist_boardingschools; Union of Ontario Indians, "An Overview of the Indian Residential School System," https://www.anishinabek.ca/wp-content/uploads/2016/07/An-Overview-of-the-IRS-System-Booklet.pdf; Peter Read, "The Stolen Generation: The Removal of Aboriginal Children in New South Wales 1883 to 1969," Department of Aboriginal Affairs (Australia), 2006, https://web.archive.org/web/20060820150941/http://www.daa.nsw.gov.au/publications/StolenGenerations.pdf.

Hawaiians who oppose the TMT for cultural-religious reasons is not convincing. More significantly, this piece fails to mention that Crowell is the father-in-law of Charles Long, CEO/president of Private Security Group Inc., whom TMT awarded a $3 million security contract, and that Long and his wife are the executive officers of Pacific Realty International, which manages the rental property that Ige and his wife own.[27]

Baybayan is described as "a vocal advocate for the [TMT] project and its advancement of astronomy and education" and a Hōkūleʻa canoe navigator. Hōkūleʻaʻs voyages in the late 1970s were part of the revitalization movement of Hawaiian culture. But Baybayan was "only one of four individuals that Papa Mau Piailug graduated into the rank of master navigator . . . and that others of that rank, including Nainoa Thompson, have spoken out in support of protecting Mauna Kea."[28] Nor did the piece clarify that Baybayan "work[ed] for the ʻImiloa Astronomy Center, which has received funding from Gordon Moore, one of the Thirty Meter Telescope funders."[29]

In this section, I have outlined the ways that developers' efforts to build the TMT, the DLNR's role in facilitating this project, and the fact that the University of Hawaiʻi and the astronomy community took advantage of the initial agreement constitute injustices against ʻŌiwi: religious bias and discrimination, destruction of cultural and natural resources, and desecration of sacred sites.

---

[27] Kingi Gilbert, "Governor Ige, Charles Long & the TMT $3mil Security Contract," September 8, 2019; Mahealani Richardson, "High-Profile Attorney Threatens to Sue over 'Vicious' TMT Rumors," Hawaiʻi News Now, September 11, 2019, https://www.hawaiinewsnow.com/2019/09/12/high-profileattorney-threatens-sue-over-vicious-tmt-rumors/.

[28] Kealoha Pisciotta, "Not the Whole Story about TMT," *Hawaiʻi Tribune Herald*, May 9, 2013.

[29] Pisciotta, "Not the Whole Story about TMT."

Sacred Mountain, Sacred Conduct

Religious practices informed the 2019 movement right from the start. At sunset on July 12, 2019, in response to a kāhea (call) the leaders had sent out to the ʻŌiwi community and our allies, about one hundred people showed up at Spencer Beach Park on Hawaiʻi Island, including those who flew in from other islands. There, they invited us to engage in a nonviolent direct action to prevent further desecration of Mauna Kea. Following this announcement, leader Kalani Flores performed a chant of protection for us. The leaders then outlined the plan of action. A small group of kiaʻi drove to Puʻuhuluhulu (a thicketed cinder cone) where they camped out in the parking lot at the hill's base. Others, like myself, arrived the next morning after preparing the supplies—camping gear, water, food, and so on—that we would need to hold space. Early that same morning, Mangauil led a procession of twenty to thirty kiaʻi as he performed a protective ritual along the perimeters of the area that the kiaʻi and the Royal Order of Kamehameha I had established as the puʻuhonua (refuge)— Puʻuhonua o Puʻuhuluhulu—"for the purpose of protecting sacred Maunakea."[30] Because the camp served a sacred purpose, it required a ritual of protection. Members of the Royal Order took every day turns standing guard at the camp's entrance. A few decades earlier, they had constructed an ahu (an altar made of stacked stones) to conduct rituals to honor the Mauna and the akua associated with it, and before standing guard, they held a ritual at the ahu every day at dawn. On July 15, a hundred or more people participated in a twelve-hour prayer vigil on the lava plain and at the Ahu. Participants chanted traditional pule (prayers) every hour on the hour.

---

[30] Puʻuhonua o Puʻuhuluhulu homepage, https://puuhuluhulu.com.

"Sacred mountain, sacred conduct" is a phrase that Pua Case, another leader, frequently repeated to kiaʻi and visitors alike. Because violence in speech or action is not in keeping with sacred conduct, the movement can also be characterized as nonviolent. To my mind, Case's simple phrase best encapsulates the spirit of the movement and the gist of the more complex concept known as "kapu aloha," a code of conduct for on and off the Mauna. This concept was especially instrumental to the success of the 2019 movement.

Kapu aloha is founded on two traditional concepts, "kapu" and "aloha." Mary Kawena Pukui compiled a Hawaiian dictionary with the assistance of linguist Samuel H. Elbert, and there they give this definition for "kapu": "Taboo, prohibition; special privilege or exemption from ordinary taboo; sacredness; prohibited, forbidden; sacred, holy, consecrated; no trespassing, keep out."[31] I would add that "kapu," in the sense of prohibitions, restrictions, or interdictions, can be practical in nature, such as no fishing during spawning season, or pertain to the sacred—whether person, place, thing, or practice—which is set apart because of its sacredness. "Aloha" is a capacious concept whose many nuanced meanings are not perfectly captured by any single English-language definition. Pukui and Elbert's entry for "aloha" gives the following definitions: "Aloha, love, affection, compassion, mercy, sympathy, pity, kindness, sentiment, grace, charity; greeting, salutation, regards; sweetheart, lover, loved one; beloved, loving, kind, compassionate, charitable, lovable; to love, be fond of; to show kindness, mercy, pity, charity, affection; to venerate; to remember with affection; to greet, hail."[32]

The movement had several leaders, and four of them were asked to share their understandings of kapu aloha: Hokulani Holt-Padilla, Pualani Kanakaʻole Kanahele, Andre Perez, and Case. Holt-Padilla explained,

---

[31] Pukui and Elbert, *Hawaiian Dictionary*, s.v. "kapu."
[32] Pukui and Elbert, *Hawaiian Dictionary*, s.v. "aloha."

Kapu aloha is always thinking about others, thinking about place, thinking about relationship and how to best have that happen, and to keep yourself in that discipline of thinking that what I want is not the most important thing if it does not align with these ways of behaving well with each other and with the place that we are in. So, that is at its simplest level of how we want people to be here.[33]

She noted that kapu aloha also has a functional application:

On a very practical basis, when we have a thousand, two thousand, five thousand people here, the kapu aloha is what holds us in our focus and our discipline to be able to bring only aloha to this place, and only aloha to lift up to the Mauna, and only aloha to take home with us when we go home to whatever island, whatever place we go home to.

According to Kanahele, "Kapu aloha" refers to "the idea of the way you behave should be sacred to not only yourself but the people around you ... prohibited because you are prohibited to act in a certain way." She added, "So, let's say when you come into this particular space or community of the mauna, this community of the Mauna is ruled by kapu aloha."[34]

Perez stated,

My understanding of kapu aloha is that it's rooted in discipline around aloha values, but I also understand that kapu aloha is not passive. Kapu aloha is discipline and

---

[33] Hōkūlani Holt-Padilla and Pualani Kanakaʻole Kanahele, "Kapu Aloha: Remember Your Ancestors," Puuhonua Puuhuluhulu, YouTube, September 13, 2019.

[34] Holt-Padilla and Kanahele, "Kapu Aloha."

kapu aloha keeps us at our highest individual standards on how we carry ourselves, how we conduct ourselves, how we treat people, how we engage with people in ways that are rooted in dignity and humanity.[35]

For Case, it is important to first consider that kapu aloha is rooted in ceremony, "how you conduct yourself in a ceremony":

Before we even looked at the human realm, how we're going to treat one another, how we're going to conduct ourselves, we were looking at how we are going to immerse ourselves into the space that we were going to be conducting ceremony in and with. So kapu aloha was the way in which we were going to interconnect, honor, have reverence, have respect beyond the human but to the elements—to everything you were calling, the unseen that you were asking to be here in the midst . . . that there is a manner in which one conducts themselves when they are in the sacred, you become the sacred, you take on all of those attributes, characteristics for chanters and dancers, because that is where I first learned it. . . . When we use it today, we are still in a ceremony. Standing for Mauna a Wākea, you are standing in the realm from the wao akua to the wao kanaka because the Mauna is everywhere. So when we say were are going to kapu aloha in a certain space, we are going to set a code of conduct as if we were in ceremony because we are.[36]

In the first week of the 2019 stand, the leaders placed a sign at the camp's entrance that implemented the following policies, which included kapu aloha:

---

[35] Andre Perez and Pua Case, "Kapu Aloha: A Guiding, Transformational, and Liberating Force," Puuhonua Puuhuluhulu, YouTube, September 23, 2019.

[36] Perez and Case, "Kapu Aloha."

> Please act accordingly. We are in the presence of the
> MAUNA & strive to uphold the highest sense of
> cultural protocol. KAPU ALOHA always. NO weapons,
> smoking, drugs & alcohol. MĀLAMA each other. BE
> PONO—always. Ask consent for any pictures or videos.
> Pick up any 'ōpala [trash] you see. Stay on designated
> trails & take a partner.
>   Mahalo for keeping the lāhui [people, nation] safe.

The phrase "highest sense of cultural protocol" draws attention to the ways that kiaʻi and visitors should behave in accordance with culturally informed conventions in the presence of the sacred. To mālama means to take care of someone or something. To be pono in this context means to act in a moral and ethical manner in keeping with the sacred purpose of Puʻuhonua o Puʻuhuluhulu.

This sacred purpose is what sustained us as we experienced the grueling reality of sustained nonviolent direct action. We kiaʻi chose our degree of engagement in the movement based on our comfort level and experience. The first camp meetings included a discussion about the three main levels of involvement in a nonviolent direct action, which were color-coded red, yellow, and green. Red meant that you were ready and willing to be arrested, in which case you would be part of the frontline action. Yellow meant that you preferred to avoid being arrested but would be if necessary; for example, to step into the front line if needed, or to act as legal observers for whom the risk of arrest still exists. Green meant that you did not want to be arrested and would hold space away from the frontline action while carrying out important duties such as caring for the children of frontline kiaʻi as they faced law enforcement, or bail out kiaʻi if they were arrested. Leaders worked with each group to outline strategies. The truth of the matter was that regardless of our level of engagement, we ended up being tested in every way.

Activists experience a range of feelings as they participate in direct action that can have positive or negative impacts—or both—on their mental and physical health.[37] As we learned, there are mental, spiritual, physical, and emotional dimensions to sustained nonviolent direct action. We were cognizant that our engagement is a response to an issue that is ultimately rooted in the oppression of our people and that we might experience violence. We who hold the mountain sacred for religious-cultural reasons feel morally and ethically obligated to protect it even if we risk physical harm. It becomes a question of choosing between two evils. The greater evil is failure to protect the sacred and the inevitable spiritual-emotional trauma we would experience as a result. The lesser evil is being arrested or physically harmed as we fulfill our obligation. We also had to acclimate to an elevation of sixty-six hundred feet. In July and August, the weather alternated between blazing hot during the day and bitterly cold at night. During the rainy season, the frigid cold and icy rain were constant.

We all contributed to running the camp. Who did what was an organic process—kiaʻi volunteered to carry out service according to what they were drawn to or best suited for: logistics, medical tent duty, kitchen duty, donation tent duty, supply runs, porta-potty duty, recycling duty, crosswalk duty. The first month, the thirty or so of us who camped 24/7 at the puʻuhonua often worked twelve- to sixteen-hour days. What little sleep we managed to get was under rough conditions. Our workload increased as more supporters arrived, especially on the weekends when one to three thousand people came to see the celebrities who supported us, including musicians who

---

[37] The Commons: Social Change Library, "Stress, Exhaustion, and Burnout," https://commonslibrary.org/impacts-of-activism-on-health-and-wellbeing/.

performed for us. Thankfully, at the height of the stand, the initial number of core kiaʻi increased to about one hundred, and then dropped back down to about thirty. In short, holding space was exhilarating but exhausting. When we were at our most vulnerable, some of us, myself included, would tell ourselves and each other, "Sacred mountain, sacred conduct"— drawing upon the spiritual comfort of Case's words, which gave us the strength we needed to continue when we were mentally and physically exhausted.

Marie Alohalani Brown was one of more than thirty kūpuna (Native Hawaiian elders) arrested at the start of the blockade to protest construction of the Thirty Meter Telescope on the sacred summit of Mauna Kea.
(PHOTO BY LAULANI TEALE / USED WITH PERMISSION)

Because the leaders knew that a state intervention was imminent, they continued to send a kāhea to supporters to come and hold space. Just before dawn on July 17, 2019, the leaders received word that DLNR officers and the police were headed our way, presumably to remove the kūpuna that comprised the front line, who held space in the tent that had been erected in the middle of the access road to the summit. Arrests ensued. The pain many of us felt at seeing well known and respected kūpuna, some of whom were in wheelchairs, being arrested was heart-wrenching. I was one of the younger kūpuna, and a few of these kūpuna, some of whom I knew and loved, were the same age as my own mother. I was among the last to be arrested. I opted to engage in a peaceful and legal form of resistance in Hawaiʻi—to lie on the ground and go limp. Given my height and weight, it took four officers to carry me to the police van. Once I was in the van, I was given a citation and offered the option of either being brought to Hilo and put in a holding cell or being released at Mauna Loa Access Road, about a mile down the road. I chose the latter. I immediately walked back to the kūpuna tent.

In the short time I had been away, a large number of heavily armed officers who appeared to be a special weapons and tactics (SWAT) team had arrived and formed lines on either side of the road, each line facing the large crowd that had gathered. They had also brought a large white machine, which others recognized as a Long-Range Acoustic Device (LRAD). By this time, a group of women had replaced us kūpuna as the front line. They stood in rows with arms linked, their faces bearing determined expressions. Despite the implied threat of violence, the crowd still maintained kapu aloha. Any act of violence in word or deed would have given the police an excuse to use violence to disperse us. Thankfully, the leaders and the DLNR reached an agreement, and no more arrests were made. All the police left the mountain as did the DLNR, with the exception of a few DLNR officers who remained because they were tasked with the duty to observe us from farther up the road behind the kūpuna tent.

Photos of that morning show thousands of supporters spread out on both sides of the road on the lava plains. Remarkably, during those tense hours, the crowd remained largely silent and no violence occurred. This feat was only possible because the leaders had continuously stressed the importance of kapu aloha over the last week and also that morning as everyone awaited the arrival of the DLNR officers and the police. The kapu aloha kiaʻi who used peaceful means to make sure that kapu aloha was maintained were also critically important that day.

Hoʻomana on a Sacred Mountain: Rites of Protection and Resistance

Protocol is the process of separating the sacred from the profane.[38]

Nearly two thousand years ago, our seafaring Polynesian ancestors left their homeland, navigating the ocean until they reached the islands collectively known today as Hawaiʻi. As centuries passed, our culture and language evolved to the point that we became a distinct people—the ʻŌiwi. Our islands shaped us physically, intellectually, and spiritually. Our ʻike (knowledge, experience, insight) is grounded in the realities of our island-world existence. For countless generations, our kūpuna lived in close connection to the ʻāina and observed it. Not only did we observe the ʻāina, we claim/ed kinship with it. We are part of a complex web of relationality in which all—land, sea, sky, and everything therein—are kin. This relationality is also spiritual, for we are the human relatives of the other-than-human entities of our island world, many of whom we consider akua. Our island

---

[38] Pualani Kanakaʻole Kanahele et al., "Nā Oli no ka ʻĀina o Kanakaʻole (The Chants for the Kanakaʻole Lands): A Compilation of Oli and Cultural Practices," Edith Kanakaʻole Foundation, Hilo, 2017, 3.

world—from the sky and its celestial bodies to the islands and
the ocean that surrounds them, along with the myriad natural
phenomena, features, flora, and fauna of sky, land, and sea—is
the modality by which our akua make themselves known and the
matrix of Hoʻomana.

Despite claims to the contrary, substantial and overwhelming
evidence shows that some ʻŌiwi never stopped practicing
Hoʻomana even though King Kamehameha II, persuaded by a few
powerful aliʻi, officially abolished it in 1819—even when these
same aliʻi embraced Christianity after the first American Protestant missionaries arrived in 1820, and even after the Hawaiian
Kingdom proclaimed to be a Christian nation.[39] While Hoʻomana
has evolved, like other religions evolved, its fundamental components remain the same. These core elements include but are not
limited to the following: the belief in mana, the belief in akua and
ʻaumākua, reverence for their kino lau (many forms), the belief
that the island world is animated, belief in traditional understandings of death and the afterlife, adherence to kapu concerning
the sacred and the secular, and the recognition of moʻokūʻauhau
(genealogy) as an organizational concept.

The 2019 stand for Mauna a Wākea has been a catalyst for
the resurgence of Hoʻomana. Each day, kiaʻi participated in and/
or led ʻAha (religious ceremonies) four times a day. As a consequence, hundreds of ʻŌiwi have, for the first time in their lives,
had the unprecedented opportunity—since Kamehameha II's
1810 edict—to practice our religion together in public on a
massive scale. Because thousands of visitors have witnessed or
participated in these ʻAha and because the ʻAha were videotaped
and made available to the public on websites such as Puʻuhonua o
Puʻuhuluhulu and Kākoʻo Haleakalā, there was a growing awareness around the world about Hoʻomana and the fact that it is a

---

[39] See Brown, "*Mauna Kea*."

living religion.[40] These ʻAha manifested protective mana through prayer chants and hula (in this case, a form of kinetic prayer). Early on in the movement, the daily pule and hula were collectively referred to as "protocol." In 2017, Pualani Kanakaʻole et al. published a collection of chants and culturally informed practices as an aid for cultural practitioners. In this guide, they give this explanation about a protocol's function:

> Protocol establishes and reestablishes an awareness of relationship between people, place, and things and is a conduit for intergenerational thought continuum. It provides a pervading attitude toward ecological sensitivity tantamount to mālama and aloha ʻāina. It communicates a code of behavior in respect to places, peoples and things. It is a safety device which reaches into realm of the unseen. It is a unifying mechanism giving strength to purpose.[41]

They also note, "The information in this guide is provided to support cultural practitioners and their efforts to reestablish spiritual connections with the natural environment and to elevate their practice."[42] In whatever manner kiaʻi and visitors conceived their participation in the protocols, that they served a spiritual purpose remains. In Hoʻomana, words have mana—thus, even if you are not a practitioner of Hoʻomana, by virtue of your participation in the ʻAha, you are nonetheless mana-festing to protect Mauna a Wākea.

---

[40] The name "Kākoʻo Haleakalā" [Support Haleakalā] refers to the sacred Mauna of Maui, Haleakalā, that kiaʻi have also tried to protect from the construction of telescopes. For videos of ʻAha and other Mauna-related videos, see Kākoʻo Haleakalā's Facebook page @kakoohaleakala, https://www.facebook.com/kakoohaleakala/?ref=page_internal.

[41] Kanahele et al., "Nā Oli no ka ʻĀina o Kanakaʻole," 3.

[42] Kanahele et al., "Nā Oli no ka ʻĀina o Kanakaʻole," 34.

I don't remember when or who first referred to the protocols as "'Aha," which denotes an assembly whatever its purpose, including religious ceremonies, but 'Aha soon replaced protocol as the prevalent term. Kanaka'ole, her children and their spouses, her grandchildren, and others they had trained in their hula hālau (school) were the usual leaders of the 'Aha, but other hula practitioners and trained ritualists occasionally stepped in to lead them. 'Aha were performed at sunrise, at 8 a.m., noon, and sunset on Mauna Kea Access Road, which we renamed Ala Kūpuna—Kūpuna Road—because the kūpuna tent blocked it. That we performed 'Aha four times every day for eight months underscores the sacred nature of the 2019 stand.

Sunrise 'Aha

The sunrise ceremony required kūpuna to wake up before dawn, usually at four-thirty. With the help of kāko'o (helpers) and Mauna Medics who slept in the kūpuna tent each night to assist us, we put away our bedding and cots, and replaced them with folding chairs. A kūpuna trained in ritual, Noe Noe Wong-Wilson, led the sunrise 'Aha. When Wong-Wilson had to go off mountain, she asked me and Cindy Freitas to lead it. When I objected because I was not a trained ritualist, she responded that all kia'i were being trained to become ritualists, which became quite clear the longer we were on the Mauna. Other kia'i, and even visitors, joined these morning rituals. This 'Aha was much shorter than the other three as we did not perform hula, receive offerings from visitors, or offer a full orientation for visitors. A few kia'i either blew pū (conch shells) or lengths of bamboo to open and close the ceremony for which we performed five pule.

The first two pule chants, "E ala e" and "E Kānehoalani ē," are for Kāne, a major akua. Kāne's many forms include the sun and freshwater. He is associated with procreation because without the sun and freshwater, life as we know would not be possible. Moreover, it is into his realm, the lani, that the summit of Mauna a Wākea extends—who is the reason for our stand. As we chanted these two pule, we faced the sunrise. For the next three chants, we faced the Mauna.

The third chant, "E Hō Mai," was composed by renowned hula master and cultural expert Edith Kanaka'ole. Her daughter, Pualani Kanaka'ole Kanahele, explains that this chant "calls upon the chanter to focus . . . and for knowledge to be bestowed upon the chanter."[43] The first line asks that knowledge be granted from above, a clear reference to something other-than- human that has the power to grant 'ike.

The fourth chant, "Nā 'Aumākua," asks 'aumākua to protect us and grant us 'ike, ikaika (strength), akamai (intelligence), maopopo pono (proper understanding), 'ike pāpālua (to be able to see that which is normally unseen by others), and mana. Here, when it came to the line declaring the chanter's identity, the movement's official version identified us as the descendants of the akua of Mauna a Wākea, the 'Ōiwi of Hawai'i.

The fifth chant, "E Iho Ana," is an adaptation of a prophecy by Kapihe, whom Samuel M. Kamakau, a noted nineteenth-century historian, described as,

> Ke kaula hope loa nana ka wanana hope, "E hui ana na moku, e hiolo ana na kapu akua, e iho mai ana ko ka lani, a e pii aku ana ko ka honua."

> The last seer who gave the last prophesy, "The islands will unite, the godly prohibitions shall topple, what once belonged above will be brought down, what once belonged below will be raised up."[44]

---

[43] Kanahele et al., "Nā Oli no ka 'Āina o Kanaka'ole," 2.
[44] Samuel M. Kamakau, "Ka Moolelo Hawaii," *Ka Nupepa Kuokoa*, November 3, 1870. Papakilo Database. Author's translation.

Kapihe's prophecy came true when Kamehameha II abolished Hoʻomana and when missionary descendants and white businessmen, backed by the American warship *Boston*, overthrew Queen Liliʻuokalani and the Hawaiian monarchy on January 17, 1893. But because words have power, we use Kapihe's words to overturn the status quo.

The Three Main ʻAha

The three main ʻAha followed the same format and consisted of three segments. The first was devoted to pule and hula, and the second to presentations of hoʻokupu (offerings). The third was an orientation for visitors and new kiaʻi in which whoever led it asked who was here for the first time and welcomed them, and then explained the movement's aim and conduct policies, which I have already discussed.

We performed many pule and hula during the 2019 stand. Because leaders and ritualists encouraged kiaʻi and visitors to participate in pule and hula, and because not all kiaʻi and visitors were trained in chant and hula, they taught us. Leaders posted PDFs of pule and mele hula on the Puʻuhonua o Puʻuhuluhulu website. There were kiaʻi, myself included, who did not know all of these pule by heart, which, at one point, Kekuhi Kealiikanaka-oleohaililani apparently noticed.

This famous hula master and chanter then made the most empowering statement I have ever heard in my life, which I paraphrase here: If you don't know the chants, read them off your phone—your intentions have power. In short, she taught us that we were all needed to mana-fest protection for the Mauna. She nullified any shame someone might feel because we did not know all the chants. An inability to chant pule is directly tied to a long history of religious persecution and colonial assimilation.

Her words allowed us to fully engage in the process with our dignity intact and to eventually memorize the pule.

Experts held regular classes on pule and hula, and as a result many neophytes learned some if not all the pule and hula. While we could chant pule as we stood on the lava plains next to Ala Kūpuna, dancing hula was done on the road. Every 'Aha, fifty to a hundred people, crowded onto the road, standing in rows of five to six people. By the time the 2019 stand ended, hundreds of kia'i could perform one or more hula to mana-fest protection for the Mauna. While those of us who had only learned hula on the Mauna cannot by any means call ourselves hula dancers, we can proudly say that we are kia'i who danced to protect our sacred mountain.

Drummers and singers lead the daily pule and hula ceremonies on the access road leading to Mauna Kea's summit, directly in front of the kūpuna (elders) tent blockade.
(PHOTO BY MARK CLATTERBUCK / USED WITH PERMISSION)

Because performing pule is a sacred act, leaders and ritualists asked people to refrain from videoing that portion of the 'Aha. I was granted an exception to this rule on one occasion after I asked permission to livestream this portion of the ʻAha to my students in my introductory course on Hawaiian religion. In short, pule are not entertainment for the masses, but a sacred ceremony that should be respected as such. People could, however, video the various hula that followed the pule even if hula is in this case kinetic prayer—or as Mehanaokalā Hind describes it, "Mana in motion."[45] The leaders did well to allow this because it helped our cause. It showed the world that we engaged in peaceful, traditional forms of protection and resistance based on religious beliefs and belief-related practices.

As with the sunrise ceremony, a group of kiaʻi blew pū and lengths of bamboo at the opening and closing of the main ʻAha. The pule segment lasted about twenty minutes. The pule were the same as for the sunrise ceremony with these exceptions: we only performed "E Ala e" at dawn and we did not chant "E Kānehoalani ē" for the eight o'clock or noon ʻAha, but we did chant it at sunset as we faced the setting sun. This is an added spiritual component. Chanting to the sun (Kāne) as it rises and chanting to Kāne as it sets completes a cycle (an entire day) in which we acknowledge and honor the akua to whom, by virtue of his function (procreation and sustaining life), we ultimately owe our existence. For these three ʻAha, an added chant was performed, one honoring Mauna a Wākea. Unlike the other chants, the ritualists did not teach us this one, because it was reserved for those who had learned it previously on other occasions.

Hula dancers interpret the chant for which a hula was composed. Some hula practitioners dance the hula while others use their hands to beat drums and gourds to provide the tempo. We performed several hula in the first few months, but ritualists periodically added others, for a total of eight hula. The

---

[45] Nicole Mehanaokalā Hind, "Hula: Mana in Motion," master's thesis, University of Hawaiʻi at Mānoa, 2010.

akua these hula and the mele (songs/chants) they collectively honored include Mauna a Wākea, Wākea, Papa/Haumea, Hoʻohokuikalani, Hāloa, Lilinoe, Poliahu, Waiau, Kahoupoakāne, Pele, Hiʻiakaikapoliopele, Kāne, and Kanaloa. Each hula had a specific purpose and were prayers in their own right—from simply honoring akua to asking the volcanic akua Pele to overturn the status quo.

Once the Makahiki began, the season over which the akua Lono presides, the ritualists taught us hula in honor of Lono, who has different forms.[46] Here, I share Kalei Nuʻuhiwa's cogent insights into Lono and the Makahiki:

> Lonoikamakahiki is the akua of establishing the annual calendar by feeding the stars and aligning the calendar with the star constellation Makaliʻi. Lonomakua is the akua of ritual fire and all the geological activities that occur during the Makahiki. Lononuiaākea is the akua for the celestial and atmospheric activities that transpire during the Makahiki season. The rituals, mele and pule that have been composed for these environmental expectations are rooted in generational observations to which layers upon layers of metaphor are added to describe Lono and his kino lau akua (manifestations).[47]

Certain mele and hula that we performed honor Kamapuaʻa, whose name means "Pig Child." Kamapuaʻa is a form of Lono, and they share several kino lau, including pigs, and certain flora and fauna that resemble pigs in some way such as certain types of tree

---

[46] Makahiki begins when the rising of Makaliʻi (Pleiades) in the east coincides with the sun setting in the west. See Kalei Nuʻuhiwa, "Makahiki— Nā Maka o Lono: Utilizing the Papakū Makawalu Method to Analyze Mele and Pule of Lono and the Makahiki," doctoral dissertation, University of Waikato, 2020, 12.

[47] Nuʻuhiwa. "Makahiki," i.

ferns and taro, sweet potatoes, candlenut trees, and mullet fish. In our traditions, Kamapua'a is known for overturning the status quo, which is another reason to honor him on the Mauna during Makahiki season. When Makahiki ended, we switched back to the hula we performed pre-Makahiki.

The ho'okupu portion of the three main 'Aha also had a spiritual component. Thousands of visitors but also a number of kia'i availed of the ho'okupu segment to make offerings to the kūpuna who by virtue of their frontline action had put the TMT construction on hold. It should be noted that this frontline action would not have been possible without all the leaders' skillful organization and the many other kia'i who held space. Because the line of people who wished to give ho'okupu was often very long, this segment might last an hour or even two. Ho'okupu was also informed by protocol.

First, a kapu aloha kia'i indicated where people should line up and asked if they needed a ritualist to help them through the protocol. If offerers knew proper protocol, they chanted themselves down the Ala Kūpuna toward the group of ritualists, many of whom were hula practitioners. These ritualists sat in their usual spot on woven mats, their drums and gourds ready to respond with a welcoming chant or an appropriate hula. The offerer paused about twenty or thirty feet from the woven mats. If the offerers did not know protocol for ho'okupu, a ritualist would assist them. The ritualist asked the offerers who they were and where they came from, and then led them down the road as he or she performed an impromptu chant that introduced them, which included poetic references to who they were and where they came from.

Next, the group of ritualists quickly decided on an appropriate welcoming chant or hula, which they then performed. Then, a male kia'i, adopting a position of lowered head and raised arms to show his respect, received the ho'okupu from the offerer and slowly backed away a few feet before turning around to give the hoʻokupu to Cindy Freitas who, trained in protocol, put it on a table. As Freitas taught us, when we kūpuna stood in line to greet the offerers, we were never to stand with our backs directly in front of the table. This is because in that instance, the table served a sacred purpose, which was to receive hoʻokupu— gifts given in aloha and out of respect for kiaʻi who served the Mauna. The table was decorated with small kāhili, or feathered standards, a traditional sign of rank. The offerers then went down the line of kūpuna, who touched noses with them and spoke words of aloha. Sometimes, the offering was a performance, which brought joy to all. In one instance, the hoʻokupu was an offering of newly carved kiʻi—images of akua, which merits further discussion.

Earlier in this essay, I had noted the rallying cry "Kū Kiaʻi Mauna" (Stand to protect the Mauna). In keeping with the ancient practice of noting new phenomena and granting them a name, it was not long before a ritualist identified Kū Kiaʻi Mauna as an akua—a form of Kū. Kū is an akua with many forms that bear his name. The practices and things associated with Kū forms include (but are not limited to) war and politics, fishing, farming, canoe construction, the ʻōhiʻa lehua tree (e.g., *Metrosideros macropus, collina, polymorpha*), the coconut tree, kī (*Cordyline termanalis*), and the eel. The aforementioned hoʻokupu of kiʻi akua were made as part of a project to revive the art of carving kiʻi for which Andre Perez, one of the main leaders, had received a million-dollar grant. These kiʻi represented a few major akua such as Kāne, but also included a female kiʻi to collectively represent the akua wahine (female akua) associated with the summit of Mauna a Wākea. Perez and his fellow carvers presented each kiʻi to a kahu who would then care for them— an important honor and responsibility. Pua Case's daughter, Kapualei Flores, received the female kiʻi.

Conclusion

The official 2019 stand on the Mauna lasted eight months. In March 2020, because of the pandemic, leaders disbanded kia'i for safety reasons, but a handful of kia'i decided to remain to hold space, and they continue to do so. As of this writing the Mauna movement and the TMT are at a standstill. As a result of the high-profile movement, in May 2021, a Canadian astronomy organization "declared that it cannot support the TMT unless it has the consent of Native Hawaiians."[48] More recently, in 2023, the National Science Foundation (NSF) held meetings in several communities on Hawai'i Island concerning the construction of the TMT to receive testimonies on the subject. As of 2024, the NSF is deciding whether they will fund the TMT.

Other positive outcomes include the following. As a result of coming together for a sacred purpose, the kia'i who lived on the Mauna together, whether for a short or long time, became an 'ohana (family)—the Mauna 'ohana. We shared the unique experience of living on a sacred mountain for a sacred purpose and faced many challenges together. Seasoned activists trained a new generation to one day replace them. Expert ritualists trained a new generation of ritualists to carry on. The 2019 stand marks an important moment in 'Ōiwi history—a huliau (time of change). We are in the final phase of hulihia after an intellectual and spiritual awakening, cresting a wave of change as we strive to overturn the status quo. We risk annihilation. We fight to protect the vertebrae that constitute the backbone of who we are as a people—our 'āina, ways of knowing and being, language, customs, and religious beliefs. Yet, for the first time, order may emerge from chaos—two hundred years of American hegemony

---

    [48] Tim Hurley, "Native Hawaiian Consent Needed for TMT, Canadian Group Says," *Star Advertiser*, May 19, 2021.

in our beloved islands. We adapt to historical challenges. As we look to the past for knowledge and inspiration on how to face the future, we are aware that we are tomorrow's ancestors, and future generations will look to us for guidance. This is our destiny.

4

CIRCLE OF PROTECTION
Yogis, Baptists, and Interspiritual Activists

Heidi Dhivya Berthoud and Swami Dayananda

The following reflections explore how spirituality—individual and communal, formal and informal—helped to shape the successful grassroots-led coalition to block construction of the proposed Atlantic Coast Pipeline (ACP) in Virginia from 2014 to 2020. The chapter is organized into three parts. The first part, written by Heidi Dhivya Berthoud, provides an overview of the threats posed by the ACP fracked gas pipeline and key moments of morally and spiritually grounded resistance in the fight to stop it, with a specific focus on the transformative collaboration that took place in Buckingham County between members of the Yogaville community and local Baptist congregations in opposition to the pipeline.

The second two parts narrow the spotlight by offering personal, first-person reflections from two women who played important roles in the resistance movement. In the second part, Swami Dayananda examines the ways in which her experience as a swami (monastic) of Hindu lineage at the Satchidananda Ashram–Yogaville in Virginia (SAYVA) fueled her own participation in the resistance. The third part contains the personal reflections of Heidi Dhivya Berthoud, a founding member of Friends of Buckingham and Virginia Community Rights Network. Her spiritual journey draws deeply from Integral Yoga and Gaia-centered goddess traditions, which keenly informed her involvement in the ACP resistance. Together, these narratives provide important insights into individual motivations for ecojustice work and inform broader current trends unfolding at the intersection of spirituality and frontline environmental activism in the United States.

Overview of the Atlantic Coast Pipeline Resistance in Buckingham

I'll take you to the river,
Tell you what I see,
I see the truth in the water
Shining back at me,
Everything in time,
Since the world began,
Feel it breathing the air,
Feel it buried in the land.

—Josh Vana, ACP Resistance Movement Artivist[1]

Roots of Spiritual Resistance

The ACP project was canceled on Friday July 5, 2020. The reflections of this chapter focus on the grassroots pipeline resistance movement that was based in Buckingham County, Virginia, with special attention given to the environmental justice issues related to the pipeline's proposed compressor station and the unique partnership of the Yogis, the Baptists, and many others to successfully

---

[1] Song "To the River," by Josh Vana, musician, artivist, and director of ARTivism. See The SUN SiNG Collective (#NoPipeline Anthem, #NoMVP, #NoACP).

lay siege to the Dominion Energy Corporation.[2] The two main
Buckingham stakeholder groups to join hands were the Yogaville
community[3] and what came to be known as the Union Hill neighborhood, largely centered on Union Hill Baptist Church and,
later, Union Grove Baptist Church. Local community members
formed the nonprofit organization Friends of Buckingham (FoB)
to lead the grassroots resistance in the county, working together
with over fifty organizations to stop the ACP under the umbrella
of the Allegheny–Blue Ridge Alliance (ABRA).[4]

Satchidananda Ashram–Yogaville, Virginia (hereafter SAYVA
or the ashram), located in the Piedmont of the Blue Ridge Mountains, is about forty miles south of Charlottesville.[5] The ashram
was established in 1979 by the world-renowned Yoga master and
Hindu monk Sri Swami Satchidananda (Swamiji). It is a place
for the residents, guests, and program participants to practice,
live, and share Swamiji's teachings of Integral Yoga. Integral Yoga
is a scientific system that integrates the various branches of Yoga
to bring about a complete and harmonious development of the
individual, fostering understanding of universal oneness and a
life of service. At the heart of the Ashram is the Light of Truth
Universal Shrine (LOTUS), designed in the shape of a lotus
flower. LOTUS is dedicated to interfaith understanding and the
Light within all faiths, backgrounds, and beliefs.

---

[2] Buckingham County, Virginia, is the ancestral land of the Monacan
Indian Nation.

[3] The Yogaville community includes the organization known as Satchidananda Ashram–Yogaville, Virginia (SAYVA), and the community that
developed around it. SAYVA is the international headquarters of Integral Yoga.

[4] For more, see the Friends of Buckingham website, http://www.
friendsofbuckinghamva.org/, and the Allegheny Blue Ridge Alliance
(ABRA) website, https://www.abralliance.org/.

[5] H. H. Sri Swami Satchidananda, *Heaven on Earth: My Vision of
Yogaville* (Yogaville, VA: Integral Yoga Publications, 2004).

LOTUS (Light of Truth Universal Shrine) along the James River at the
Satchidananda Ashram–Yogaville in Virginia (SAYVA).
(PHOTO BY DAVID PARRY / USED WITH PERMISSION)

Situated on 750 acres of mostly forested land along the
James River, the ashram includes a teaching academy, conference center, meeting and dining hall, library, office building,
federal credit union, organic farm, and guest accommodations.
There is a monastery for monastics. Members of the Integral
Yoga ministry live in the extended Yogaville community. As
the ashram has grown, the surrounding Yogaville community
has grown to include over 250 like-minded residents, many of
whom participate in Ashram activities and offer their services
to the ashram. Yogaville Environmental Solutions (YES) was
established to resist the ACP and to expedite the community's transition to clean energy and a sustainable future. Swami
Dayananda was a former director of YES and of the LOTUS
Center for All Faiths.

Two African American Baptist congregations led by Pastor
Paul Wilson in the Union Hill community were another key locus

of spiritual opposition to the ACP.[6] These churches are rooted in the independent Missionary Baptist tradition, where an evangelical commitment to Bible-centered preaching is wed to a vision of Jesus as a champion of racial and economic justice. Publicly raising their voices against the ACP pipeline represented a shift for these congregations who had learned to keep their heads down and not rock the boat on hot-button issues given the history of racial tension in the region. However, with Pastor Paul's leadership and the strength of the wider pipeline resistance movement, along with growing anger at the deceit being spread by Dominion to downplay the real risks and dangers that the project posed to Union Hill residents, the churchgoers ultimately felt empowered to speak out.

Notably, a number of folks who had returned to their homes after many years away stood strongest against Dominion's deceptions and bribes. "It was hard to listen to their lies: how good it would be, the jobs, and good for the environment," explains John Laury, a deacon at Union Grove Baptist Church. "They would lie as if we were too dumb to understand that they were lying. There were times it was just too much to listen to their lies and we would stand up and turn our backs, holding signs like 'Tell the truth' or 'This is a robbery.'" With his rueful smile, John adds, "Due to the damage this project would have caused to the environment—people, animals, earth—every Christian should live in resistance to this. Every spiritual leader should be in opposition to this. If this would hurt one person, whether Christian or not, all should stand in opposition."[7]

---

[6] Paul Wilson is the pastor of Union Grove Baptist Church and the former pastor of Union Hill Baptist Church. He is also a member of Friends of Buckingham. Union Grove and Union Hill are independent Missionary Baptist Churches. He is a fifth-generation funeral director and owner of the oldest African American business in Virginia. His wife, Marilyn, is the first Black woman circuit court clerk in Virginia.

[7] John Laury, Friends of Buckingham member and married to Ruby

Dominion Energy had chosen to locate the project's only Virginia-based compressor station squarely in the Union Hill community, a majority-Black neighborhood in which many trace their ancestry to enslaved persons who were forced to work on the former Variety Shade Plantation. The plantation owners' descendants sold this land to the ACP for the controversial compressor station, extending their legacy of exploitation of the Union Hill community. The blatant environmental racism in targeting the Union Hill community with the project's worst impacts—toxic emissions, deafening noise, and dangerous explosion potential—led many to frame the fight as a David-and-Goliath contest of environmental justice.

The Yogaville and Union Hill communities were joined by a rich variety of additional moral and spiritual traditions in opposing the ACP. As described in the pages that follow, individual and collective pipeline resistance arose from convictions rooted in traditions as diverse as Wicca, Indigenous spirituality, the Catholic Worker movement, engaged Buddhism, Sufism, Quakerism, the Episcopal Church, and many others. Additionally, some key leaders in the grassroots resistance movement explicitly reject any institutional religious affiliations but nonetheless speak openly about the ways in which conscience and spirituality nourish their ecojustice work.

All of these voices are key to understanding the emergence of new, extrainstitutional spiritual communities of conscience that are arising in the crucible of frontline eco-activism all across the United States today, creatively merging the wisdom and ritual

---

Laury, interviewed by Heidi Dhivya Berthoud, May 6, 2023. Many courthouse records were burned in the South after the Civil War, taking with them evidence of enslavement, and thus entitlement to reparations. John firmly believes he is descended from enslaved peoples from Variety Shade Plantation, the proposed site of the ACP compressor station.

practices of wildly diverse traditions in spirit- and moral-driven defense of one, shared, sacred Earth. At a time when religious affiliation in the United States continues to decline, with religious nones (those identifying as atheist, agnostic, or nothing in particular) now making up 30 percent of the US population, the rise of such an organic, interspiritual community around a shared commitment to the sacredness of Earth might suggest a new trend in the country's shifting spiritual landscape.[8]

The proposed ACP route was to begin in Harrison County, West Virginia. It was to draw fracked natural gas from wells in the Utica and Marcellus shale fields, then traveling southeast, through Central Virginia to its terminus in Robeson County, North Carolina, and to the Cove Point export facility in Maryland. Buckingham County is located in the heart of Virginia, in the Piedmont, with stunning views of the Blue Ridge Mountains to the west. Dominion Energy was determined to locate one of three mega compressor stations (CS) for the more-than-six-hundred-mile, forty-two-inch high-pressure fracked gas Atlantic Coast Pipeline (ACP) project here, connecting with the Transco Pipeline that runs from the Gulf Coast to New England.

The proposed locations for Dominion's three compressor stations were all chosen as sites of anticipated least resistance. This follows a worldwide corporate pattern of disproportionately locating harmful industrial activities in communities marked by a high percentage of nonwhite or low-income residents, sites for necessary environmental justice (EJ) work. In the case of the ACP, the project's three compressor stations were sited for installation in a low-income white Appalachian community in West Virginia,

---

[8] For more on current trends in religious self-identification among the US population, see Gregory A. Smith, Pew Research Center (online), "About Three-in-Ten U.S. Adults Are Now Religiously Unaffiliated," December 14, 2021.

a predominantly Black community in Union Hill, Virginia, and the home of the Lumbee Nation in Eastern North Carolina.

Dominion gained eminent domain permission by the Federal Energy Regulatory Commission (FERC) to take land for private gain for the ACP, even though the gas was heading for export terminals rather than for domestic consumption. The project was racist, land-destroying, water-contaminating, air-poisoning, community-fracturing, and climate-destroying. Local communities were being forced to shoulder risks that were all to help Dominion ensure continued dependence on fossil fuels for the next forty years and to ensure that stockholders could benefit from a Virginia State Corporation Commission (SCC)-guaranteed 15 percent rate of return for their investment.[9]

Dominion originally considered siting the Buckingham CS in Nelson County, by the James River crossing on the north shore, at Wingina, formerly known as Monahassanugh, one of five main villages of the Monacan Tribe.[10] Another site was a white neighborhood in Buckingham. In the end, the compressor station was sited for Union Hill, a predominantly Black community. This decision also rerouted the pipeline to within a mile of the LOTUS Temple. The Three Sisters resistance camp, discussed later in this chapter, was set up at that proposed river crossing site in 2018.

Union Hill: Racial and Environmental Justice

The pursuit of environmental justice for the Union Hill community was a key driver of our movement's work to stop the ACP. Our primary contribution to the enforcement of environmental

---

[9] Paula C. Squires, "Pipeline Battle," *Virginia Business*, July 28, 2017.

[10] Reverend Dhyani Simonini to Kimberly Bose, Federal Energy Regulatory Commission, November 8, 2015. FERC Docket Number PF 15-6. See FoB website, "Dhyani Simonini FERC Letters: Defending First People's Burial Grounds."

justice regulations was community participatory research that uncovered deliberately erased historic and demographic household evidence for the Union Hill site that Dominion chose for the compressor station.

Reverend Lakshmi Fjord, PhD, longtime practicing anthropologist and Integral Yoga minister, helmed this environmental justice campaign.[11] Fjord focuses her ministry and anthropology practices on elevating the cultural expertise of Black and Indigenous communities within community-guided research in an effort to protect our air, land, water, and all beings of Mother Earth.

African American historian Charles White spent forty-five years researching the history of Black people in Buckingham County.[12] Combining White's findings, interviews with longtime Black family members in the Union Hill neighborhood, and archival materials on the Variety Shade Plantation, Fjord successfully documented the existence of the Union Hill Rural Historic District, named after the Union Hill Baptist Church built by free Blacks in 1868. In 2016, the district received "Most Endangered Historic Place" status from Preservation Virginia.

This critical work countered flagrant attempts by Dominion and the FERC to erase the neighborhood's historic African American heritage and significant preexisting health conditions of local residents in an effort to expedite approval of the massive CS in the community. In late 2016, Fjord organized a door-to-door, ethnographic household study with frontline Black elders

---

[11] Material for this section drawn from an interview with Lakshmi Fjord by Heidi Dhivya Berthoud, May 2023. For more information on the participatory research project in Union Hill led by Dr. Fjord, see Heidi Dhivya Berthoud and Lakshmi Fjord, "Retrospective: EJ Played a Pivotal Role with the ACP," Friends of Buckingham website, December 16, 2023.

[12] See Charles W. White, *The Hidden and the Forgotten: Contributions of Buckingham Blacks to American History* (1985; repr., Meherrin, VA: Lamp Post Publicity, 2017).

that documented an 84 percent African American majority in and around the ACP's proposed compressor station site, with many also claiming Indigenous heritage and direct lineage from Union Hill's free Black founders.

The white supremacist violence that Fjord witnessed at the Unite the Right Rally in Charlottesville in August 2017 motivated her to organize the Charlottesville People's Tribunal on Human Rights and Environmental Justice Impacts of Fracking related to the ACP and MVP (Mountain Valley Pipeline) projects. Synchronistically, then–Virginia governor Terry McAuliffe launched the Advisory Council on Environmental Justice (ACEJ) by executive order two days after the tribunal. Pastor Paul Wilson, Swami Dayananda, Friends of Buckingham president and cofounder Chad Oba, and other Union Hill residents spoke during public comments at the first ACEJ meeting. ACEJ's notable membership included Rev. Faith Harris, a theologian focused on ecological justice and director of Virginia Interfaith Power and Light (VAIPL), and Beth Roach, Nottoway Nation, currently with Sierra Club and cofounder of the Alliance of Native Seedkeepers.

Prominent social justice activist and Yale Divinity School theologian Rev. William Barber II and former vice president Al Gore, founder of Climate Reality, teamed up to boost our work with a large public event at Buckingham Middle School in February 2019. Besides making a national impact, their visit to the community was also felt on a deeply personal level for many in the movement. Ella Rose, an African American elder who was born in Union Hill, describes a profound spiritual experience she had that day:

> Reverend Barber came to my house, because I am so close to the CS site. I said to Bishop Barber, "Would you please bless my home?" He came in and blessed my

home. Everyone packed in, including former vice president Al Gore and his daughter Karenna Gore. Reverend Barber took me by the hand and we walked around the kitchen. As he was saying a prayer, my body levitated. I was still walking, but I could feel it. He then said, "Now there's a song after the blessing." We sang that song all the way through. Right today, I cannot remember a word of the song. That motivated me to just keep on advocating, keep on speaking. It gave me spiritual power, right down in my soul. I get choked up when I be telling that story. I have seen people on television levitating and having an out-of-body experience.[13]

In October 2019, a joint legal challenge to the proposed CS permit was heard in the US Court of Appeals for the Fourth Circuit. On January 7, 2020, the judges' published decision overturned Dominion's air permit in Union Hill, a huge environmental justice win and a major turning point for the fight against the ACP. The momentous decision marked the eighth time that a federal court or federal agency had revoked or suspended ACP permits. On July 1, 2020, the Virginia Environmental Justice Act, which our coalition helped to get in place, established a commission to investigate incidents of environmental injustice and coordinate government efforts to ensure that minorities and low-income citizens are not disproportionately subjected to environmental hazards. On Friday, July 5, 2020, Dominion and Duke Energy canceled the ACP.

---

[13] Ella Rose, cofounder of Friends of Buckingham, was born in the Union Hill neighborhood and later retired to her home in Buckingham after fifty-one years away. She had two years to enjoy family and friends before the ACP decided her backyard was a good route for the pipeline, less than half a mile from the CS site. Interviewed by Heidi Dhivya Berthoud, June 11, 2023.

Reflecting on this history, Jeeva Abbate (Salish and Kootenai), director of Yogaville Environmental Solutions (YES), said,

> I had a powerful realization through this work about how marginalized minority and poor people are by powerful corporate interests that place profit before people and our planet. In the end, it was our fight for environmental justice for Union Hill that allowed us to cancel the CS permit and defeat Dominion. Our partnership with our African American Baptist neighbors was a transcendent experience for me. In working together, marching together, speaking together, and praying and singing together for environmental justice, we transcended our religious differences and established deep friendships that continue. This reality underscored my viewpoint that there can be one Truth, but many Paths to the Truth.[14]

Three Sisters Resistance Camp

On Saturday morning, January 20, 2018, Dominion began tree cutting on Buckingham pipeline easements to make way for construction, even before the necessary permits were approved. Pipeline opponents rushed to the site near Yogaville. The trucks all had out-of-state plates, undercutting the industry's promise to create local jobs. That night, Yogaville community member Jai Ram Eyth set up the first tent on the ACP right-of-way on the family property of Peter Max, the prominent artist who invited Swami Satchidananda for his first visit to the United States in 1966. And so began the Three Sisters Resistance Camp that would last for the next twenty-two months.

---

[14] Jeeva Abbate (SAYVA Board of Trustees, FoB member), interview by Heidi Dhivya Berthoud, May 19, 2023.

The ACP was sited to cross the James River, from Nelson County into Buckingham County, just upstream from LOTUS Temple's river frontage. Libra Max, Peter's daughter and an animal rights activist, gave permission to set up a resistance camp on the family's land. Jai Ram was a steady presence for the duration. Virginia Student Environmental Coalition (VSEC) students were a major force at the camp, showing up twenty to thirty strong in the height of the camp, hailing from universities across the state. A large majority were young women. The students took time to process gender-identity agreements among the camp participants, along with how to coordinate the operation of the camp and how to interface with Dominion and local law enforcement.[15]

The agreed-upon name for the camp, Three Sisters, was a reflection of the tangible urgency felt by diverse peoples who came to work together just as beans, corn, and squash support each other as they grow. They were there to protect the sacred—to protect the balance of life, the land, water, and air—in the face of such a powerful existential threat. "We built a community," says Jai Ram, "so disparate, and yet remarkably cohesive, confident, and very motivated were the predominantly student activists."[16] For Jai Ram, steeped in Nature and the interconnectedness of all things, Frank Lloyd Wright's words "I spell God: Nature" were a compelling force motivating his dedication.

Another remarkable force at the camp was the group Veterans for Peace that came from Charlottesville to build two

[15] One of the first films about the ACP resistance movement was created by VSEC students. See *Won't Pipe Down* (dir. Marley McDonald, Dan McNew, Art Pekun, and Abby Riggleman, 2015), http://www.wont-pipedown.com/.

[16] Jai Ram Eyth (Yogaville community member, landscaper, river outfitter, naturalist, FoB member), interview by Heidi Dhivya Berthoud, July 2, 2023.

sturdy tree stands on the ACP right-of-way to house tree-sitters to stall pipeline construction. They also helped to restore an historic corn crib located on the easement to create another obstacle for Dominion to navigate, a project led by Freeman Allan and Scott Ziemer. Freeman's activism was partly rooted in a hitchhiking experience he had in college, when he was abducted by two Klansmen who were convinced he was an outside agitator and who were ready to throw him into an alligator bayou. This was the summer of 1965, after Freedom Riders were murdered by the Klan in his home state of Mississippi. Years later, he would join a call for military vets to assist Indigenous Water Protectors at Standing Rock in North Dakota. He explains, "As a Quaker Buddhist Pagan, each tradition places stewardship of Earth as a core precept, which for me is the same as environmental justice. I venerate Mother Earth as Goddess and work to convert our planet from patriarchy to partnership values which sustain and cleanse the natural world."[17]

The Three Sisters resistance campers had many adventures. They endured a blizzard, a tornado, being surveilled by helicopters, and fending off illegal surveyors and unwarranted policing. Dominion hired a local deputy to fly a drone over the camp. Campers called Buckingham sheriff Kidd, who sent out an officer to apprehend the deputy. Other challenges at the camp came from the inside. The students focused heavily on ensuring a culture of equity and inclusion within the camp, while the elders were more focused on completing concrete tasks such as building the tree sits. Some of the campers wanted to build a wickiup on the drill

---

[17] Richard "Freeman" Allan (author, veteran, environmental activist, iconologist, FoB member), interview by Heidi Dhivya Berthoud, May 2023. See Allan, *A History of Racism in Charlottesville: A Journey towards Understanding* (Charlottesville, VA: Foundation for American Heritage Voices, 2023), https://vacommunityrights.org/two-new-powerful-local-books-reviewing-racism-in-charlottesville/.

pad site to raise awareness of the threat posed by drilling, as well as to offer blessings. An Indigenous woman who served as one of the camp's leaders objected to the cultural appropriation of the act, so the structure was not built. Wearing of Native regalia by non-Native participants caused further conflict. There was also conflict over the use of Sanskrit names by those on the Yoga path. Tensions arose over accusations of racism. In all these ways, the camp is a poignant case study in both the abundant possibilities and unavoidable obstacles that accompany intensive community-building experiments across interfaith and multicultural lines.

Jai Ram noted a turning point toward the end of the camp in late fall 2019. The ACP had submitted paperwork condemning the land for the drill pad, clearing the way for horizontal directional drilling under the river. "When we looked at the paperwork," he said, "we found it was the wrong parcels, which meant they would have to redo the whole months-long process." When the campers realized the land was no longer under threat, many of the well-seasoned resistance campers moved to the more urgent Yellow Finch resistance camp, blockading the Mountain Valley Pipeline (MVP) in Montgomery County, Virginia, which was being built at the time despite powerful local resistance. Though the Three Sisters Camp soon closed down, it served as a site of intimate community building and soul-searching for a diverse group of pipeline fighters who were motivated by an intense commitment to defend the land they loved against the abuse of immoral corporate power.

Circle of Protection

One of the highlights of our work together was the creation of the Circle of Protection, which became essential and magnetic monthly gatherings for stressed pipeline resisters to lift up our spirits with song, interfaith prayer, testimony, and shared food. The circles drew people from across the state. It was a space to focus on community nourishment and support rather than to talk business.

It was conceived in March 2018 by a group of women gathered at the Three Sisters Resistance Camp, sitting in a circle on the good Earth, down on the James River floodplain, grounded in the beauty of Buckingham countryside. Sue Frankel-Streit, a member of the Catholic Worker movement, had been delivering supplies to the camp from the Louisa Food Bank and urged direct action to hinder pipeline construction and suggested a vigil. Kim Williams and Joan Wages, also Catholic Workers from Virginia, concurred on the need to draw attention to Buckingham. They were experienced, intrepid activists with passionate convictions to act upon grave wrongs, deeply dedicated to love with justice. They were willing to put their lives on the line, having endured multiple arrests for bold civil disobedience, such as lockdowns on pipeline earthmoving equipment and incapacitating a B-52 war plane armed with cluster bombs headed to Iraq.

We started out simply enough, setting a date to initially meet at the proposed compressor station site on South James River Highway, where the ACP was proposed to intersect with the Transco Pipeline, which runs from the Gulf Coast to New England. With banners and signs, we gathered at the site. We prayed, sang, danced, read poetry, heard testimonials, and shared meals.

Much to our great relief, Kay Ferguson generously took leadership of the circles and other rallies "like a good stage manager," allowing others to simply show up, network, and be nourished together. She remembers being "pregnant with my first child when I cut my teeth on the 1980s women's action for nuclear disarmament with Helen Haldicott." She brought the force of

ARTivism to our movement. Steeped in years of theater, she brought in ecomusicians and huge street puppets that bridged the gaps between ages, faiths, and geographical distances. Evelyn Dent, a well-loved Afro-Indigenous elder of the Union Hill Community, was a regular participant—a pianist, guitarist, and singer-songwriter, crooning out the blues and gospel at our events. Ferguson's vision was to "first touch the heart, then the head, then the feet, refilling well springs."[18]

Evelyn Dent, a member of Union Grove Baptist Church, leads a gospel song during a pipeline resistance rally.   (PHOTO BY DAVID PARRY / USED WITH PERMISSION)

The Circle of Protection was powered by the Sun Bus, a van with a solar panel on the roof. This also made the gatherings very portable, traveling to MVP sites in addition to ACP sites. The circle brought together people who, as Kay Ferguson noted, were

---

[18] Kay Ferguson (founder of ARTivism), interview by Heidi Dhivya Berthoud, May 16, 2023.

"tired of talking heads." She wisely consolidated messages and memes such as, "We are all Union Hill" and "This is a Robbery."

"I have fond memories of leading a slow Wiccan spiral dance under the shade trees at Union Hill Baptist Church," says Heidi Dhivya Berthoud. "I was thrilled and frankly surprised to see so many people rise to participate, including elderly Black Baptist congregants like John Laury. Together we sang, 'Spiraling into the Center, the Center of the Wheel. We are the weavers, we are the woven ones, we are the dreamers, we are the dream.'"

John Laury recalls,

> The Circles of Protection started in prayer, holding hands, testifying, fellowshiping, breaking bread together. It was spiritually based. We asked God to come in, we asked the Holy Spirit to come in. When the Holy Spirit came in, I'd say we had an A+. We were in very good company. We are our brothers' keepers. We must tell the truth. It may not be popular, but that's beside the point. On our journey on this Earth, we have to please God. We answer to God. Personally, some say there are many ways to God. The Bible tells us you can only get there through Christ. But we worked together.[19]

He was not the only Baptist whose beliefs were stretched by his experience of interfaith eco-activism. Along with twenty-one other ACP activists, Pastor Paul Wilson was arrested in October 2016, while protesting the pipeline at the governor's mansion. In fulfillment of his court-mandated community service, he chose to volunteer at the ashram and ended up staying a week. He recalls, "I could feel the [interfaith] LOTUS Temple was a place of Spirit and peace. I went to the Christian altar. I was shaking and

---

[19] John Laury, interview by Heidi Dhivya Berthoud, May 6, 2023.

crying. . . . I know there are different paths to God and eternal life. I believe that other paths lead to the one I'm on. I believe in free will. It's my job to preach, to inform, and let the people decide."[20]

Kim Williams of Norfolk, Virginia, where the seawater is rising and the land is sinking, traveled far to take part in the Circles of Protection. She had heard a young Black woman from her local chapter of Virginia Organizing refer to Union Hill as "Virginia's Standing Rock." With other Catholic Workers who were following the Indigenous-led pipeline resistance movement at Standing Rock, Williams was moved "to take action to oppose the ongoing colonization of the local descendants of the formerly enslaved by the descendants of the former owners of Variety Shade Plantation, who had sold the compressor station land to Dominion."[21]

Warrior Women, Earth Protectors

While fighting the fossil fuel industry here in Virginia, like everywhere, women played an outsized role in the struggle for creation care. Trending globally, women lead frontlines ecojustice work despite the disproportionate risks they face compared with men.[22]

---

[20] Paul Wilson, interview by Heidi Dhivya Berthoud, July 3, 2023.

[21] Kim Williams, interview by Heidi Dhivya Berthoud, April 23, 2023. A member of the Catholic Worker movement and Mothers Out Front, Williams has been arrested many times for nonviolent direct action (NVDA) such as chaining herself to a backhoe on a pipeline worksite.

[22] For example, see V'cenza Cirefice and Lynda Sullivan, "Women on the Frontlines of Resistance to Extractivism," *Policy and Practice: A Development Education Review* 29 (Autumn 2019): 78–99. For an exploration of the disproportionate harms faced by women in the wake of environmental degradation, see Karen Bell, "Bread and Roses: A Gender Perspective on Environmental Justice and Public Health," *International Journal of Environmental Research and Public Health* 13, no. 10 (October 2016), https://www.mdpi.com/1660-4601/13/10/1005.

Here we present a sampling of women's voices arising from the front lines of our six-year-long campaign against the ACP. Recurring themes of sacrifice, fierce defense of life, and a willingness to collaborate across differences emerge in their reflections.

"Certainly men care," says Friends of Buckingham (FoB) president Chad Oba. "But women care more." She continues,

> We carry life, or the capacity to, and there's something about that. I feel responsible. Women have forever made sacrifices. We just do it. We just take it on. We don't do it for the fame or money that drives the dominant culture. We know how to work together, bear pain, make sacrifices. There was a lot more at stake than our personal needs. We had personal conflicts. We had to keep going. We didn't have time to work things out thoroughly. There is something noble about confronting something bigger than you. Women do that well.[23]

Jessica Sims, a key field organizer with FoB, shares a similar perspective when she says that "women approach issues with a level of empathy essential in ultimate caring about the human impacts [of polluting industries], which are not abstract." She adds bluntly, "More broadly, men want to stay in power."[24]

Irene Leech was raised on her family's large cattle farm in central Buckingham, land she feels "responsible for passing onto the next generation" in "as good or better" shape as when she lived there. Dominion's proposed route for the ACP would have bisected that farm for a mile stretch, placing all its buildings within

---

[23] Chad Oba (cofounder and president of FoB, retired mental health worker, Union Hill resident), interview by Heidi Dhivya Berthoud, July 2, 2023.

[24] Jessica Sims (field organizer with Appalachian Voices, former field organizer with Virginia Sierra Club, longtime essential aide to FoB), interview by Heidi Dhivya Berthoud, June 16, 2023.

the pipeline's blast zone. Today, she lives on another farm in Montgomery County, Virginia, located four miles from a major compressor station site for yet another fracked gas pipeline— the highly contentious Mountain Valley Pipeline (MVP). She observed,

> Most farmers operate with respect for the earth. They take care of it, continue to care, don't use it up, keeping it viable for generations. Our view of our relationship to the earth is similar to Indigenous peoples. The pipeline experience highlighted that most of society doesn't have this relationship, doesn't feel a lasting connection to land. It's a tradable commodity. Our ancestors pushed Indigenous peoples off their land. Dominion didn't attempt to understand our connections or our needs.

She links Creation Care with the fight for women's rights and well-being around the world: "Environmental justice is what we do: advocacy and justice, racial equity, hunger and poverty, women's ministry, interfaith work." A year into the pipeline fight, she went to Guatemala with women from her Presbyterian church "to advocate for communities who had been protesting peacefully for three years against US and Canadian mining companies who just took their land with the help of their own government." There, they experienced how "the protesters are predominantly women in a very patriarchal culture. The police, mostly men, armed with automatic weapons, were not there for our security. Many times, here and there, those who make the time to do the work are women. Women fight more selflessly and for others."[25]

Marie Flowers says she aspires to live the best of her Catholic faith. Spontaneous and fearless in speaking truth to inequities,

---

[25] Irene Leech (associate professor of consumer studies at Virginia Tech, FoB cofounder), interview by Heidi Dhivya Berthoud, June 13, 2023.

she is a reflexively protective mother, always ready to defend the innocent and the vulnerable. She says, "People don't know how to stand up for themselves, and have no hope for tomorrow. The rewards in volunteering are in meeting the best people, because they give from their hearts." She is always ready to pitch in where she can, serving numerous organizations and bridging divides across the county. She was a constant presence at local supervisor meetings during the ACP fight. With her quirky humor and compassionate insight, she would win people over to do the right thing. At one event she collected seventy out of ninety signatures for a petition. She is extraordinary in her bighearted love and caring for all peoples, animals, and nature. She's also not afraid to hold her own faith tradition to account: "The Catholic Church has a lot of sins. This pope is trying to teach what Jesus taught— to love one another, even the rich. I've seen it change over the years since I was a child. Before, the emphasis was to obey the Ten Commandments, to pass judgment. [But now] Pope Francis cares more about speaking up for the poor and Mother Earth."[26]

Ruby Laury, a member of Union Grove Baptist Church, appeals directly to the Bible when explaining her motivation for pursuing this work:

> When I found out from Chad [Oba] how harmful fracking would be—not only to us humans but also animals, wildlife, and plants—that's when I got involved. There are many scriptures in the Bible that specifically tell us that we are stewards of the Earth, that we have a responsibility to care for it. Not only for ourselves, but for our future generations. One of the scriptures I

---

[26] Marie Flowers (FoB cofounder, devout Catholic, Garden Club treasurer, Buckingham Democratic Committee treasurer, Ellis Acres & Curdsville Community Centers, Historic Village), interview by Heidi Dhivya Berthoud, June 12, 2023.

found was Deuteronomy 11:12: "A land for which the
LORD your God cares. The eyes of the LORD, your God,
are always on it from the beginning of the year to the
very end of the year." Another scripture was Genesis
2:15: "The LORD God took the man and put him in the
Garden of Eden to work it and take care of it." It takes a
lot for me to get going. When Dominion thought that
we were just going to roll over and they could walk all
over us, it got my dander up. It's not right. The Lord
made us stewards. We are to help take care of the Earth.
We had to stand up and do what the Lord wanted us to
do, which was to take care of the environment, the land.
I had to get up the courage to get up to speak.[27]

Ada Washington, a quiet, steady, and dedicated FoB council
member, with her sister Mary Rose installed a banner high above
the Union Grove Baptist Church choir that reads, "Stand up for
what is right, even if you have to stand alone." They, along with
a handful of remaining Union Hill community folks, continued
to stand firmly against the injustice of the ACP, even while most
of their neighbors fell for the divisive, desperate bribes offered by
Dominion after the company realized our grassroots movement
was a force to be reckoned with.

Nonviolence was a near-universal theme among the women
leaders of our frontlines movement. "For me, nonviolence is
absolutely necessary. It's a human reaction to want to protect
and defend. Violence perpetuates violence," says Chad Oba.
Her story also highlights the role that both spirituality and an
intersectional vision of justice play for many women in the
movement, and also for some who have chosen to be unaffiliated
with religious institutions. She shares the following:

---

[27] Ruby Laury (Union Grove Baptist Church member, FoB cofounder),
interview by Heidi Dhivya Berthoud, May 6, 2023.

I've stayed away from organized spiritual traditions, though I have forayed into them, starting with Christianity. I never had anyone say it to me in a way that made sense. I do have a Sufi teacher, Asha Greer, who encouraged my activism, holding me accountable, saying I could not drop this work. Actually, she joined us too, attending rallies, becoming a legal observer [for our actions] after the killing of George Floyd. My way is of the heart. How can you see suffering and not want to do something about it? I have to respond to it if I am really to run it through my heart. Environmental justice is directly related to the heart. Being in the company of others who act on their convictions, I became much more aware of what it means to be white and privileged. I've developed relationships with Black neighbors in Union Hill. I wasn't aware of who I was in relation to them before the ACP.[28]

Kim Williams and Sue Frankel-Streit are both members of the Catholic Worker movement who have played various roles in the ACP resistance movement.[29] Williams cites Genesis when reflecting on her own experience of defending Creation, saying,

We are to be caretakers of the Earth. It is not ours to use and abuse. Creation is meant to be shared; it is no one's domain. Jesus says we are called to be in the world, but not of the world and the domination system that could put

---

[28] Oba, interview.

[29] The Catholic Workers were cofounded by lay Catholic leaders Dorothy Day and Peter Maurin in the 1930s on the principles of "a preferential option for the poor," the pursuit of social justice, and a radical commitment to pacifism based on the teachings of Jesus. Small farming communes and Houses of Hospitality to serve those in need of food and housing became trademarks of this decentralized religious movement, with roughly two hundred Catholic Worker communities around the world today.

Church members hung this banner of resistance inside Union Grove Baptist Church at a time when divisions were running high in the community over pipeline construction. (photo by david parry / used with permission)

you on the cross. This government leaves people out. The church has many injustices. The patriarchy will end. It is not love. I live as if it has ended. Jesus has nothing to do with the 1493 Doctrine of Discovery. The early church was about nonviolence and refused to bow to Caesar. The saints have tried to call back the church to the original teachings to love and nonviolence. This is the work we do.[30]

Frankel-Streit connected her activist experience to her maternal experience:

As a mother, I have a sense of being responsible for the caretaking of life. There is historical imagery of earth as a mother. Earth has provided so much for us. I have found resonance with women trying to protect that. A

---

[30] Williams, interview.

circle as opposed to a straight line. Circle of Protection is feminine. We are all One. Injury to one is injury to all. Direct action, generally speaking, is taken to confront violence. Things that cause violence, that are systemic, are easy to overlook because they are so big. . . . There are so many ways institutions can inflict violence.[31]

She explains that a commitment to nonviolence does not mean never breaking the law, or never using force in the pursuit of peace. Indeed, Catholic Workers have a long history of radical work in the service of peace and justice, employing civil disobedience to confront unjust political and economic systems. In 1991, Sue Frankel-Streit was part of an antiwar Catholic Worker action that took place on the Griffiss Air Force Base in New York. The small group of peace activists disabled a B-52 bomber by hammering a crack in its fuselage. The bomber was armed with cluster-bombs, preparing for an imminent aerial assault on downtown Baghdad during the US-led Gulf War. She and three others spent a year in jail for taking action against the Iraq War.[32] "There's a place for yelling and property destruction" in spiritually grounded peace work, she maintains. "No justice, no peace. In the name of good order, a lot of atrocities have been left unaddressed."

ACP activists were arrested for direct actions. Some did community service, some paid fines, but none did jail time. Learning about the bold, impassioned, righteous actions and sacrifices of Catholic Workers put our various offerings of service into perspective, stretching and challenging us.

---

[31] Sue Frankel-Streit (Little Flower Catholic Worker Farm, Louisa County, VA), interviewed by Heidi Dhivya Berthoud, May 9, 2023.

[32] See Sue Frankel-Streit with Bill Frankel-Streit, "Reflections on the ANZUS Plowshares 20 Years Later," The Nuclear Resister (online), January 1, 2011.

The voices highlighted here are only a small sampling of the many women who provided leadership to our grassroots movement through their deep moral conviction and spiritual practice. The remainder of the chapter now shifts to offering more extended, personal narratives of how religion, spirituality, and ritual practice motivated and informed the eco-activism of two key women leaders of the ACP resistance movement. First, Swami Dayananda's story illustrates the way established religious communities—most notably Swamis and Baptists—formed unlikely alliances to stop the desecration posed by the ACP, forging cooperation across divergent theologies through a shared love for the sacredness of Earth. Second, Heidi Dhivya discusses participation in this ecojustice movement with commitment to the struggle against ACP, fueled by ancient wisdom traditions and deep spiritual convictions that are intentionally located outside institutional religious frameworks.

The ACP resistance became the crucible in which traditional and nontraditional commitments to the sacred formed a new, eclectic, transformative community united both by outrage at corporate oppression and a shared defense of Mother Earth. In this way, their stories, while deeply personal, shed light on broader trends emerging in spiritually grounded eco-activist movements across the United States today.

Personal Reflections of Swami Dayananda

Shinto Roots in Japan

I was born in Japan, where many homes had Shinto along with Buddhist altars. Shinto is the Indigenous faith of Japanese people who believe in the presence of Kami (divine entities) coming through many forms. On the narrow roads, especially in the countryside and small villages and towns, I would see food and drink offerings to statues of foxes at the entrance of the shrines or street altars where people clap their hands and bow in deep respect. Kami may be defined as spirits, deities, and divine beings. They represent various elements in nature, such as the mountains, rivers, trees, animals, and rocks, as well as concepts such as creativity, protection, good fortune, and fertility.

My mother took me to Shinto shrines where the entrance (Torii) had a thick, beautifully entwined rope (Shimenawa) and white rice paper made into a zigzag pattern of lightning attached to the rope. Torii symbolizes a gateway into the sacred from the mundane space, with the Shimenawa signifying purification by entering into the presence of Kami.

In the mountains, I saw the same Shimenawa around large, impressive trees or big, distinctive rocks. Even in the middle of the city streets, some very old large trees would be protected and honored with Shimenawa. I also saw Torii built in the bodies of water, like lakes, rivers, and the ocean, without understanding its meaning. As a child, I did not pay much attention or ask any questions about what I saw. It was a part of daily life.

Years later, in America, I experienced the sacredness of nature through the practice of Yoga and through facing the threat of environmental destruction by the fossil fuel industry.

A Black Baptist Preacher and a Swami

"This is my spiritual sister, Swami Dayananda!" This is how Pastor Paul Wilson introduced me to another Baptist preacher at the Allegheny–Blue Ridge Alliance conference in 2015. I was pleasantly surprised. It was not something a Baptist pastor would normally say about a Yogi, who is also a swami (monk) of Hindu heritage.

During the first year of our collaboration to oppose the pipeline, we quickly forged a strong bond through our common determination and dedication to protect our communities and the environment.[33] I heard Pastor Paul speak often of the public's need for the truth behind the safety and health hazards of the compressor station, which he felt was not forthcoming from Dominion. His commitment to protect the Union Hill community never wavered.

I would often go to the Sunday morning church services where Pastor Paul preached. I felt his complete faith in God and felt in one spirit with him and the congregation as we sang hymns and gospel songs, connecting at a level beyond our different nationalities, cultures, traditions, and religions.

One of the most memorable times with Pastor Paul was the first time he came to visit the ashram. After he prayed at the LOTUS temple, he remained silent and thoughtful for some time. He then said, "I have been putting my God in a box. This is a holy place. I had a real experience of God here."

Another memorable time was when Pastor Paul welcomed Krishna Das (KD), a renowned chant master of American yoga, to Union Hill Church. KD has been coming to the ashram annually for chanting retreats for many years. In May 2018, he agreed to chant at Union Hill in support of racial and environmental justice.

The church was packed with Yogaville community members and a handful of church members. KD sat cross-legged on the floor in front of the pulpit and began playing the harmonium, a rare sight and sound in a Baptist church. He began, "Jaya Ram, Jaya Ram, Jaya Jaya Ram Om. . . ." KD built up the energy slowly, repeating and chanting faster and faster for this call-and-response chant.

After some time of chanting, Pastor Paul asked me nervously, "What is he saying? At our church, we always know what we are saying or singing and understand the meaning."

---

[33] Gregory S. Schneider, "The Baptists and the Yogis Join Together to Fight a Pipeline," *Washington Post*, August 18, 2018.

I told him the meaning of the chant: "Rama is the name of God, and Jai means victory. So we are chanting 'Victory to God, Victory to God.'" Pastor Paul smiled approvingly and relaxed. I felt deeply relieved, thankful for our mutual understanding of the universality of devotion to God, no matter what names we use.

It was then that KD began singing the popular gospel lyric, "Jesus is on the main line, tell him what you want!" Pastor Paul, children, and adults, all stood up, singing and dancing. We took the roof off of that church.

Nonviolence

> Nonviolence is the most powerful way to counter oppression and establish freedom and justice.—Dr. Martin Luther King Jr.

I visited Dr. Martin Luther King Jr.'s museum in Atlanta when attending the North American Interfaith Network (NAIN) conference in 2012. I saw Mahatma Gandhi's statue right outside of the museum. *What is Gandhi's statue doing here?* I wondered, then completely ignorant of the connection between MLK and Gandhi.

Fasting and prayer were main components of Satyagraha as adopted by Gandhi, with other elements being noncooperation, civil disobedience, and worker strikes. During his seminary years, MLK learned of Gandhi's teachings and his practices of truthfulness (Satya) and nonviolence (ahimsa). Deeply inspired, he adopted the methods of Satyagraha in his fight against racial discrimination in the United States.

As I started learning more about environmental justice, I read about MLK's beloved community and how he saw the deep connection between the teachings of Christian love and Hindu nonviolence. Jeeva Abbate, a fellow Yogi of Indigenous ancestry, and I served closely together with our common love for the Yogaville and Union Hill communities.

When facing what feels like an insurmountable force, spiritual teachings through Yoga have taught me to pray, surrendering the result to the higher consciousness. I was grateful that, wherever we had an event with Pastor Paul and the Union Hill congregation, we would always begin with prayers that naturally helped me remember the power of nonviolence.

Ahimsa is one of the values I follow at the ashram as a spiritual seeker in order to remain peaceful in "thoughts, words, and deeds" at all times. It is easier to observe nonviolence in the confines of the ashram, a secluded and protected place for spiritual pursuits. While engaged in the work of resisting the ACP, I suddenly found myself in the public, speaking at meetings, marching on city streets, protesting in front of the governor's mansion, marching across a bridge in Richmond, Virginia, and around the White House in Washington, DC.

Fortunately we did not have any major physical violence during the public events in which we participated. I was part of many peaceful protests and experienced the power of our constitutional rights to protest peacefully.

When Pastor Paul invited me to speak at Union Hill Baptist Church, I was inspired to speak on the common belief in nonviolence by MLK of the Christian tradition and Gandhi of the Hindu tradition. In the church, there was a group of grassroots activists of many faiths, including Christians and Yoga practitioners. Instead of just admiring Gandhi and MLK, I challenged us to be just like them. There were a lot of "amens" and "hallelujahs," giving me the blessed experience of spontaneous vibrant interactions with the congregation.

The great teachings of ahimsa, nonviolence, came to play an important part as the basis for my activist participation. Early on, a few sangha members expressed concerns that I was straying from my monastic path by getting involved in politics while expressing public opposition to the pipeline. They felt that, as a monk, my service was to stay inward, meditate and pray, and focus on the duties at the ashram. I respected their concern for my spiritual journey, and seriously reflected on whether to continue or to stop my pipeline resistance work. But it took no time for me to recognize that this engagement was not about politics but about ahimsa, one of the foundational teachings in the Yoga Sutras.

There would have been great harm to the Yogaville community if the pipeline had come as close as it was planned. It was my duty to do what I could to protect our community along with the other concerned community members.

My teacher, Swami Satchidananda, taught that if violence and harm were being done, you must do what you could to stop it. Years ago, he advised those protesting the war in Vietnam to not lose their own peace in the process. Do what we can, maintaining peace and practicing nonviolence, if we really want to be of service in restoring peace.

Swamiji was a trailblazer. He was called a "revolutionary monk" due to his activism against the dowry system in the 1950s in Sri Lanka. He spoke at the First Earth Day in 1970 in New York City, and he participated in many peace initiatives. In 1980 and 1986, he was invited to be a peace envoy from the United States to the Soviet Union. I see my service to stop the ACP as an extension of that legacy today in Yogaville and Buckingham County.

Sacred Rivers

For Hindus, each river is a manifestation of the Divine. They are sacred and purifying. It is customary for Hindus to make pilgrimages to sacred rivers and take ritual baths for purification. Bhakti Yoga, a branch of yogic practices, is the yoga of the heart.

Those of a devotional nature offer chanting and pujas (Hindu worship services) to the chosen form of their God, gurus, and other objects of worship such as mountains and rivers. Arati is an offering of light before sacred images to infuse the light with love, energy, and blessings of deities. Rivers are considered to be goddesses or gods in India, and Arati is offered to them. At the completion of these Arati, the light is offered to all those present to receive the blessings of the sacred rivers.

I offered an Arati to the James River as part of an interfaith service to support a group of people canoeing down the river to deliver a letter to the governor in Richmond, Virginia, urging him to oppose the pipeline. The body of the moving water felt cool as it made the gentle swirling movement around my feet. The river water touched me with its sacredness and blessed me with reverence and awe.

I had a similar experience at Standing Rock in 2016, where over five hundred members of the clergy responded to the call of an Episcopal priest. We gathered there, at the edge of the Standing Rock Sioux Reservation in North Dakota, in solidarity with the Indigenous people who were protecting their land and the water from the Dakota Access Pipeline.

I recognized that ACP's cancellation was not the end of my journey to engage in protesting against fossil fuel projects and advocating for a just transition to renewable energy. In August 2023, I accepted an invitation to offer Arati at Greenbriar River, close to where the Mountain Valley Pipeline (MVP) was proposed to cross. Protect Our Water, Heritage, Rights (POWHR) invited me to join in the offering of interfaith prayers. Crystal Cavalier-Keck (Occaneechi Band of the Saponi Nation) and Jason Crazy Bear Keck (Louisiana Band of Choctaw) offered prayers at the Haw River, North Carolina, in September 2023. They invited me to their interfaith prayers, and I had the opportunity to offer an Arati to the Haw River.

Interfaith Supporters and Events

Rev. Faith Harris, the executive director of the Virginia chapter of Interfaith Power and Light (VAIPL), based in Richmond, was very supportive of our work to stop the ACP. The mission of VAIPL is to "collaborate among people of faith and conscience to grow healthy communities by advancing climate and environmental justice."[34] Kendyl Crawford, former director of VAIPL, attended hearings and rallies with us. The Muslim mother of a VAIPL board member offered Islamic prayers on the street in front of the building where Dominion was meeting with its investors. Pastor Paul offered a Christian blessing, and I recited Hindu prayers in Sanskrit.

Another profound interfaith gathering was at the Richmond Quaker Meeting House and was organized by Barb Adams. Rev. Weston Mathews of Grace Episcopal Church and the late Rev. Robert Dilday offered vital support through their organization, the Interfaith Alliance for Climate Justice (IACJ), which also offered financial assistance to grassroots activists. The Right Reverend Susan Goff, Episcopal bishop of the Diocese of Virginia, was offered solar panel installations on diocesan building rooftops by Dominion in an effort to buy her silence. She declined the offer after visiting Union Hill and Yogaville, experiencing the situation with her own eyes. Her moral fortitude and integrity are remembered with great respect, love, and gratitude.

William Barber and Al Gore: Faith, Science,
and Environmental Justice

In early summer of 2018, I attended a Poor People's Campaign conference in Baltimore, wishing to meet and speak with Bishop William Barber II to bring his attention to the environmental

---

[34] "Mission," Virginia Interfaith Power and Light (online), https://vaipl.org/about-us/our-mission/.

justice issue at Union Hill. Bishop Barber is a civil rights leader who has served as president of Repairers of the Breach and cochair of the Poor People's Campaign. Through social media, I was aware of his powerful presence and the movement he has created, which connects the issues of poverty, systemic racism, the war economy, and our climate crisis. Between workshops, I had the chance to speak to him about the pipeline that threatened Union Hill.

In August 2018, Pastor Paul, his wife, Marilyn, and I traveled to Greensboro, North Carolina, to join an event at Bishop Barber's church. Former vice president Al Gore was the guest speaker. There, Pastor Paul introduced himself to Bishop Barber and spoke to him about the threat to his people's church and the neighborhood in Union Hill. Bishop Barber told him he is aware of the situation and told Pastor Paul to contact him again.

Karenna Gore, Al Gore's daughter, and I had met in early November at an event on climate change and how local grassroots groups are standing up to ACP that was organized by Sam Rasoul, one of the two Muslim representatives in the Virginia General Assembly. Later that month, I met her again at the 2018 convening of the Parliament of the World's Religions in Toronto. She listened with great compassion about the situation facing Union Hill residents and Yogaville, telling me that she would get back to me if she could offer any help.

Karenna has been involved in fighting fracked gas pipelines, mainly the Constitution Pipeline in New York and Spectra AIM in Massachusetts. The Center for Earth Ethics, where she is the director, explores the moral and spiritual dimensions of the climate crisis and work in interfaith dialogue. Knowing these fights and feeling passionately aligned with our struggle, she found our experience deeply inspiring. In February 2019, Karenna called to say that Bishop Barber and former vice president Gore could come to Buckingham in two weeks if we could get ready. I was struck by her humility, emphasizing that they would only come if our local communities wanted them and if they could be of service to our grassroots efforts to stop the pipeline.

Our coalition met the challenge of pulling together this large public event at Buckingham Middle School. At the Moral Call for Ecological Justice in Buckingham, Bishop Barber's powerful spiritual presence and his resounding speech for the marginalized residents in Union Hill captured the hearts of the audience gathered. He said of the pipeline company: "What they're doing is wrong legally, it's wrong scientifically, and it's wrong morally!" Al Gore followed Bishop Barber, calling the ACP project a "reckless, racist rip-off." He complemented Bishop Barber's spiritual call to action with scientific facts about the toxicity of the pipeline, the compressor station, and the threat of fossil fuels.

The event was picked up by national media outlets. Reverend Barber prompted us to follow up this event by walking across the Robert E. Lee Bridge in Richmond in continued protest against the pipeline. Karenna Gore and Reverend Barber's son, William Barber III, joined us in May 2019 for the march. This march occurred in the tradition of the 1968 Poor People's Campaign march to Washington, DC, and I had the honor to collaborate with VAIPL to organize an interfaith prayer event to conclude the march.

Inspired by these events, some of us attended Climate Reality Training in Atlanta, led by Al Gore and attended by Bishop Barber and other clergy of various faiths. Not long before the event, I had decided to grow hemp for healing medicine after learning how quickly hemp plants reach maturity and how effectively they sequester carbon. At the end of the training, I had the honor of participating in an interfaith prayer at Ebenezer Baptist Church, where MLK and his father were both pastors.

After giving my all to the ACP, becoming a restorative farmer gave me a connection to the Earth that was missing and brought me profound healing. This was also a reawakening to my Shinto roots. Currently, the farm is being established as a nonprofit organization for creating vegetable and medicinal herb community gardens, protecting and enriching our corner of Mother Earth through restorative agriculture and sustainability.

Finding Hope for the Future in the Spirit of Youths

In June 2023, I felt compelled to join those working to stop the MVP at a protest at the White House. These were dear friends with whom I had the chance to work closely to stop both the ACP and MVP. Congress had just fast-tracked the MVP's construction by slipping a provision into the national debt ceiling bill (the Fiscal Responsibility Act) to expedite the project after a string of serious safety and environmental violations had effectively brought the project to a halt. The bill included language that ordered all federal agencies to simply issue any outstanding permits without further consideration, stripping federal courts of the right to consider legal challenges to those permits. In July, the Supreme Court followed suit by preemptively dismissing a key hold on the project by the US Court of Appeals for the Fourth Circuit due to environmental impacts on the Jefferson National Forest.[35] I was in disbelief as to how far the fossil fuel industry's influence reaches. All this dampened my usual positive attitude, and it felt like there was nothing more one could do.

---

[35] See Maxine Joselow, "How a Fossil Fuel Pipeline Helped Grease the Debt Ceiling Deal," *Washington Post*, May 31, 2023. For more on the Supreme Court's role in fast-tracking the MVP, see Amy Howe, "Supreme Court Rules in Favor of Mountain Valley Pipeline," SCOTUSblog, July 27, 2023.

Swami Dayananda stands in front of the US Supreme Court building in
Washington, DC, for a case involving the Atlantic Coast Pipeline. Cases involving
spiritually guided eco-activism are regularly ending up in the federal courts,
where judges seldom defend the religious freedom claims of ecojustice groups.
(PHOTO BY DAVID PARRY / USED WITH PERMISSION)

Nevertheless, I joined the Climate March in New York
City in September, along with the MVP coalition. There were
interfaith prayers at the start of the march, setting a peaceful
and nonviolent tone. I walked with the faith groups along with
seventy thousand others, young and old.

At the end of the Climate March week, I left New York
newly encouraged by the activities of a well-organized group
called Start: Empowerment. Founded by bright young women in
their twenties, they remarked, "We are educating young people."
I asked who the younger people were, because, to me, the
founders themselves were the young people! She answered that
they educate kids ranging in age from eight to twelve while they
are still curious, open, and eager to learn. The answer took my
breath away, and I found new hope. These young people helped

me realize that it's time for me to shift my attention to what teens and young adults have been doing about climate change, collaborate with them, and support their leadership.

Youths have taken the lead in the climate movement and are taking charge of their own future. Emerging climate movements by younger generations are spiritually grounded in how they care deeply about the intersections of social, racial, and climate justice. I have faith that, just as the Yogis and the Baptists came together in the spirit, youths now and in the future will come together even more broadly, finding new solutions through spiritual unity for justice.

Personal Reflections of Heidi Dhivya Berthoud

I'm honored to offer this telling of the successful Atlantic Coast Pipeline (ACP) resistance story, drawing this tale out of the depths of our travails and placing it alongside these other chapters of heroic struggles, all to protect what we love. The foremost challenge for me in this writing project was finding the time to write in the midst of yet another intensive fight to stop new, industrial-scale metallic mining from coming to Buckingham County, Virginia, or to any part of the state. Also, the quandary of any storyteller is leaving out the many inspiring untold dramas that made our collective success possible. Gathering our stories from twenty interviews for this chapter and listening to the remembering of what deeply moves us to do this work makes my heart sing. There was much pleasure, and also sadness, in reconnecting with folks to recall their trials that drew forth the best and most enduring in us—that is, what it took to weather a six-year epic conflict with the Atlantic Coast Pipeline.

Wisdom Teachings of Yoga

> May we meditate on the effulgent light (truth, beauty, wisdom) of the worshipful One Who gave birth to all the worlds. And may that One direct our mind rays to the paths of goodness, right understanding.
>
> —Gayatri Mantram, from the *Rig Veda*.
> This rendering honors the goddess Gayatri

It is my great fortune to have found the wisdom teachings and regenerative lifestyle practices of Yoga, including hatha, meditation, and prayer—all of which are essential for supporting a healthy immune system and for countering the long-term stressors of water protecting, land defending, and pipeline fighting.

One of the hallmark teachings for me of Integral Yoga is "One Truth, Many Paths." The Light of Truth Universal Shrine (LOTUS temple) embodies this wisdom. In the shape of a lotus flower, it symbolizes our ability to grow in beauty out of the mud. This is an honoring of common ground and of the beauty and wisdom of our many differences. It aligns well with the current pressing need to understand and support biodiversity and make peace, not war, with the many divergent ways of the world. As Swami Satchidananda, the founder of Integral Yoga, would say, "Would you really be satisfied with only daisies in the field?" Such simple but profound teachings drew me to Integral Yoga, a pioneer of the interfaith movement in the 1960s. I was honored to direct numerous interfaith ceremonies at the ashram, observing our common inner light, while celebrating our outer diversity in prayer and sacred music.

Swamiji encouraged us to embrace the faith we grew up with, not to reject it for Yoga—which is a healthy, balanced way of life for many, a science for some, and a religion for still others.

I believe that being steeped in this open, uplifting, respectful perspective on all faiths and lifeways made it easier for us from the Yogaville sangha (community) to reach out to others. It also helps in being respectful of others' limitations or aversions to religious traditions and fosters the collaboration that was so vital for our movement. The first rallies I attended in Richmond were regularly inaugurated with prayer by clergy, mostly Christian. Later, other traditions were included: Indigenous, Jewish, Hindu, Muslim, Buddhist. For me, seeing mainstream faiths stand up for social and ecojustice was a welcome surprise and created an aura of protection, connection, and solidarity.

The pressures of barely keeping up with each new drama exacted tolls on relationships and our health. We were strongly motivated to rise above our personal differences in order to serve the larger good. Many in our local resistance movement talk of still dealing with PTSD. What it takes to be an activist is a heart cracked open by the pain of feeling the sadness, suffering, existential threat, and injustices of the climate crisis and then answering the compelling call. This alone is a powerful unifying force.

Most of us were volunteers, giving all we had and more. Selfless service—called seva in Sanskrit or Karma Yoga—is another core Yoga wisdom teaching that sustained me through the demanding years of the ACP struggle. Staying present, right action, not being attached to the fruits of the work: each of these concepts conjures helpful memories of Tibetan monks creating beautiful mandalas with colorful sand on the Fralin Art Museum floor. The final action is to sweep it up and move on to the next creation, reflecting the cycles of life, death, rebirth. Three simple guiding words given by Swamiji go together well: "easeful, peaceful, useful." This is another way of thinking about ahimsa, or nonviolence. One can be most useful, and not part of the problem, when being easeful and peaceful. Moreover, while it's agreeable to be easeful and peaceful, it is more beneficial when that action is made useful.

The *Bhagavad Gita* (The Great Song) is a crown jewel of the Vedic tradition from which Yoga evolved. This is an allegorical story of life as a battlefield that feeds my understanding and acceptance of the tasks and roles of pipeline resistance that come before me. Arjuna, who is born into the warrior class, has chosen Lord Krishna as his primary support to face the agonizing conflicts before him. Krishna asks Arjuna to draw his chariot up between the two battle lines to survey the field of opponents. All are relatives, loved ones, teachers, elders on both sides. While in conflict, can we see Dominion Energy as our relatives?

I call on Native wisdom, too, that challenges me to see Dominion as a good enemy who makes us strong. And indeed they did. For eighteen chapters, Krishna encourages Arjuna to fight this battle, while Arjuna comes up with really good reasons why not to. One argument from Krishna is that, if Arjuna doesn't fight, all life as we know it, with all its long-developed and complex interrelationships, will be destroyed and chaos will ensue. To do battle is Arjuna's dharma, his life's right relationship. We, as pipeline fighters and Mother Earth lovers, also know too much to walk away.

I found that the reverence for the Divine Feminine in the Integral Yoga tradition deeply informed my worldview. The mother is the baby's first guru. Mother Nature, Annapurna, is the manifest; the unmanifest is the Father. It is only the Mother who knows who the true Father is. Mother Nature points the way to the Father. Much wisdom is wrapped up in these simple words, which pillar my quest to transform the abusive ways our patriarchal culture has devolved to treat Mother Earth and her children, both human and other than human. Goddess Saraswati inspires, with two hands playing a veena (music being a universal language), one hand holding pearls (of wisdom), and another holding a book, meaning that even the goddess continues learning. These sacred stories and truths are bedrocks that sustained me through my own struggles on the battlefield with Dominion and the ACP.

I Take Refuge in Our Mother

My parents infused me with a deep love for and attunement with Mother Nature via the joys of gardening and hardy outdoor sports, including skating, skiing, hiking, bicycling, and ocean body surfing, along with a profound sense of fairness and justice. My parents were not political activists, but they were actively serviceful to their family, friends, and community. This, in part, naturally led me to the Twin Oaks community in Louisa, Virginia, where I lived for six years (1975–1981) in my early twenties, after finishing up college. I had an extraordinary opportunity to comanage the organic farm, which was a full-bodied transformative experience, heightening my Earth connections. I was waking up to both the wonders of farming and the fraught world of politics with the help of books like *One Straw Revolution, Malabar Farm, The Gift of Good Land, The Only Dance There Is,* and *The Spiral Dance.* These were all metamorphic remedies for my soul.

Twin Oaks is a richly progressive, egalitarian, secular, intentional community of conscience that I found to be inherently spiritual. I got to enjoy Wiccan celebrations at Twin Oaks and in nearby settings. Wiccan ritual was for me an essential extension of feminism, of deep ecology, working with and living close to the land and animals. Since my heritage is European Christianity, it was easy to align with a profound tradition hailing from Indigenous peoples of Eurasia.

Life led me not far from Twin Oaks in Louisa County, to Yogaville in Buckingham County. I continued celebrating, and then organizing, the 8 Wiccan Sabbats each year at Yogaville, thanks to the community's openness to interfaith practices. Sabbat simply means a pause from the mundane to observe the sacred. We hold most Sabbat celebrations under the open sky, calling in the guardians and elements, tuning into the seasons and the cycles of letting go, so as to make way for the new, the next Turning of the Wheel.

By the time the ACP came knocking at my door in 2014, I had long been nurtured by the healing powers of Yoga and, with that fortification, saw that a workhorse was needed to cover the housekeeping of Friends of Buckingham. That was my direct-action contribution. Someone had to do the newsletter and website, organize meetings, and conduct baseline testing (water, air, health) and stream monitoring. I also got trained as a legal observer by a local chapter of the National Lawyers Guild. I was moved by the presence of legal observers at previous demonstrations and saw how they helped to deescalate tensions for demonstrators and the police by bringing a sense of fair witness, accountability, and civil rights. Typically we only went where we were invited by activist groups, and we were trained to maintain neutrality with all present.

In the years leading up to my work resisting the pipeline, I had done a deep dive into the fascinating and controversial legacy of Miriam the Magdalene, even following her trail on pilgrimage in southern France.[36] The Divine Feminine was missing in my Protestant upbringing in the Union Congregational Church.[37]

---

[36] For recent translations and commentary on the Gospel of Mary Magdala, see Jean-Yves Leloup, trans., *The Gospel of Mary Magdalene* (Rochester, VT: Inner Traditions, 2002); Jehanne de Quillan, trans., *The Gospel of the Beloved Companion, the Complete Gospel of Mary Magdalene* (CreateSpace, 2010); Karen L. King, trans., *The Gospel of Mary of Magdala: Jesus and the First Woman Apostle* (Salem, OR: Polebridge Press, 2003).

[37] I was raised in a Union Congregational church but didn't continue

Fortified with the profound truths of Wicca, Yoga, and Indigenous practices and studies, I was able to open to Herstory, which had great significance for me in further understanding how far from the Garden we of the white Christian patriarchal dominator culture had roamed.

Magdala, in Aramaic, means tower, a high place used by a shepherd to watch over the flock, a bishop of the people.[38] Miriam, and all other women, have been in exile from the dominant story of the patriarchal tradition of Christianity. This original, erased and forgotten, nonhierarchical tradition was coopted by Roman imperialism and yet resisted and survived underground for two millennia, resurfacing in the last seventy-five years. This epic story feeds my heretical fires and my understanding of how "We've got to get ourselves back to the Garden," as Joni Mitchell famously sang. This retrospective underscores the archetypal story of oppression and persecution concurrent with eternal yearning for peace with justice.

The Hebrew prophet Isaiah offers this vision of the future: "For Sion's sake, I will not be silent until her vindication shines forth like the dawn.... No longer shall she be called 'abandoned' or her lands 'desolate,' but she shall be called 'beloved' and her lands 'espoused'" (Isaiah 62:1–4). Can we imagine what it would be like: how different to live in a world that values partnership versus competition or to have happily married couples modeling healthy, balanced relationships at the helm of religious traditions and nations?

---

after high school. I was happy to discover, while directing an interfaith ceremony at Yogaville, that my childhood church became part of the United Church of Christ, a leading church in the early antiabolition movement.

[38] Magdal-eder, tower of the flock. See Margaret Starbird, *The Woman with the Alabaster Jar: Mary Magdalen and the Holy Grail* (Rochester, VT: Bear and Company, 1993), 51.

In antiquity, the bride, the queen, represented the land and the people, the ekklesia, the church, the sangha.[39] She was the sacred container, the Holy Grail, of the national identity. She conferred on the king the power and strength of the nation, of the Creation vested in her as our queen.[40] Seeing the results of five thousand years of patriarchy gone so wrong, I look for other ways to improve our world, such as the Oneida, a matrilineal Indigenous nation, where the women are the wisdom leaders, where they continue to assert the "original contracts."

Rematriation, returning to the Mother, offers an appealing way forward. It's a new word for me, yet holds a familiar longing. The Rematriation Project defines the concept like this: "Unlike the legal term 'repatriate,' which signifies a simple transfer of ownership, 'rematriate' means something more profound: a restoration of right reciprocal relationships and a true action of decolonization, aimed not just at righting a past wrong but transforming our collective future."[41]

> We all come from the Mother,
> And to Her we shall return,
> Like a drop of rain,
> Flowing to the Ocean:
> Isis, Astarte, Diana,
> Hecate, Demeter, Kali, Innana,
> Miriam, Sky Woman, White Buffalo Calf Woman,
> Pele, Pachamama....[42]

---

[39] Starbird, *Woman with the Alabaster Jar*, chapter 2.

[40] For more, see Michael Baigent, Richard Leigh, and Henry Lincoln, *Holy Blood, Holy Grail* (New York: Bantam Dell, 1982).

[41] For an excellent discussion of rematriation rooted in an Indigenous paradigm, see "Rematriate," *All My Relations* (podcast), April 6, 2023.

[42] Wiccan ceremonial song.

Ours is a civilization out of balance; this is the psychological and cosmological genesis of our deep ecology in crisis. The Earth was understood to be the partner of God, the sacred vessel that contains divinity, the Holy Grail. The restoration of the Bride, the feminine, would heal the schism between spirit and matter, Sophia and Logos; it would also heal the wounded psyche of both female and male, healing the wasteland and causing the desert to bloom. This grand myth waters my soul and feeds my activism. I learn from and feel kinship with many other cultures that esteem Pachamama, Mother Earth. Certainly our future as a species depends on mending and embracing this sacred union with all of Creation.

Rights of Nature, Continuing the Heretical Path

"Hmmm," said Debra White Plume (Lakota), "so municipalities are the white man's reservations. The only difference is, we know we're on reservations."[43]

Hearing the words "Rights of Nature" for the first time was an epiphany for me, as well as for others in our movement. A fundamental paradigm shift is urgently needed in the dominant colonial, capitalist, consumer culture in order to recognize our interdependence with Nature and to respect our need to live in harmony with the natural world. This also means securing legal protections

---

[43] These words were spoken at a Community Environmental Legal Defense Fund (CELDF) Democracy School just off the Pine Ridge Reservation, South Dakota. See "Remembering Debra White Plume," CELDF Newsletter (online), December 6, 2020. CELDF Democracy School instructor Ben Price adds, "That was it. I could imagine no better explanation of how commoners in the United States have been politically, economically, and legally subordinated to the corporate class. Only, most Americans choose to ignore this structure."

for Nature through the recognition of Rights of Nature and the authority of local communities to assert those rights.

In the fall of 2017, three years into the ACP fight, the Charlottesville Unitarian Church and the grassroots ecojustice organization Friends of Nelson hosted two Rights of Nature events. The Rights of Nature movement, rooted in the Indigenous conviction that we are not separate from or superior to Nature, makes empirical sense of the environmental crisis. It asserts that human separation from Nature is a prime cause of suffering. This aligns easily with the Integral Yoga view of valuing the whole, while respecting and enjoying the differences. We needed a clear-eyed, comprehensive worldview and guidance to understand how we got here and to navigate the madness and the oppressive magnitude of this fossil-foolish fight. We are all relatives, so who would relatives sacrifice, and for what?

The global Rights of Nature movement shows us how corporations have coopted the regulatory system by permitting—and thus legalizing—pollution, rather than stopping it. Industry, with its vast advantage of money and lobbying power, has literally written the rules of the game. The ACP saga awakened us to the settler-colonial imperial project, a small taste of what Indigenous people have been experiencing for the last five hundred years, thanks, in large part, to the Doctrine of Discovery. This doctrine is rooted in a series of papal bulls issued in the late fifteenth century by which the Roman Catholic Church established religious, political, and legal justification for colonization and seizure of lands not inhabited by Christians.[44] This became

---

[44] For a discussion of the Doctrine of Discovery, see Roxanne Dunbar-Ortiz, *An Indigenous People's History of the United States* (Boston: Beacon Press, 2014), 197–217; and Steven Newcomb (Shawnee/Lenape), *Pagans in the Promised Land: Decoding the Doctrine of Christian Discovery* (Chicago: Chicago Review Press, 2008). In March 2023, the Vatican formally repudi-

entrenched in our global legal system and justification for Manifest Destiny all around the world.

Environmental injustice is grounded in moral disparity and greed. The Lakota word "wasicu" says it all: one who takes more than they need. The dominant culture has lost its reverence for the sacredness of all life. We can thank the ACP for teaching us to connect ecological disaster with wealth disparities, poverty, capitalism, corporatization, consumerism, settler-colonization, genocide, racism, white privilege, and militarization. The reality that our country was founded on these sins was making painful sense.

As national Community Rights Network president Susie Beiersdorfer puts it, "We don't just have a pipeline problem. We have a democracy problem."[45]

In spite of how it appears, with the courts having denied permits for the ACP project eight times, it was not the legal or regulatory system that actually protected us or stopped the pipeline project. It was "death by a thousand cuts" brought about by a broad alliance of deeply dedicated peoples. That we allow industry to poison anywhere, that we are willing to make *any* community a sacrifice zone, is a key to understanding how we have lost our moral compass. We have long forgotten our Rites of Nature, and thus in the eleventh hour of the Sixth Extinction, we cry out to protect the Rights of Nature.

I knew my soul's call for a higher justice was being answered, and I was initially clueless as to the depth of this movement. It was thrilling to see many of us light up to this way of understanding, a beacon in the pipeline darkness. For others it was

---

ated the Doctrine of Discovery. But its impact still persists, codified into law around the world.

[45] Susie Beiersdorfer, National Community Rights Network president, "Episode 6," *We the People,* September 20, 2019, online video, 1:52.

a distraction that interfered with the need to stay focused on working with the confounded regulatory system. While it was a welcome lifesaver, it was also a juggling act to learn about and follow the Rights of Nature path, all the while navigating the regulatory system that the corporate playbook bids us to follow. I did not choose either/or, and walked both paths, exhausting and exhilarating as that was.

We, heretics of obedience to the corporate coopted regulatory system, hosted a Democracy School in January 2018, taught by the Community Environmental Legal Defense Fund (CELDF), pioneers of the Rights of Nature movement. Learning that our global legal system is based on property law laid bare the systemic structure of the ecological crisis: the commodification and legal enslavement of Nature as property to be bought and sold. With stratification of wealth comes privatization and fragmentation; enslavement of land, animals, men, women, and children; and the enclosing of the commons by the hegemonic minority.[46] We are urgently called to emancipate Nature, returning to right relationship with both the human and nonhuman world.

Hosting a Democracy School led to the birth of Buckingham: We the People (BWTP) with the mission to write a Community Bill of Rights to protect the Rights of Nature of the James River Watershed from fossil fuel infrastructure. This was a community-building, educational tool to assert our inherent rights and responsibilities as a natural community to not just survive but to regenerate, flourish, and naturally evolve and to challenge the injustice of illegitimate corporate rights that impede local and direct democracy. We knew it would not be well received in our county, but we did it anyway.

---

[46] Ben Price, *How Wealth Rules the World: Saving Our Communities and Freedoms from the Dictatorship of Property* (Oakland, CA: Berrett-Koehler, 2019).

BWTP would morph into the Virginia Community Rights Network (VACRN) in March 2020, which Mindy Zlotnick, Kenda Hanuman, and I cofounded. VACRN partnered with Friends of Buckingham (FoB) in 2020 to counter yet another extractive industry that threatened our community by asserting a local rights-based ordinance to protect the James River watershed from the toxic trespass of metallic mining.

The daunting demands of attention to minutiae such as learning about and navigating the unjust legal system ironically can lead us far from the Garden in the quest to champion our beloved Mother. This movement's high moral compass inspires us to carry on. My roots in Yoga, Wicca, and the embrace of the Divine Feminine nourish the deep knowing of a higher natural law of right relations, celebrating diversity while anchored in unity. For this I prostrate before the great wisdom teachings that are guiding lights to making "peace with justice" possible. As the wheel turns, may these musings serve to benefit Nature's inter-relational web.

5

Earth Quaker Action Team
Spirit in Action

Lina Blount and Eileen Flanagan

Surrounded by police, the chorus of voices was starting to grow hoarse from chanting, "Sweep, sweep, sweep out corruption!" and "No KXL pipeline!" in the frigid March air. Earth Quaker Action Team (EQAT) had organized this 2014 civil disobedience action to support the national campaign against the Keystone XL (KXL) pipeline, which had come to symbolize the reckless expansion of the fossil fuel industry despite climate scientists warning against extracting the dirty Tar Sands oil the pipeline was intended to transport from Alberta across the continental United States. Inspired in part by Indigenous resistance to Tar Sands extraction, the action was designed to pressure the Obama administration to stop the pipeline. Forty protesters from a range of local groups had blocked the three main doors of the Philadelphia Federal Building with their bodies and brooms—props that dramatized the dirty dealing of the State Department, which hired an oil industry firm to evaluate the pipeline's potential environmental impact. Another 160 people supported from beyond the metal barricades the police had erected. The police had made a few arrests at the northern door and then paused after a group of reinforcements breached the barricades to strengthen the group of activists there. As tensions escalated, the protesters and police both felt agitated.

Sensing that a change was needed, and remembering a previous action where silent prayer had shifted the energy, fifty-two-year-old Eileen Flanagan leaned over to twenty-three-year-old Lina Blount, a fellow EQAT board member, and whispered, "Let's call for worship." Lina nodded and said, "You do it." Trying to project her hoarse voice over the chaotic scene, Eileen invited the crowd to silent prayer, which transformed the mood, as well as the dynamic between the police and protesters.

Many in the crowd were familiar with the Quaker tradition of silent worship, which dates back to the seventeenth century in Philadelphia. While some branches of Quakerism eventually adopted clergy, the branch dominant in the Northeast (known as the liberal unprogrammed tradition) worships by settling into silence without an appointed minister or planned service. Some describe this worship as a deep listening for the guidance of God, Christ, or Spirit, while some use less theist language in a tradition that is theologically broad. In unprogrammed worship, there is no clergy, and anyone can offer a "message" to the gathered meeting when they feel led by Spirit to speak out of the silence. In the midst of the chaotic KXL action, Eileen invited the crowd into this type of worship, acknowledging that the group included people of different faiths, as well as those not associated with a religious tradition. She invited people to reflect on what humanity was doing to the Earth and to pray for the Earth as well as future generations, including the children of the police and the corporate executives who were putting short-term profits above their children's futures.

Eileen's invitation was only heard by those immediately around her, but as the silence of those initial few began, it grew

EQAT participants regularly turn to the Quaker practice of silent worship during protests for climate justice to ground their action in Spirit, as shown during a mass action in 2024.

(PHOTO BY RACHEL WARRINER @RAYEPHOTO ON INSTAGRAM / USED WITH PERMISSION)

to encompass the full group at the north door, then moved across the plaza to the center door, which was blocked by a Jewish group that included several rabbis. They felt the shift in energy and stopped their chanting, as the silence spread to all two hundred protesters. Later, those who had been at the other doors described the almost physical sensation of the silence settling over them. The silence became so "loud" we could hear the clicking of press cameras and the sound of the police turning off their radio, while even some police bowed their heads. Afterward, people present had widely different estimates of how long the silence had lasted, but it ended when Lina, sensing it was time, began singing "Guide My Feet," a civil rights hymn by Bernice Johnson Reagon. Matthew Armstead, one of the action leads and staff with EQAT, leaned over the

barricade and told us to start moving, so we joined hands
with others at the north door. Walking slowly in a circle, still
blocking the doors, we sang,

> Guide my feet
> While I run this race
> Guide my feet
> While I run this race
> Guide my feet
> While I run this race
> 'Cause I don't want to run this race in vain.

The song was picked up across the plaza. What had just a few
minutes prior been a growing sense of frantic energy was shifted
by the worship and song. Quakers call this a "gathered meeting,"
where we feel palpably connected by Spirit.

Our voices revived, and we felt more physically present,
grounded in our purpose. Suddenly, the balance of power in
the space had shifted from those with structural authority, the
police, to those of us asserting moral authority and conviction.
The police, who initially seemed reluctant to arrest more people,
tried to regain control by resuming the arrests, starting with Lina
and Eileen (the coauthors of this chapter), and others who seemed
to be giving the group energy and leadership. For us, the purpose
of the action was not to get arrested, though some mistakenly talk
about civil disobedience this way. The purpose was to pressure
the Obama administration, and being put in handcuffs, even if
only for a day, was a way to dramatize our refusal to go along with
business as usual in the face of the climate crisis. We could feel
that we had done what we came to do. The group's spirits stayed
high through an afternoon in the Federal Building jail, as twenty-
nine arrestees sang to each person who joined them. Afterward,

many spoke about the profound feeling of stillness and clarity that the worship had brought out of the chaos of the moment.

The KXL action story is a rich example of how worship and connecting to the sacred are not just rituals of protest, but grounding and guiding practices that can change what a group perceives as possible in any given moment of resistance. For EQAT, the moment grew out of our foundational principles, which are rooted in Quaker beliefs: that our faith calls on us to live our values, that there is "that of God" or the sacred in everyone and everything, that "way opens" or Spirit gives us signs to head in certain directions, that God is constantly speaking to us in "continuing revelation," and that our spiritual lives and leadership are deeply communal.[1]

Beginnings

Long before there was a term for it, Quakers engaged in what we now call noncooperation, a form of nonviolent direct action that involves directly and nonviolently challenging injustice by refusing to go along with it. In the nineteenth century, English Quakers refused to pay tithes to the Church of England, which they felt was entwined with oppressive state power and unfaithful to the teachings of Jesus. Passionately preaching that each person could connect to God directly (including women and non-Christians), they were imprisoned by the thousands. In colonial America, Quakers such as Mary Dyer were hanged by Puritans for continuing to worship and preach in defiance

---

[1] For more on Quaker spirituality, its connection to social issues, and how it has evolved over the centuries, see Marcelle Martin, *Our Life Is Love: The Quaker Spiritual Journey* (San Francisco: Inner Light Books, 2016). For a compilation of primary sources, see Jessamyn West, ed., *The Quaker Reader* (Wallingford, PA: Pendle Hill Publications, 1992).

of Protestant law. While many seventeenth-century Quakers participated in enslaving people of African descent, a few courageously and persistently challenged the practice, making it taboo for American Quakers by the end of the eighteenth century. By the nineteenth century, Quakers played a significant role in the abolitionist movement, boycotting goods made by enslaved people, and in some cases breaking the law to protect those escaping from slavery. In the twentieth century, Quakers (also known as Friends) continued to use civil disobedience to demand the vote for women, civil rights for Blacks, and the end of nuclear weapons testing, among other issues.[2]

By the early twenty-first century, few American Quakers were engaged in such bold, risky action, though many liked to boast of Quakers' role in past movements (often downplaying their early complicity with slaveholding and colonialism, or racism within the women's suffrage movement). Many Friends did engage in social issues—writing letters to elected officials, standing in silent vigil against the wars in Iraq and Afghanistan, or attending large marches. Individual ecological practices, like composting food scraps or driving a Prius, were popular among American Quakers. The national network Quaker Earthcare Witness, founded in the 1980s under the name Friends Committee on Unity with Nature, highlighted the connection between environmental destruction and the inequitable distribution of the world's resources, reminding Friends of the Quaker traditions of finding the Divine in the natural world and living

---

[2] For a summary of Quaker involvement in social justice issues in the United States, see Susan Sachs Goldman, *Friends in Deed: The Story of Quaker Social Reform in America* (Highmark Press, 2012). For a more in-depth and less flattering exploration of American Quakers' work on racial justice, see Donna McDaniel and Vanessa Julye, *Fit for Freedom, Not for Friendship: Quakers, African Americans, and the Myth of Racial Justice* (Philadelphia: Quaker Press of FGC, 2018).

simply.[3] As concern about climate change rose, some Quaker organizations renovated their old buildings to be more green, including Friends Committee on National Legislation, which also lobbied on climate change. Still, few Quakers were using noncooperation as a strategy to address protection of the Earth.

In 2009, the annual gathering of Philadelphia Yearly Meeting, the regional body of over one hundred Quaker congregations, met around the theme of environmental and climate justice. One of several speakers, longtime Quaker activist George Lakey, asked the audience, "If we really believe that climate change is going to be catastrophic, shouldn't we use the kind of strategies that have worked historically?" Many in the crowd, including Eileen, were moved by his stories of past Quaker movements that used nonviolent direct action and his belief that Friends could play this role again in confronting the causes of climate change. During the deep silent worship that followed, one Friend stood and said, "I'm ready to hear the most radical thing that you can tell us to do." Another said, "Show me the way." Many later described it as a "gathered meeting," worship where many feel the movement of the Spirit.

After the speech, a small group made plans to meet with George to explore what they might do. After some group discernment, Earth Quaker Action Team (EQAT, pronounced "equate") was founded in 2010 to apply the Quaker tradition of nonviolent resistance to the work of building a just and sustainable economy. The next step was to discern a focused campaign that would enable them to learn the skills of nonviolent direct action while actually making a difference. Understanding that

---

[3] For the Quaker theological roots of environmental concerns, see Douglas Gwyn, *A Sustainable Life: Quaker Faith and Practice in the Renewal of Creation* (Philadelphia: Quaker Press of FGC, 2014); and Cherice Bock and Christy Randazzo, *Quakers, Ecology, and the Light* (Leiden: Brill, 2023).

climate change was caused by many actors, especially the fossil fuel industry and the other corporations that prop up their profits, EQAT looked for a specific corporation that might be sensitive to pressure from a small band of southeastern Pennsylvania Quakers. The group also looked for an issue that clearly connected climate change and justice, preferably an issue where we could join an existing movement rather than trying to start one from scratch. Pennsylvania-based PNC Bank's financing of mountaintop removal coal mining emerged as such an issue, and the group came to easy unity around it, which Quakers use as one sign that they are following Spirit.

Founded in the early 1980s through the merger of Provident National Corporation, a largely Quaker bank, and the Pittsburgh National Corporation, PNC bragged about its Quaker roots and green business practices. At the same time, it was one of the largest financiers of mountaintop removal coal mining, a horrific, capital-intensive practice that involves blowing up mountaintops to get hard-to-reach coal, while poisoning the water of already exploited Appalachian communities. The felling of forests and burning of coal both contribute to climate change. There had been some history of Quakers working in Appalachia, and a long history of Appalachians advocating for themselves, which continued as people courageously defended their communities and the beautiful mountains where their ancestors were buried. The inaugural EQAT campaign targeting PNC was named Bank Like Appalachia Matters! (BLAM!). As EQAT started holding disruptive and creative actions at PNC locations, others joined, including Lina, who was a student at nearby Bryn Mawr College, and Eileen.

Through group discernment, prophetic risk taking, and mutual support, the BLAM! campaign grew from a small band of Philadelphia-based Quakers to a campaign that held over

125 actions in thirteen states, ultimately pressuring PNC to stop financing mountaintop removal coal mining. Over the five years of the campaign, there were many moments of gathered worship and Spirit-led discernment in action, though often in smaller groups than the 2014 KXL solidarity action, which was a brief detour from our relentless focus on PNC. EQAT grew to include people of many faiths and no faiths, while continuing to employ the Quaker practice of silent worship, listening inwardly for guidance in group decisions, and drawing on other Quaker principles. The board, which employed an adapted form of Quaker-style group discernment, gradually became younger and less dominated by Quakers. Still, listening for Spirit, grounding in Spirit, and trying to live our values while honoring "that of God" in all creation were central parts of how EQAT executed action plans, oriented ourselves to our campaign targets, and created community with each other.

Integrity in Action

Integrity is a core Quaker value. Historically, many Friends have refused to make vows in court or swear oaths in other settings. Although not all Quakers consider themselves to be Christian, the ever-evolving community-crafted guide to Quaker principles, known as *Quaker Faith & Practice*, calls on Friends to be "honest and truthful in all you say and do" and to embrace Jesus's prohibition against swearing oaths, since "taking oaths implies a double standard of truth."[4] As Wilmer Cooper writes in *The Testimony of Integrity in the Religious Society of Friends*, "Friends'

---

[4] See *Quaker Faith and Practice: The Book of Christian Discipline of the Yearly Meeting of the Religious Society of Friends (Quakers) in Britain*, 5th ed. (London: Britain Yearly Meeting of the Society of Friends), 01.02.37.

concern was that followers of Christ should be known for telling the truth all the time, and not just when one was called before a judge and sworn to tell the truth."[5] Even when abolitionist Friends aided those escaping slavery, they instructed their children to hide them, so they could truthfully say they hadn't seen any runaway slaves if asked by the police.

This historical Quaker commitment to integrity was part of the reason Quaker banks and other businesses had been so successful. They had gained a reputation for honest dealing. This history gave EQAT some leverage to challenge PNC's public image, since the bank advertised its Quaker roots on its website, claiming also to be a green bank while financing a practice that was devastating to the Appalachian environment and contributing to climate change. PNC's Quaker roots also meant that a good number of Quaker organizations as well as many Quaker congregations and individuals still had their funds saved with the bank. This gave Quakers an easy form of noncooperation, moving our money, which fit with the Quaker emphasis on integrity. Many Quaker congregations already had investment policies, such as not buying stock in companies that made weapons, so the idea of aligning our finances with our values was not unfamiliar. But unlike these quiet acts of integrity, EQAT (like early Friends) encouraged people to make their witness public, inviting supporters to come with signs explaining that a person or group was closing their PNC account because of the bank's role in the destruction of mountains. In some cases, such account closings were covered in local papers. Over time, the amount EQAT was able to track totaled at least $3 million

---

[5] Wilmer Cooper, *The Testimony of Integrity in the Religious Society of Friends*, Pendle Hill Pamphlet 296 (1991; repr. Wallingford, PA: Pendle Hill, 2015), "The Quaker Practice of Integrity."

moved, a pittance to a bank that netted over $4 billion a year, but a significant sum for a small religious community. More importantly in terms of strategy, Quakers moving their money out of the bank challenged PNC's public image, which we knew was very valuable to them.

It wasn't possible to physically interrupt the electronic flow of the bank's money to coal companies the way some activists were trying to physically interrupt the building of pipelines. Instead, EQAT experimented with creative and symbolic ways to interrupt "business as usual" at the bank, sometimes risking arrest by refusing to leave bank property, but often by transgressing social norms, like singing in bank lobbies and leaving before arrests were made. The intention to act with integrity ourselves challenged us to reflect on how we were designing actions, especially around the question of how transparent to be about our plans.

One such example arose in late 2013. The secular national youth climate conference PowerShift had chosen Pittsburgh for its annual gathering, which just happened to be the location of PNC's national headquarters. EQAT decided to make use of the coincidence, offering NVDA training at PowerShift, and announcing a series of actions at PNC branches around the city on the last day of the gathering. By 2013, a strong cohort of college students had joined the BLAM! campaign. One of them observed that her experience of student activism involved a lot of shouting, and she loved that EQAT actions challenged her to be bold and creative, not just loud. Another college student said that she had been moved by EQAT's use of silence, which was easy for newcomers to join, so maybe we should center our PowerShift actions in Quaker-style worship. She suggested we bring small plastic lights in the shape of candles to visually express that what we were doing was spiritual. That became the blueprint for a day that ultimately included seventeen actions, most of them Quaker worship in bank lobbies at PNC branches across the city. Front-line leaders from Appalachia came to join the day of action and in some places spoke out of the silent worship about the harm that mountaintop removal coal mining was doing to their communities. A Pittsburgh Quaker who attended said with tears in his eyes that it was some of the deepest worship he had experienced.

Members of EQAT are arrested during a BLAM! campaign action at a PNC Bank in Pittsburgh. The movement's commitment to nonviolent, joyful activism is reflected in the faces of the "truth tellers."   (CREDIT: EQAT / USED WITH PERMISSION)

The integrity question arose around the final action of the day, the only one planned to include civil disobedience. By the afternoon, momentum and word of the actions was building. PNC branches were starting to lock their doors when they saw us coming. At other locations, security guards began screening people at the door, offending some customers whom the guards thought looked more like protesters. As EQATers approached the final action, which was to take place at a branch in the base of the US Steel Building, it became clear that this final location was one of the many that now had a security guard at the door. As the seven risking arrest discussed what to do, the question of integrity and truth-telling became central. Was it okay to lie to get past the guard, in the name of a higher good? The group ranged in age from their early twenties to late seventies with a mixture of Quakers and non-Quakers. It was one of the non-Quaker Bryn Mawr students who pointed out that the message they had settled on for this particular action was "Tell the Truth," a challenge to PNC to acknowledge the harm their investments were doing. The student spoke powerfully about the fact that they shouldn't lie if they were asking PNC to tell the truth. The group agreed.

They decided that each individual would say what they felt led to say to the guard at the door, guided by the value of integrity in their hearts. The person delivering large photos (for those risking arrest to hold during the action) told the security guard she was there to "meet Friends." Despite the bundle under her arm, the guard waved her past. Another EQAT member, whose role was to speak to the manager and explain the purpose of the action, said that he had "business with the bank." Without lying, every one of the team made it past the security guard and into the bank. Once inside, they took up position in front of the branch doors, holding the photos of decimated mountains and brown polluted water. As police gathered, one of the group called the curious onlookers and police into silent worship for the lives lost in Appalachia and the impact of mountaintop removal on health, jobs, and climate change. A profound silence descended, joined by everyone in the lobby. This is the incident that inspired Eileen to call for silent worship during the KXL action a few months later, as described at the outset of this chapter.

As in the KXL action, the police felt challenged by this assertion of moral authority and the fact that the activists seemed to have more control over the space than they did. Although fifty chanting, anti-fracking protesters nearby had taken over an office, hoping to be arrested, the seven silent truth-tellers were the only action arrests in Pittsburgh that day. After the rest of us sang to the seven as they were escorted in handcuffs to police vans, Eileen turned and saw one of the young PowerShift participants weeping. "I've never sung before," he tried to explain. Eileen understood it to be an understandable response to the powerful movement of the Spirit that day.

Leadership and Learning

Shared leadership and training were among the practices that attracted young people to EQAT. Since many of those who founded the organization didn't have much nonviolent direct-action experience themselves, much time was put into training and preparation for each action, especially in the early years. The approach to training was deeply influenced by the philosophy of Training for Change (TFC), which George Lakey had founded decades before EQAT, and which had influenced several other EQAT leaders. A Philadelphia-based organization that trains activists, TFC's method incorporates ideas from Paulo Freire and gestalt psychology models of experiential education. EQAT likewise embraces a culture that recognizes that the knowledge needed is inherently within the group, and the learning cycle is about sharing an experience, reflecting on that experience, then generalizing the lessons from the experience in such a way that they might be applied moving forward. As a result, EQAT has an almost fastidious commitment to debriefing actions, which we do by asking people in every role what they noticed, what worked and what didn't work, what it felt like to confront authority physically or spiritually, and what people might do differently.

In addition to pressuring PNC on their home turf, the PowerShift actions put almost everyone on their "growth edge," a phrase EQAT uses to express the idea that we all need to grow our skills, courage, and leadership in order to have a hope of slowing climate change.

One of the great things about executing seventeen actions in one day was that it widened the number of people who held action roles. Some were action leads or police liaisons for the first time. Others became song leaders or spiritual anchors, a role we assign to support the group's spiritual grounding.

In the meeting for worship that is held weekly in unprogrammed Quaker congregations, there is usually someone who has "care of meeting," a person appointed to pray for the whole group. Often this person comes early or takes extra steps to assure their own spiritual grounding. In EQAT, spiritual anchors likewise hold the spiritual grounding of the group. Often before an action, the spiritual anchor leads the group in a breathing exercise or some other centering practice. Especially when we are expecting police or anything that might upset or distract participants, we encourage them to look to the spiritual anchor for regrounding. People are invited to this role because of the energy they bring, regardless of their age or religious affiliation.

Eileen was reminded of how countercultural EQAT's approach to roles was after the PowerShift action, when she gave a ride home to someone from a large, secular nonprofit. He had noticed that at the rally outside the civil disobedience action, Matthew Armstead—EQAT's charismatic staff person— had handed the megaphone to Lina, by then a recent college graduate. Unscripted, Lina had passionately shared about the environmental impacts PNC's investments were making in Appalachia and why we were called to act. On the ride from Pittsburgh back to Philadelphia, the observer asked Eileen,

"Did Matthew really just hand the megaphone to Lina?" "Sure," Eileen replied, surprised by the question. "He just handed the megaphone to her?" he repeated incredulously. Eileen suddenly realized that her companion came from a hierarchical nonprofit culture where the executive director gets the megaphone and then passes it to another executive director. Our practice not only empowered more people to take on leadership, but it resulted in more inspired speaking, since no one was giving their usual canned talking points. Such an approach also encourages younger and antipatriarchal leadership.

In Quakerism, the term "clerk" describes a leadership role that involves listening to and shepherding the group rather than directing it. Four of the first five people to serve as EQAT board clerks were female, including Eileen and Lina. Although George was the most well-known of the founders, men were a minority of the board throughout the BLAM! campaign. Cis, hetero-sexual white men were a tiny minority, even though EQAT was majority white. Queer members occasionally commented that the organizational culture was not demonstrably queer, but their presence and leadership, including trans and gender-noncon-forming people on the board, helped to distinguish EQAT from large "big green" environmental organizations, which often had cis, straight, white male leadership. The age diversity of EQAT leaders was also unusual, with the board including people from their twenties to their seventies, and all learning from each other. Over the course of the campaign, as some of the founders left the board, the average age of board members dropped significantly.

Although not framed in religious terms, all of these aspects of organizational culture are deeply influenced by Quaker faith and practice, especially the tenet that there is "that of God in every person," so anyone can be a channel for divine wisdom. This included women from the seventeenth century who traveled throughout England spreading the Quaker message. The idea that Spirit can communicate with people of all ages informs Quaker approaches to education and decision-making. Today, in a congregation's monthly business meeting, which is grounded in worship, anyone might have an insight into the values reflected in the budget, even if they are not on the finance committee. Although it is acknowledged that some people have particular skills or gifts, leadership in the unprogrammed tradition rotates among volunteers. EQAT, likewise, has term limits for board members, and encourages feedback from the wider community when a major decision is being considered, even when the ultimate decider is the board. Clarity about the EQAT board's role in major decisions, and a provision in the bylaws that allows the board to vote if there is no consensus, are departures from the practice of local Quaker congregations and regional bodies (called "monthly meetings" and "yearly meetings," respectively). While these communities use a group process of spiritual discernment that can be quite slow, EQAT seeks consensus guided by Spirit, while recognizing the danger of a prolonged and excessively open process for a type of activism that is sure to invoke fear and could attract infiltrators.

EQAT's decision making is also implicitly influenced by the concept of continuing revelation. Like Pentecostal Christians, Bahá'ís, and members of many other religious groups, Quakers hold that the Divine continues to communicate with us, so our understanding of God's will may evolve over time. That is why *Faith and Practice*, the guidebook drafted by each yearly meeting, is regularly revised, using a communal discernment process to identify our best, collective, and current understanding of our faith. Looking at different *Faith and Practice* editions over the centuries shows the evolution of attitudes toward slavery, same-sex marriage, and many other issues. Although the language of continuing revelation is not explicitly used in EQAT, there is an openness to new spiritual guidance, especially in action, that might be different from what we had previously discerned or planned.

Over time, we realized that action planning went best with a small dedicated group, which we call a "core team." Around four or five people, only one a staff member, meet regularly to strategize and design a given action and then manage the logistics and implementation. Ideally the group is composed of people with varying levels of experience and different strengths, such as a visionary as well as a detail-oriented implementer. The core team is intentionally a place where newer volunteers are invited into leadership. That way, new folks can learn experientially from teammates who have been in the campaign longer, while building relationships with them. And more experienced volunteers are forced to repeatedly see actions and messaging with fresh eyes. The core team also lessens the common activist problem of a few people doing most of the work month after month.

The beauty of both experiential learning and continuing revelation is that they happen in community, and everyone has access to wisdom, knowledge, and the sacred. It is through the dynamic flow of individual discernment, action, and then group discernment and action that individual-, group-, and systemic-level change can happen, and love and justice can be nourished and realized. Though not everyone in EQAT is a Quaker, many have experienced the way that individual action and discernment transform and are transformed through community.

Supporting Individual Leadings

Continuing revelation often starts with the experience of particular individuals willing to follow what Quakers call a "leading," and then share their learning with the group. In the summer of

2013, Lina had the opportunity to heed the solidarity call of the Dene, Metis, and the Keepers of the Athabasca and join the annual Tar Sands Healing Walk against the extraction of dirty tar sands oil in Fort McMurray, Alberta. Indigenous peoples near Fort McMurray had been organizing healing walks since 2010, but had made it known they wanted the 2013 gathering to be a large one, inviting Anishinaabe leader Winona LaDuke, Naomi Klein, and Bill McKibben to join them. Lina had been connected to the effort through an activist at the first annual student fossil fuel divestment convergence at Swarthmore College that spring, and was inspired by the work of the Idle No More movement of Indigenous leaders that had erupted throughout Canada and the United States that same year. Lina felt a strong call to go, and she committed to a support role with a small team of people who would continue south from Fort McMurray, walking along the proposed route of the Keystone XL pipeline. But Lina was uncertain about how to open herself up to the experience, be most helpful, or honor the invitation. After one EQAT meeting, Lina spoke to Eileen about her leading to join the Healing Walk and her uncertainty about how to meet that call. Lina knew she was asking for some kind of help or support, but wasn't even fully sure what she was asking for. Eileen's eyes lit up as she suggested that Lina might benefit from what Quakers call a "Clearness Committee." Without knowing what she was getting herself into, Lina said yes to the invitation.

About a week later Lina gathered with Eileen and four other EQATers who identified as Quaker. Starting with silent worship, they invited Lina into the Clearness Committee process with them. As the focus person, Lina described the situation she was facing and her uncertainties, as well as her desire to follow the solidarity call. After listening attentively, they all settled into more silent worship. Then, out of the silence, different people asked open-ended questions. Lina was instructed not to answer each question in turn, but to listen to the questions and sit with them, and share only the answers that arose in her. Through this contemplative dance of worship, asking and discerning answers, Lina felt the fears about the unknowns slip away, and gained a sense of gratitude and clarity that following the leading was the most important thread. The committee left her with guiding questions that helped to ground her experience at the healing walk. Eileen reached out to Quakers in Montana, who agreed to pray for Lina as she walked across their large state. Upon her return, Lina sat with the clearness group again to share and reflect on her experience. It was a profound gift that launched her on a deepening commitment in her Quaker faith, which she had first encountered in EQAT actions.

That same summer, Lina was invited to join the EQAT board, and her experience from the Clearness Committee and Healing Walk continued to inform her leadership in that capacity. When the invitation to support the Keystone XL Action Pledge was being discussed, Lina was a strong advocate for EQAT stepping up to support the effort.

Another individual leading that helped the group to grow occurred in the summer of 2014. Matthew Armstead was both on staff with EQAT and a regular trainer with TFC, which serves activist organizations by supporting their learning. TFC received a request from Black activists in Ferguson, Missouri, during the uprising against the police murder of Michael Brown, a young Black man whose body was left in the streets for hours. Grass-roots activists in Ferguson had been thrown into the national spotlight, while experiencing increased police repression. Matthew was already sensing an inner call to support them when TFC shared that they were seeking trainers of color with experience working with youth, especially those with experience in street theatre, civil disobedience, or spiritual counseling. Amazingly, this list perfectly described Matthew. They briefly resisted, but soon realized they were called to go to Ferguson. They also realized they couldn't afford to take three weeks off from their EQAT job without organizational support, so Matthew reached out to Eileen and other board leaders.

While supporting Matthew to go to Ferguson might not initially seem aligned with the goals of the BLAM! campaign, the EQAT board felt clear that it could be a sign of continuing revelation that the group should heed, especially since EQAT had begun conversations on racial justice but hadn't figured out how to incorporate it into BLAM! The feeling was so clear and strong among the group members that they moved unanimously to pay Matthew's salary during their three-week trip. TFC paid for Matthew's transportation. A few EQAT leaders served with others on a support committee for Matthew, checking in with them from Ferguson and debriefing with them afterward. Volunteers stepped up to do much of Matthew's EQAT job, which at the time included preparation for two major actions.

Matthew returned profoundly touched by their experience in Ferguson and more open to discussing racial dynamics within EQAT, which they had initially resisted as one of the few Black members. Matthew's learning deepened and expanded a thread of continuing revelation within EQAT around racial justice. EQAT had never been an exclusively white organization, and EQATers of color and a few white EQATers had long and dedicated individual experiences around racial justice work. But EQAT as an organization did not talk much about racial justice in the early years, even though climate change is inherently a racial justice issue. Some Quakers of color questioned why EQAT had chosen to stand in solidarity with the predominantly white people of Appalachia instead of taking on environmental racism in our own predominantly Black city. Over time, the group grappled with how to bring racial justice work into the mainstream of the group and out of the margins in a way that was not affirmation seeking or virtue signaling, but instead grounded in radical solidarity. That work grew over the coming years, especially once we won the BLAM! campaign and chose a subsequent campaign with a strong focus on racial justice.

Dealing with Conflict

Many predominantly white and middle-class groups resist having open conflict, preferring to bury differences under a veneer of niceness.[6] This is a particular struggle for contemporary US Quakers, whose historic commitment to peace is often confused with unanimity and passivity. Erica Thorne, a TFC trainer whom we hired as a consultant to help us work on race, told us that if we wanted to be able to discuss racism, first we needed to get more comfortable with conflict. During retreats, we explored how our families had dealt with or avoided conflict. During one daylong strategy session, we set up the discussion to encourage more open disagreement within EQAT.

This invitation to conflict helped us as we talked more openly about racism on the societal, group, and individual levels. We experimented with making room in our regular debriefs to reflect on how identity or positionality might have played out in how an action was perceived or received. We offered trainings on how to be a more welcoming community—and what got in the way. We also held sessions on implicit racial bias and economic inequality along racial lines. Still, many of our white members found it difficult to confront each other when someone said something that revealed racial bias, which was tiring for our staff of color.

---

[6] See, for example, Thomas Kochman, *Black and White Styles in Conflict* (Chicago: University of Chicago Press, 1983).

Despite our mission as a direct-action group, discomfort with confrontation was something that had come up in our direct-action planning when it involved confronting individuals. Two years into the campaign, PNC made a declaration that they would no longer invest in companies that drew more than half of their income from mountaintop removal coal mining, which was misleading since no such companies existed. It became clear that actions in PNC Bank branches would not be adequate to persuade the powerful corporation to change their practices. Called to take action with an urgency that matched the scale of destruction and injustice in Appalachia, EQAT contemplated what Spirit-guided escalation might look like. The idea arose to challenge specific PNC board members and executives at their private residences and in public forums, such as events at which they were being honored for personal philanthropy. While most EQATers were supportive of disrupting board meetings, several questioned whether it might be too aggressive—perhaps even "violent"—to confront individual PNC leaders in their private or not-explicitly PNC-connected lives, a tactic generally called "bird-dogging."

While Quaker and non-Quaker members of EQAT broadly agreed on our commitment to nonviolence, the disagreement over bird-dogging forced people to put into words their differing understandings of what constitutes violence and acknowledge that some of their discomfort stemmed from their own fears of engaging in such a confrontational tactic. One EQAT board member spoke clearly and passionately about how it was actually from a depth of love and seeing "that of God" in the PNC leaders that he called on them to do better, that he believed deeply in their humanity and capacity to change, even if that meant showing up to deliver the news at their homes. One adaptation that helped the reluctant become willing to accept this approach was that we stopped using the term bird-dogging, with its hunting connotations, and adopted a new term, "spotlighting," which tapped the Quaker metaphor of light that is often used as a synonym for Spirit. Still, some chose not to participate in spotlighting actions. Others we found needed extra support, since breaking social norms of politeness and privacy stirred up many feelings.

One instance of spotlighting was made possible by the strong transcontinental connections Quakers hold, especially as a relatively small religious community. We knew that climate-concerned Friends in Britain had been following the work of EQAT, so when we learned that a PNC board member, Jane Pepper, would be leading a garden tour of England, we reached out and asked them to spotlight her during her trip. Pepper had led the Pennsylvania Horticultural Society and was the PNC board member with the most green image. As such, we particularly challenged her to use her role to raise the issue of the bank's financing of mountaintop removal coal mining. Although she evaded our "Be Brave" signs at the Philadelphia airport on the day of her tour's departure, she was met at her English hotel by three white-haired Quakers who offered her chocolates and literature on mountaintop removal. It was an effective example of escalating pressure on PNC leaders while drawing on Quaker strengths and values. Despite some discomfort with the escalatory tactic of challenging individual PNC board members and executives, in hindsight many saw evidence that it led to the "way opening" that enabled a critical turning point in the BLAM! campaign.

Way Opening

Way opening is a Quaker concept closely related to continuing revelation, though it refers to outward circumstances that fall into place in a way that feels miraculous or like a sign from Spirit.

This is particularly meaningful when the circumstances shift in a way that reaffirms inward spiritual guidance, like Matthew's leading to go to Ferguson arising just as EQAT was questioning what a predominantly white group working on mountaintop removal coal mining could do to support racial justice. Contemporary Quaker writer Brent Bill explains in his book *Sacred Compass*, "God works within and around us, leading, guiding, and opening the way, sometimes when we least expect or feel it. The idea of being led and guided implies movement.... *As way opens* implies a deep way of developing our spiritual insight, making major decisions, and planning."[7]

It had felt at least fortuitous, possibly miraculous, when EQAT learned that PowerShift had chosen Pittsburgh for its fall 2013 conference, in contrast to previous years when it met in Washington, DC. Over the following year, a series of coincidences unfolded that, as they came together, felt clearly like way opening. For one, in late 2013, a Quaker adult in Philadelphia told Eileen that there were Quaker teenagers in Florida who felt led to get involved with EQAT. Some had traveled to Appalachia to see mountaintop removal for themselves. One had even undergone a clearness process to get her entire yearly meeting's support for her leading, a clear example of an individual leading moving the group. Eileen was touched by this story and reached out to Florida Quakers, though she had no idea how to involve the teenagers in the Pennsylvania-based BLAM! campaign. Then, in early 2014, PNC announced that it was moving its annual shareholder meeting to, of all places, Tampa.

EQAT had attended three previous PNC shareholder meetings, the first year speaking powerfully during the question-

---

[7] J. Brent Bill, *Sacred Compass: The Way of Spiritual Discernment* (Brewster, MA: Paraclete Press, 2008), 1.

and-answer period, the second year handing out fliers about mountaintop removal coal mining to the board as they arrived. In spring 2013, after approving spotlighting, EQAT escalated tactics within the shareholder meeting. Willing to risk arrest, thirteen EQAT members used legal proxies to enter the meeting, which seemed to include more security personnel than protesters. EQAT held its own meeting for worship during the corporate meeting, and assigned each participant a board member to address by name. As the bank tried to conduct its business, EQATers stood up one by one from a place of grounded worship to ask the board members how they could support the destruction in Appalachia. After each address, the group sang the old union song, "Which Side Are You On?" In addition to posing a challenging question, the song was also a nod to Appalachian labor history. Amid some confusion, the PNC CEO called their legally mandated annual meeting to an abrupt halt just seventeen minutes after it began. Since business reporters cover the shareholder meetings of major companies, our action was picked up by the Associated Press and was reported in one hundred newspapers, even though the bank had chosen not to have us arrested.

Clearly PNC hoped to avoid a repeat of this situation by moving the following year's meeting to Florida, a state where, we soon learned, it is illegal to disrupt a shareholder meeting or even hold up a sign during a meeting. But it was also the only state outside of the Northeast where EQAT had a group of Quakers eager to take action in support of the campaign. More serendipity helped us to mobilize them. It turned out that the regional gathering of southeastern Quakers was meeting the weekend before the shareholder meeting, so Matthew and another EQATer flew down early to conduct an intergenerational training in nonviolent direct action. Author Brent Bill was the keynote speaker, and he agreed to promote the action in his talk. The organization, SumOfUs, heard about the coincidences around the Tampa shareholder meeting and offered to pay travel expenses for a few other EQATers as well, so four of us were able to support an action that included an intergenerational group of Quakers from seven Florida monthly meetings.

One of the biggest questions that arose during the planning was what to do in the action itself. We weren't particularly interested in risking arrest so far from Philadelphia, where we didn't have a friendly lawyer on call. We also wanted to do something the young people could fully participate in without alarming their parents with the risk of arrest. And we didn't want to simply repeat what we had done the year before, so we settled on the idea of standing up to silently worship with T-shirts that explained our purpose. It was simple and would achieve our purpose, showing PNC that they couldn't run away from the results of their investments.

When the day came, PNC used an obscure rule about proxies to exclude everyone whose proxy came from shares purchased through a broker. Only Eileen and Matthew had proxies from shares bought directly from the company, but Matthew was illegitimately locked out, meaning that Eileen entered the meeting alone. When she sat down at an aisle seat, the meeting was well underway, and she could see that management was flying through the agenda, presumably to minimize whatever disruption EQAT had planned. She tried to ground herself, remembering her insistence at the training the night before that the act of praying during the meeting would only be meaningful if they actually prayed. In other words, it was not an act. She decided to time her witness to coincide with the only item on PNC's agenda related to climate change, a shareholder resolution asking them to track the carbon cost of their investments. When the negative vote was announced, Eileen stood up and removed her blazer and scarf to reveal a white T-shirt that said in green letters, "Praying for PNC to act responsibly" on one side, and "No $$$ for mountaintop removal" on the other. The CEO ended the meeting almost immediately, making it even shorter than the previous year's, a total of fifteen minutes.

Eileen closed her eyes as people began shuffling out of the hotel conference room. The head of PNC security stood behind her, as she remembered that she was there to pray. An image came to her of the Appalachian Mountains and Dustin White, a West Virginia activist who had shown her the devastation first-hand. In the silence, she felt a profound sense of connection to Dustin, those mountains, and people the world over who were suffering from the destruction of the Earth and its climate. When the room grew quiet, she exited and found Matthew and the Florida Quakers, their jackets removed, worshiping in silence in their matching T-shirts, positioned so those leaving the meeting would have to pass them. We all walked through the hotel lobby singing and then joined the larger group holding a rally on the hotel sidewalk, where people of all ages had taken turns giving their own speeches on the issue of mountaintop removal.

The way opening around the Tampa action had a significant impact on the campaign. As it happened, the annual national gathering of unprogrammed Quakers, which moves across the country from year to year, was scheduled in the summer of 2014 to meet on a college campus outside of Pittsburgh, a convenient drive to PNC's corporate headquarters. EQAT had already planned to take advantage of this serendipity and was renting six buses to bring Quakers from across the country to PNC's downtown locations. The Florida teenagers came to the gathering and played an important role in galvanizing other youth and adults who had not heard of the campaign. Again we planned dispersed meetings for worship around the city, so people could experience worship as direct action, and then regathered for our largest rally ever at PNC headquarters.

Afterward, Matthew mapped out where in the United States the two hundred participants had come from, and EQAT organized four regional trainings to empower those people to lead their own BLAM! actions at PNC branches across the country. Each new action-planning team was assigned an experienced coach. We also took advantage of the People's Climate March in September of that year, knowing that Quakers from many places would be attending. The day before the march, we offered a nonviolent direct-action training and then held actions at two Manhattan branches of PNC Bank, helping to build the connection that national Quakers felt to the campaign. Three months later, in December 2014, we held our largest day of action so far, holding space at thirty-one PNC locations in thirteen states and the District of Columbia. Influenced by the young people in Florida and the extreme threat of rising seas there, we named the day of action Flood PNC. Teenage girls from Florida served as action lead and police liaison with colorful signs depicting the rising sea level threatening their state, while volunteers across the country stepped into new and empowering roles.

A few months later, in March 2015, PNC announced that it would pull away from financing mountaintop removal coal mining, something it said it would never do at the beginning of the campaign.

Conclusion

Although EQAT members were well aware that limiting the financing of mountaintop removal coal mining was only a piece of the long struggle to end that horrific practice, they celebrated the campaign's end by focusing on what they had learned that could be carried forward in subsequent campaigns. In addition to the concrete skills of direct action, lessons included the power of noncooperation with injustice and the power of cooperating with each other, even amid conflict. Ultimately, the Quaker concepts that shaped the life of EQAT through and beyond the BLAM! campaign—the idea that action itself is worship, the importance of integrity, telling the truth amid holding "that of God" in everyone, following way opening or signs from Spirit, and being open to continuing revelation—are collective and communal practices enriched both by those who identify as Quaker and those who do not. They continue to bind us as a community as we continue to nonviolently and prayerfully challenge corporations profiting from the desecration of the Earth and its climate.

How we chose our next two campaigns exemplifies how we have tried to apply these practices over the years. Even before we heard that PNC Bank was going to change its mountaintop removal policy, Eileen had an intuition that EQAT would win the BLAM! campaign and asked Lina to lead a preliminary conversation about what we might be called to next. From that first conversation, a few themes emerged that persisted through a discernment process that lasted a few months. One was that we wanted a campaign that explicitly challenged racial injustice. Another was that we wanted to try a "solutions campaign," one that didn't just protest something bad but that pushed for positive solutions to the climate crisis. Inspired by Black and Brown communities that were leading the way in promoting renewable energy as a job creator, we explored how that might work in our region, with Philadelphia being one of the poorest big cities in the United States. Through a combination of research and paying attention to our inward guidance, we decided to target southeastern Pennsylvania's largest electric utility, PECO, which lagged far behind other utilities in renewable energy use. We called the campaign Power Local Green Jobs.

Way opened early on when we learned that another organization wanted to join us, Philadelphians Organized to Witness Empower and Rebuild (POWER), a Black-led interfaith group that was making a difference on a variety of justice issues in Philadelphia. That partnership helped EQAT to become much more aware of and comfortable talking about racial injustice, while making POWER members more comfortable talking about the impacts of climate change. By showing up together in nonviolent direct action, the Power Local Green Jobs campaign pressured PECO to take several important steps, including establishing a solar department, making solar hookups easier for contractors, and giving at least two hundred thousand dollars to solar jobs training programs that prioritize people in low-income communities. Although PECO eventually pledged to procure more of its tiny amount of solar energy locally, we were unable to build enough pressure to fundamentally change the way the company buys energy. Eventually, we felt it was a matter of integrity to admit that we would not be able to win our ambitious goal of 20 percent locally owned solar by 2025. Way opened once again in 2021, just as the board was considering whether we should move on, and what we might focus on instead.

An international coalition of groups working on fossil fuel financing reached out to EQAT about joining a new campaign against the global asset manager Vanguard, which is based in the suburbs of Philadelphia, making us a logical choice to anchor the nonviolent direct-action wing of the campaign. As extremely large investors, asset managers have the power to pressure fossil fuel companies in a new direction, and most are not using it. Vanguard in particular is one of the world's top investors in coal, oil, and gas, but has one of the worst voting records when it comes to shareholder resolutions that could move fossil fuel and other climate-warming companies. Returning to a financial target played to EQAT's strength—moral clarity—as opposed to a utility, where the muddy waters of utility regulation and an out-of-date grid often blunted our moral message. We also loved the idea of being part of a global coalition, which would be a new learning experience, while we could continue to highlight racial injustice, given the companies in Vanguard's portfolio.

EQAT members enact a playful skit outside Vanguard's headquarters during a mass action. The morality-play parody highlighted the company's habit of listening to the proverbial devil—rather than the angel—on its shoulder when making corporate policy decisions. (PHOTO BY DAVID PARRY / USED WITH PERMISSION)

In 2021, Eileen had followed a leading to spend a month in Minnesota as part of the Stop Line 3 campaign (see chapter 1) and was motivated to learn that Vanguard was the number-one investor in the responsible oil pipeline company, Enbridge. It was also a top investor in Duke Energy, which attempted to build the Atlantic Coast Pipeline from West Virginia through Virginia and into North Carolina (see chapter 4), and Williams Partners, which built the Atlantic Sunrise Pipeline in Pennsylvania (see chapter 2). In EQAT's southeastern Pennsylvania region,

Vanguard was a top investor in many of the companies that polluted the air and water along the Delaware River, especially those in Chester, south of Philadelphia. A majority-Black town, Chester had long resisted the numerous polluting industries—including an incinerator, a chemical company, a paper mill, and a nearby oil refinery—all of which are Vanguard investments, either directly or indirectly through a parent company. When rumors emerged that a new liquified natural gas plant was being considered for Chester, our volunteer research team, which had been learning the new skill of following the money, found that several of the involved companies were in Vanguard's portfolio.

Worshippers hold prayerful space in the driveway of Vanguard's headquarters near Philadelphia. Silent worship continues to be a cornerstone of EQAT's eco-activism as its attention shifts to Vanguard.

(PHOTO BY RACHEL WARRINER @RAYEPHOTO ON INSTAGRAM / USED WITH PERMISSION)

In this ongoing campaign, we continue to learn while applying lessons from the BLAM! and Power Local Green Jobs campaigns. We have held silent worship in Vanguard's driveway and in front of the CEO's home, holding him in prayer along with the people around the world harmed by the investments he oversees. In other acts of noncooperation, we have pledged to move our money out of Vanguard, drawing on the Quaker principle of integrity. We made that announcement at a joint action with Chester Residents Concerned for Quality Living, gathered in front of the Covanta incinerator that causes innumerable health problems for their community. We have also held actions focused on youth, enlivened by a new generation of young people, and hosted Indigenous leaders from Peru who are fighting an oil company whose expansion is financed by bonds bought by Vanguard. Each time we step onto Vanguard's manicured campus, we have the chance to remember that by following the leadings of Spirit, we are part of a movement much larger than ourselves, connected by Spirit, air, water, and the flow of money to people everywhere who are working for a just and sustainable future.

Epilogue
A Call to Join the Work of Sacred Resistance

Mark Clatterbuck

As noted in the Introduction, this project is driven by a desire to inspire and embolden more spiritually grounded eco-activism in an age of ongoing corporate violence against the Earth. With that hope in mind, this brief epilogue highlights three principles of eco-activism that mark every campaign featured in the preceding chapters. I offer these reflections as guidelines for individuals and groups that are currently engaged in the work of defending the Earth, as well as those who might be feeling the tug of activism for the first time.

Be Bold

The first way that each of these movements acted boldly was in their choice of targets. Despite being grassroots movements with relatively limited financial and material resources, they each chose to confront multibillion-dollar environmental threats. This alone indicates a strategic approach that is worth noting and emulating.

A tried-and-true practice of the worst offenders against the environment is to shift blame away from themselves and onto the rest of us. Mimicking the strategy of the tobacco industry, fossil fuel giants like ExxonMobil and BP have spent decades running elaborate propaganda campaigns to frame climate change as a consumer problem rather than a problem of corporate tyranny. They even popularized the "carbon footprint" concept as a savvy strategy for laying primary responsibility for the climate catastrophe on me and you, rather than on the handful of global fossil fuel giants responsible for more than half of the world's industrial emissions. The true climate criminals prefer to keep us feeling guilty about that extra straw we used at the diner last week, rather than feeling furious at them for burning our children's future for the sake of billionaire profits today.

The grassroots movements in this book dared to move beyond guilt over straws in order to confront the true culprits of environmental violence: multibillion-dollar corporate assaults on the Earth and the financial institutions backing them. The fact that three of the movements examined in this book succeeded in stopping the project they targeted, while the other two caused substantial delays and called national attention to the major industrial dangers that they faced, should serve as motivation for other grassroots movements to believe that they are capable of tackling even the biggest threats.

A second way these movements demonstrated boldness was by engaging in direct action. They did not simply talk about the importance of environmental justice with their neighbors, nor did they stop at writing letters to the editor or calling their lawmakers. They chose to keep going, putting their bodies on the front lines of climate action to defend the sacred.

Having said that, most of the campaigns did not begin with members risking arrest and building blockades. Instead, participants generally had a steep learning curve to travel before committing to civil disobedience. Most of the campaigns described in this book spent a great deal of time convincing members that the regulatory system would not be their salvation. It was only when a critical mass of the movement reached this conclusion that the direct-action phase of the campaign could begin.

Minority groups and marginalized communities—e.g., Indigenous elders, Black women, trans youth, those in poverty—tend to know intuitively that "the system" was never intended to protect people like them. Personal experience has long taught them that politicians, regulators, law enforcement, and the courts do not serve the interests of everyone equally. Instead, and above all else, these structures were designed by those in power to protect their own privilege and wealth. Environmental policy is no exception. The reason federal and state regulatory agencies—including state Departments of Environmental Protection—so spectacularly "fail" to rein in corporate greed and halt large-scale environmental destruction is that their primary job is not to protect the Earth or local communities. To the contrary, their raison d'être is to issue permits that legalize industrial harm that would otherwise be illegal if it were not for their intervention.

This reality explains why Hawai'i's Department of Land and Natural Resources (DLNR) went out of its way to help TMT circumvent rules put in place to protect Mauna Kea and Native Hawaiian cultural practices. It also explains why, despite widespread grassroots resistance and religious opposition to a new pipeline in the state, the Pennsylvania Department of Environmental Protection chose not to deny a key project permit when it became clear that the pipeline would violate state and federal clean air standards. Instead, the agency fabricated a workaround for the industry to proceed with the project by magically applying clean air "credits" from a different state. The five case studies in this volume offer many more examples of similarly disturbing regulatory actions.

Direct action tends to be the course of last resort, meaning that participants must first come to the conclusion that other paths of resistance are insufficient to stop the harm. That is the moment direct-action organizing kicks into gear. For those who have generally benefited from the US political, regulatory, and legal system, it can take awhile to reach that realization.

In 2016, when the #NoDAPL campaign was in full swing, I happened to be in New Jersey, attending a community meeting of mostly white residents who were discussing the dangers of a new, high-volume fossil fuel pipeline proposed to run through their neighborhoods. Many expressed shock and anger when they learned that the government could simply issue a permit for a private corporation to take their land, against their will, to locate a dangerous corporate project right beside their homes. At that point, the chief of a local Indigenous tribe approached the microphone. With a glint of amusement in his eyes at the realization belatedly dawning on the audience, he dryly quipped, "It looks like we're all on the reservation now."

A common sentiment that I hear from movement organizers following a direct-action campaign is regret that they weren't bolder from the start. While acknowledging the necessity of the educational journey, they wish it hadn't taken two or three years to help participants grasp the futility of appealing to regulatory bodies for protection when those agencies are literally designed to facilitate corporate harm. Those precious years of hesitation, before arriving at direct action, sometimes allowed the industry all the time they needed to inflict their damage. Perhaps the stories contained in this book can expedite the direct-action timeline for future movements, allowing for bolder and more effective resistance from the start.

Be Joyful

The pervasive sense of joy emanating from each of these communities is one of the deepest impressions I carry from the time I spent among the five movements featured in this project.

Joy was ubiquitous and contagious—from children playing in resistance camps, to ebullient dancers holding space while performing pule and hula, to the calm smiles on Quaker faces during silent-worship sit-ins in front of confused bank lobby tellers. Put another way: the movements were driven more by a joyful defense of what they loved than by a desperate opposition to what they feared or hated. That underlying motivation translated into a lively, often playful spirit animating these campaigns.

One of my favorite memories serving as direct-action lead with Lancaster Against Pipelines came during a tense standoff with pipeline workers and law enforcement at an active construction site after we had disrupted several other sites earlier in the day. Three women in their fifties and sixties, all local residents, had locked themselves together in front of tree-clearing machinery, bringing the equipment to a grinding halt. Twenty state troopers marched single file into the construction zone to cut the women out of their lock boxes and arrest them, when suddenly laughter filled the air. I later learned that the "criminals" had been cracking menopause jokes with the male troopers midarrest.

It may sound counterintuitive to highlight the role that joy played in movements marked by the weight of ecological devastation, trauma-inducing stress, and militarized confrontations with law enforcement. But it's precisely against this backdrop of aggression, intimidation, and militarization that joy emerges as the unsung superpower of sacred resistance.

Indeed, the modern playbook for industry attacks on grassroots eco-activist movements came straight out of Standing Rock. During the #NoDAPL campaign of 2016–2017, the Texas pipeline company Energy Transfer hired Tiger Swan to oversee its security operations. Tiger Swan, which was founded by an ex–Special Forces army officer, specializes in counterterrorism and counterinsurgency tactics. The firm honed its practices during the US wars in Afghanistan and Iraq before establishing itself as the go-to source for US-based oil and gas companies forcing unwanted pipelines through resistant communities. At Standing Rock, their aggressive tactics against Water Protectors included aerial surveillance, radio eavesdropping, undercover personnel, sending infiltrators into the resistance camps, and logging intelligence reports on movement leaders. They also ran an extensive propaganda campaign using fake social media accounts to discredit and malign prominent members of the resistance, referring to pipeline opponents as domestic terrorists and "jihadists." All of this was done in seamless coordination with taxpayer-funded local, state, and federal law enforcement agencies, which waged an increasingly militarized offensive against ceremonially grounded Water Protectors.

The movements in this book, to varying degrees, faced excessive police force, surveillance, mass arrests, and inflated criminal charges. This was particularly true for the #StopLine3 movement, which sustained more than one thousand arrests. Furthermore, in the wake of Standing Rock, industry lobbyists have successfully pressured lawmakers in twenty-four states to introduce sweeping antiprotest legislation that hypercriminalizes grassroots resistance against so-called critical infrastructure projects like pipelines. They've been enacted in seventeen of those states. These laws turn misdemeanor protests into felonies, level eye-popping fines, and impose extensive jail sentences for even peaceful grassroots resistance. One recent law proposed in Pennsylvania to target a group of Catholic nuns blockading a gas pipeline specifically outlaws "the holding of vigils or religious services" that might interfere with pipeline construction. In some cases, these laws even protect violent industry sympathizers who, for example, drive their vehicles into peaceful protesters.

These efforts bring us back to the jarring juxtaposition of the infectious joy that pervaded the communities examined in this book. For so many of the participants I met during this project, the pervasive joy that was found in these communities kept them engaged in the work of eco-activism, despite the dangers and stressors they endured. Joy also proved to be incredibly disarming for industry advocates and their allies, who were largely unsuccessful in their efforts to portray participants as angry, unpredictable, dangerous actors.

Be Disciplined

Many factors came together to make each of the movements in this book highly effective and nationally recognized models of eco-activism. Arguably, the most important distinction that was shared by all five movements was their clear articulation of core principles of conduct, including a highly disciplined adherence to those principles.

At Mauna Kea, this principle was captured in the ubiquitous motto "Kapu aloha, always." As described in chapter 3, kapu embodies sacredness, taboo, consecration; aloha embodies compassion, kindness, love, affection. As such, kapu aloha was a call for participants to behave in a manner consistent with aloha values while being in the presence of the sacred. As movement leader Pua Case explains, kapu aloha is "how you conduct yourself in a ceremony." This is why she repeated the mantra "sacred mountain, sacred conduct" at virtually every gathering that took place on the Mauna during the months-long blockade. Participants understood that any action undertaken for the protection of Mauna Kea—whether greeting guests, interacting with police, performing chants, serving meals, or picking up trash—was to be guided by kapu aloha. No activity related to this work of sacred resistance in defense of the Mauna fell outside the binding obligations of kapu aloha.

Lancaster Against Pipelines and the Adorers of the Blood of Christ were likewise committed to principles of nonviolence, right conduct, and a posture of love even when coming face-to-face with those inflicting violence on the Earth. During each briefing that took place immediately before launching a direct action, one of the movement leaders would walk around the circle, look each participant in the eye, and ask, "Is your heart in a good place today? Are you fully confident that you will remain peaceful no matter the level of escalation we face today? Are you motivated by love rather than rage as you enter this action?" Those who were feeling less than confident were invited to take a step back and return when they were better prepared to align their actions with the movement's principles.

For ecojustice movements anchored in the conviction that their work constitutes a sacred duty analogous to religious ceremony, highly disciplined behavior is a natural consequence. Although participants came from a variety of spiritual traditions, all five movements in this project benefited from the fact that the majority were familiar with sacred conduct and ceremonial behavior and were habituated to performing tasks in alignment with that interior posture. Similarly, members were also generally accustomed to operating within tightly accountable ceremonial communities or religious congregations, where each person has a role to play and the success of the whole depends on properly attending to one's duties.

These tendencies proved to be an enormous strength in each of the campaigns. The tightly knit, highly disciplined nature of these movements made them largely impervious to industry attempts at intimidating leaders and other members, exploiting divisions within the movements, or portraying the movements as violent or dangerous in an effort to undermine public support for their resistance. These movements demonstrate why building strong, disciplined, spiritually anchored communities is such a powerful tool of grassroots activism.

Looking Ahead

Extraordinary acts of communal resistance will be required to confront the corporate ecoviolence fueling the global climate crisis. While religious communities have a mixed track record when it comes to environmental justice, the preceding case studies offer compelling examples of what spiritually grounded activism can achieve in the face of major threats to the natural world. Recalling the words of Kanaka ʻŌiwi (Native Hawaiian) elder Marie Alohalani Brown on the role of Hoʻomana (the ancient belief system of the islands) in the Mauna Kea movement, "As we look to the past for knowledge and inspiration on how to face the future, we are aware that we are tomorrow's ancestors, and future generations will look to us for guidance. This is our destiny." It is going to take all of us to embrace a sense of spirit-guided destiny to ensure a livable future for those who come behind us.

CONTRIBUTORS

Heidi Dhivya Berthoud was on the front lines of the Atlantic Coast Pipeline struggle (2014–2020), serving as secretary of Friends of Buckingham and cofounder of the Virginia Community Rights Network. She moved to the egalitarian Twin Oaks Community in the late 1970s, where organic farming and Wicca deepened her understanding of right relationship. She resides with her husband and three cats in Central Virginia (occupied Monacan land) by the James River in the extended Yogaville Community. She is a massage and yoga therapist and teacher.

Lina Blount is an organizer, trainer, and nonviolent action strategist who has been working on environmental justice campaigns in the Philadelphia area for over fifteen years, currently as the director of strategy and partnerships with the Earth Quaker Action Team. Lina has also worked with the Divestment Student Network and spent years as a canvas director and anti-fracking organizer in Pennsylvania. Lina considers herself Quaker and the Earth Quaker Action Team her primary spiritual community.

Marie Alohalani Brown ('Ōiwi) is a professor of Hawaiian religion at the University of Hawai'i–Mānoa. Her books include *Ka Po'e Mo'o Akua: Hawaiian Reptilian Water Deities* (2020); *Facing the Spears of Change: The Life and Legacy of John Papa 'Ī'ī* (2016); *The Penguin Book of Mermaids* with Cristina Bacchilega (2018); and a children's book on Hawaiian mythology (in production) with Make Me A World, a Penguin Random House imprint.

Mark Clatterbuck is associate professor of religion and codirector of the Native American & Indigenous Studies Program at Montclair State University. His 2017 book *Crow Jesus* (University of Oklahoma Press) explores the complex legacy of Christian missions among the Apsáalooke Nation in Montana. He cofounded Lancaster Against Pipelines, a grassroots direct-action movement that fights the fracked gas industry in Pennsylvania. He lives with his family in the Susquehanna River Hills.

Swami Dayananda is a monastic student of Swami Satchidananda living in Yogaville, Buckingham, Virginia. She served with LOTUS Center for All Faiths and Yogaville Environmental Solutions and collaborated with Union Hill Baptist Church and Friends of Buckingham to stop the Atlantic Coast Pipeline (ACP). Today she continues to pursue climate justice and her yogic lifestyle through vermiculture, composting, organic vegetables, and healing herbs. Her wish for the health and well-being of people and planet is to promote plant-based food and sustainable energy.

Eileen Flanagan is an award-winning Quaker author and speaker. As an Earth Quaker Action Team leader, she has over a decade of experience building spiritually grounded campaigns for climate justice. Ahead of the 2020 election, she was the trainings coordinator for Choose Democracy, which trained nearly ten thousand people in nonviolent strategies to prevent a coup. Her upcoming book, *Common Ground*, is about how overcoming our divisions can help us build a movement for a more just and sustainable world.

Winona LaDuke is an enrolled member of the Mississippi Band of Anishinaabe and lives on the White Earth Reservation (Minnesota). She is an internationally recognized activist, organizer, economist, entrepreneur, writer, and farmer. She has worked to defend wild rice, promote land back, and reclaim

Native culture and economy on the White Earth Reservation and across the United States. She has been working to defeat the permitting of Line 3 since 2015. She has played key roles in establishing numerous organizations that promote Indigenous rights, including the Indigenous Women's Network, the White Earth Land Recovery Project, the Anishinaabeg Agriculture Institute, Akiing, and Honor the Earth. She twice ran as vice president on the Green Party ticket. In 2023, she opened the Giiwedinong Museum of Treaties and Culture to celebrate the work of Water Protectors everywhere.

Julia Nerbonne is executive director of Minnesota Interfaith Power & Light (MNIPL). She is an adjunct assistant professor in the Department of Fisheries, Wildlife and Conservation Biology at the University of Minnesota. She has a PhD in conservation biology from the University of Minnesota. Since 1998, she has taught environmental justice and sustainability studies while bringing students into the world of social movements. Before MNIPL, she was cofounder and acting director of MN350. She is a white Minnesotan of European descent and an Episcopalian. In her organizing work, she seeks to center Indigenous world-views throughout Minnesota and the nation.

David Parry is an associate professor of media and communications at Saint Joseph's University in Pennsylvania where he researches and teaches about media, power, and social change. As a photographer he makes images of community and civic actions that resist injustice and pursue social change. He has spent time with pipeline resisters, community schools, civic organizations, protesters, and electoral campaigns that are working to craft a better future. His work can be viewed at www.outsidetheimage.com.

INDEX